Compliance with Decisions of the Dispute Settlement Bodies of the UN Convention on the Law of the Sea

The Law of the Sea

Volumes published in this Brill Research Perspectives title are listed at *brill.com/rpls*

Compliance with Decisions of the Dispute Settlement Bodies of the UN Convention on the Law of the Sea

By

Natalie Klein
Jack McNally

BRILL

LEIDEN | BOSTON

This paperback book edition is simultaneously published as issue 4.3–4 of *Law of the Sea*,
DOI:10.1163/24519359-12340011.

Typeface for the Latin, Greek, and Cyrillic scripts: "Brill". See and download: brill.com/brill-typeface.

ISBN 978-90-04-68989-3 (paperback)
ISBN 978-90-04-68990-9 (e-book)
DOI 10.1163/9789004689909

This book is printed on acid-free paper and produced in a sustainable manner.

Contents

Compliance with Decisions of the Dispute Settlement Bodies of the UN Convention on the Law of the Sea

Natalie Klein | ORCID: 0000-0001-9838-4302
Faculty of Law and Justice, UNSW Sydney

Jack McNally | ORCID: 0009-0003-8680-4359
Faculty of Law and Justice, UNSW Sydney

Abstract

The UN Convention on the Law of the Sea ('UNCLOS') not only establishes a suite of maritime zones and sets out the rights and duties of States therein, but it is also one of the few multilateral treaties that includes a complex dispute settlement regime creating compulsory jurisdiction for disputes relating to its interpretation or application. Given that the UNCLOS dispute settlement regime has now been in operation for close to 30 years, it is timely to consider whether the cases instituted under the regime are resulting in decisions with which the parties comply. This study is the first to examine compliance in relation to all judgments issued pursuant to the UNCLOS compulsory dispute settlement regime to date.

Keywords

UN Convention on the Law of the Sea ('UNCLOS') – International Tribunal for the Law of the Sea ('ITLOS') – international courts and tribunals – compliance and non-compliance – international dispute settlement

 | DOI:10.1163/9789004689909_002

List of Abbreviations and Acronyms

Annex VII tribunal	Tribunal constituted under the provisions of Annex VII of the *United Nations Convention on the Law of the Sea*
BIOT	British Indian Ocean Territory
CCSBT	Commission for the Conservation of Southern Bluefin Tuna
CLCS	Commission on the Limits of the Continental Shelf
CMATS Treaty	*Treaty between Australia and the Democratic Republic of Timor-Leste on Certain Maritime Arrangements in the Timor Sea*
COLREGS	*Convention on the International Regulations for Preventing Collisions at Sea*
EEZ	Exclusive Economic Zone
GDP	Gross domestic product
ICJ	International Court of Justice
IMO	International Maritime Organization
ITLOS	International Tribunal for the Law of the Sea
MOX	Mixed oxide fuel
MPA	Marine Protected Area
Nm	Nautical mile
PCA	Permanent Court of Arbitration
SRFC	Sub-Regional Fisheries Commission
UN	United Nations
UNCITRAL	United Nations Commission on International Trade Law
UNCLOS or Convention	*United Nations Convention on the Law of the Sea*
WTO	World Trade Organization

List of Abbreviated Case Names

ARA *Libertad*, Annex VII	ARA *Libertad* (*Argentina v. Ghana*), Termination of Proceedings, Order of 11 November 2013, PCA Case No. 2013-11
ARA *Libertad*, Provisional Measures	ARA *Libertad* (*Argentina v. Ghana*), Provisional Measures, Order of 15 December 2012, ITLOS *Reports* 2012

Arctic Sunrise, Compensation	*Arctic Sunrise* (*Netherlands v. Russian Federation*), Compensation, Award of 10 July 2017, PCA Case No. 2014-02
Arctic Sunrise, Jurisdiction	*Arctic Sunrise* (*Netherlands v. Russian Federation*), Jurisdiction, Award of 26 November 2014, PCA Case No. 2014-02
Arctic Sunrise, Merits	*Arctic Sunrise* (*Netherlands v. Russian Federation*), Merits, Award of 14 August 2015, PCA Case No. 2014-02
Arctic Sunrise, Provisional Measures	*Arctic Sunrise* (*Netherlands v. Russian Federation*), Provisional Measures, Order of 22 November 2013, *ITLOS Reports* 2013
Atlanto-Scandian Herring	*Atlanto-Scandian Herring* (*Denmark in respect of the Faroe Islands v. the European Union*), Termination Order of 23 September 2014, PCA Case No. 2013-30
Barbados v. Trinidad and Tobago	*Barbados v. Trinidad and Tobago*, Merits, Award of 11 April 2006, 27 *RIAA* 147
Bay of Bengal Arbitration	*Bay of Bengal Maritime Boundary Arbitration* (*Bangladesh v. India*), Merits, Award of 7 July 2014, PCA Case No. 2010-16.
Bay of Bengal Delimitation	*Delimitation of the Maritime Boundary between Bangladesh and Myanmar in the Bay of Bengal* (*Bangladesh/Myanmar*), Merits, Judgment of 14 March 2012, *ITLOS Reports* 2012
Camouco	*Camouco* (*Panama v. France*), Prompt Release, Judgment of 7 February 2000, *ITLOS Reports* 2000
Chagos Advisory Opinion	*Legal Consequences of the Separation of the Chagos Archipelago from Mauritius in 1965*, Advisory Opinion, *ICJ Reports* 2019
Chagos MPA	*Chagos Marine Protected Area Arbitration* (*Mauritius v. United Kingdom*), Merits, Award of 18 March 2015, PCA Case No. 2011-03
Chaisiri Reefer 2	*Chaisiri Reefer 2* (*Panama v. Yemen*), Prompt Release, Order 2001/4 of 13 July 2001
Coastal State Rights	*Coastal State Rights in the Black Sea, Sea of Azov, and Kerch Strait* (*Ukraine v. Russian Federation*), Preliminary Objections, Award of 21 February 2020, PCA Case No. 2017-16

Detention of Ukrainian Naval Vessels and Servicemen	*Detention of Ukrainian Naval Vessels and Servicemen (Ukraine v. Russian Federation)*, Preliminary Objections, Award of 27 June 2022, PCA Case No. 2019-28
Duzgit Integrity, Compensation	*Duzgit Integrity (Malta v. São Tomé and Príncipe)*, Compensation, Award of 18 December 2019, PCA Case No. 2014-07
Duzgit Integrity, Merits	*Duzgit Integrity (Malta v. São Tomé and Príncipe)*, Merits, Award of 5 September 2016, PCA Case No. 2014-07
Enrica Lexie, Annex VII Provisional Measures	*Enrica Lexie (Italy v. India)*, Provisional Measures, Order of 29 April 2016, PCA Case No. 2015-28
Enrica Lexie, ITLOS Provisional Measures	*Enrica Lexie (Italy v. India)*, Provisional Measures, Order of 24 August 2015, *ITLOS Reports* 2015
Enrica Lexie, Merits	*Enrica Lexie (Italy v. India)*, Merits, Award of 21 May 2020, PCA Case No. 2015-28
Ghana/Côte d'Ivoire, Merits	*Delimitation of the Maritime Boundary between Ghana and Côte d'Ivoire in the Atlantic Ocean (Ghana/Côte d'Ivoire)*, Merits, Judgment of 23 September 2017, *ITLOS Reports* 2017
Ghana/Côte d'Ivoire, Provisional Measures	*Delimitation of the Maritime Boundary between Ghana and Côte d'Ivoire in the Atlantic Ocean (Ghana/Côte d'Ivoire)*, Provisional Measures, Order of 25 April 2015, *ITLOS Reports* 2015
Grand Prince	*Grand Prince (Belize v. France)*, Prompt Release, Judgment of 20 April 2001, *ITLOS Reports* 2001
Guyana v. Suriname	*Guyana v. Suriname*, Merits, Award of 17 September 2007, 30 *RIAA* 1
Heroic Idun	*Heroic Idun (Marshall Islands v. Equatorial Guinea)*, Prompt Release, Order 2022/3 of 15 November 2022
Hoshinmaru	*Hoshinmaru (Japan v. Russian Federation)*, Prompt Release, Judgment of 6 August 2007, *ITLOS Reports* 2007

Juno Trader	*Juno Trader* (*Saint Vincent and the Grenadines v. Guinea-Bissau*), Prompt Release, Judgment of 18 December 2004, *ITLOS Reports* 2004
Land Reclamation, Merits	*Land Reclamation by Singapore in and around the Straits of Johor* (*Malaysia v. Singapore*), Merits, Award on Agreed Terms of 1 September 2005, 27 *RIAA* 133
Land Reclamation, Provisional Measures	*Land Reclamation by Singapore in and around the Straits of Johor* (*Malaysia v. Singapore*), Provisional Measures, Order of 8 October 2003, *ITLOS Reports* 2003
Louisa, Merits	*M/V Louisa* (*Saint Vincent and the Grenadines v. Spain*), Merits, Judgment of 28 May 2013, *ITLOS Reports* 2013
Louisa, Provisional Measures	*M/V Louisa* (*Saint Vincent and the Grenadines v. Spain*), Provisional Measures, Order of 23 December 2010, *ITLOS Reports* 2010
Mauritius/Maldives	*Delimitation of the Maritime Boundary between Mauritius and Maldives in the Indian Ocean* (*Mauritius/Maldives*), Preliminary Objections, Judgment of 28 January 2021, General List No. 28
Mauritius/Maldives, Merits	*Delimitation of the Maritime Boundary between Mauritius and Maldives in the Indian Ocean* (*Mauritius/Maldives*), Judgment of 28 April 2023, General List No. 28
Monte Confurco	*Monte Confurco* (*Seychelles v. France*), Prompt Release, Judgment of 18 December 2000, *ITLOS Reports* 2000
MOX Plant, Annex VII Provisional Measures	*MOX Plant* (*Ireland v. United Kingdom*), Provisional Measures, Order No. 3 of 24 June 2003, PCA Case No. 2002-01.
MOX Plant, Provisional Measures	*MOX Plant* (*Ireland v. United Kingdom*), Provisional Measures, Order of 3 December 2001, *ITLOS Reports* 2001
Norstar, Merits	*M/V Norstar* (*Panama v. Italy*), Merits, Judgment of 10 April 2019, *ITLOS Reports* 2019

Norstar, Provisional Measures	*M/V Norstar (Panama v. Italy)*, Preliminary Objections, Judgment of 4 November 2016, *ITLOS Reports* 2016
Qatar v. Bahrain	*Maritime Delimitation and Territorial Questions between Qatar and Bahrain (Qatar v. Bahrain)*, Judgment, *ICJ Reports* 1994
Saiga	*M/V Saiga (Saint Vincent and the Grenadines v. Guinea)*, Prompt Release, Judgment of 4 December 1997, *ITLOS Reports* 1997
Saiga (No. 2), Merits	*M/V Saiga (No. 2) (Saint Vincent and the Grenadines v. Guinea)*, Merits, Judgment of 1 July 1999, *ITLOS Reports* 1999
Saiga (No. 2), Provisional Measures	*M/V Saiga (No. 2) (Saint Vincent and the Grenadines v. Guinea)*, Provisional Measures, Order of 11 March 1998, *ITLOS Reports* 1998
San Padre Pio	*M/T San Padre Pio (Switzerland v. Nigeria)*, Provisional Measures, Order of 6 July 2019, *ITLOS Reports* 2019
San Padre Pio (No. 2)	*M/T San Padre Pio (No. 2) (Switzerland/Nigeria)*, Merits, Order 2021/6 of 29 December 2021
South China Sea	*South China Sea Arbitration (Philippines v. China)*, Merits, Award of 12 July 2016, PCA Case No. 2013-19
South China Sea, Jurisdiction and Admissibility	*South China Sea Arbitration (Philippines v. China)*, Jurisdiction and Admissibility, Award of 29 October 2015, PCA Case No. 2013-19
Southern Bluefin Tuna, Jurisdiction and Admissibility	*Southern Bluefin Tuna (New Zealand v. Japan; Australia v. Japan)*, Jurisdiction and Admissibility, Decision of August 2000, 23 *RIAA* 1
Southern Bluefin Tuna, Provisional Measures	*Southern Bluefin Tuna Cases (New Zealand v. Japan; Australia v. Japan)*, Provisional Measures, Order of 27 August 1999, *ITLOS Reports* 1999
SRFC Advisory Opinion	*Request for an Advisory Opinion submitted by the Sub-Regional Fisheries Commission (SRFC) (Request for Advisory Opinion submitted to the Tribunal)*, Advisory Opinion of 2 April 2015, *ITLOS Reports* 2015

Three Ukrainian Naval Vessels	*Detention of Three Ukrainian Naval Vessels (Ukraine v. Russian Federation)*, Provisional Measures, Order of 25 May 2019, *ITLOS Reports* 2019
Timor Sea Conciliation	*Conciliation between the Democratic Republic of Timor-Leste and the Commonwealth of Australia*, Report and Recommendations of the Compulsory Conciliation Commission, 9 May 2018, PCA Case No. 2016-10
Tomimaru	*Tomimaru (Japan v. Russian Federation)*, Prompt Release, Judgment of 6 August 2007, *ITLOS Reports* 2007
Virginia G	*M/V Virginia G (Panama/Guinea-Bissau)*, Merits, Judgment of 14 April 2014, *ITLOS Reports* 2014
Volga	*Volga (Russian Federation v. Australia)*, Prompt Release, Judgment of 23 December 2002, *ITLOS Reports* 2002

Acknowledgments

Funding for work on this publication was provided by the UNSW Sydney's SHARP scheme and is gratefully acknowledged. The inspiration for this project came from an invitation to present on the topic at the National University of Singapore's Centre for International Law celebration of the 40th anniversary of UNCLOS in 2022. That presentation was published as a short essay in Nilufer Oral and Tara Davenport (eds), *UNCLOS at 40: Essays in Honour of Ambassador Koh* (NUS Press, 2024). The findings in that essay have since been updated and significantly elaborated upon for the purposes of this publication.

All data concerning cases and post-judgment compliance reflects the understanding of the authors as at 1 September 2022. Digital resources cited herein were each last accessed on 1 September 2022. The text was updated in pre-production to reflect new proceedings relating to the *Heroic Idun* and merits judgment in *Mauritius/Maldives*, as well as the addition of *Request for an Advisory Opinion submitted by the Commission of Small Island States on Climate Change and International Law* to the Tribunal's list of cases.

1 Introduction to Dispute Settlement under the UN Convention on the Law of the Sea

1.1 *Introduction*

The question of compliance with international law is one of the discipline's "most central questions".[1] It is, however, a vexed question. In this book, we do not seek to answer theoretical questions of *how* and *why* States comply with international law. Instead, the object of this book is to compile the empirical evidence to determine, as a matter of fact, *whether* States have complied with certain of their obligations under international law. Whether States have complied with decisions of international courts and tribunals may provide an indication, albeit not the only indication, of how well international dispute settlement procedures are performing in relation to the international legal system within which they sit.

For the purposes of this study, we limit our focus to the question of compliance with the decisions rendered by the dispute settlement bodies established under one of international law's most important and widely ratified instruments, the UN Convention on the Law of the Sea ('UNCLOS' or 'Convention').[2] The Convention, which was opened for signature in December 1982 and entered into force in November 1994,[3] has now passed its 40th anniversary and has close to 170 parties, including the European Union.[4] It is commonly referred to as "the constitution of the oceans".[5] In light of its constitutive nature, the dispute settlement system in Part XV of UNCLOS is essential for the Convention's operation.[6] The dispute settlement bodies created pursuant to Part XV of the Convention have issued nearly 50 decisions. Upon this

1 A. T. Guzman, 'A Compliance-Based Theory of International Law' (2002) 90 *California Law Review* 1825, 1873.

2 United Nations Convention on the Law of the Sea, adopted 10 December 1982, entered into force 16 November 1994, 1833 UNTS 397.

3 The Convention came into force in November 1994, being a year following the 60th ratification of the Convention (by Guyana): UNCLOS, Art. 308(1).

4 165 United Nations member States, the Cook Islands, Niue, Palestine, and the European Union.

5 A label applied even during the time it was being negotiated. See E. M. Borgese, 'A Constitution for the Oceans: Comments and Suggestions regarding Part XI of the Informal Composite Negotiating Text' (1978) 15 *San Diego Law Review* 371. The President of the negotiations also made this observation at the time the Convention was adopted. See T. T. B. Koh, 'A Constitution for the Oceans' (Speech at the Third United Nations Conference on the Law of the Sea, Montego Bay, 11 December 1982).

6 As Klein has previously discussed: N. Klein, *Dispute Settlement in the UN Convention on the Law of the Sea* (Cambridge University Press, 2005), 25–26.

anniversary, and with increasing case law concerning the interpretation or application of the Convention, it is timely to investigate the extent to which these decisions have been complied with by States party to the Convention. We find that the compliance record can be positively viewed, but that compliance is only one factor among many in assessments of UNCLOS dispute settlement.

This information should assist States in their decision-making as to possible avenues to pursue in resolving disputes relating to the Convention. Other scholars interested in international dispute settlement may be able to compare the UNCLOS dispute settlement system with the operation of other international courts and tribunals.[7] Such analysis is likely to contribute to debates relating more broadly to compliance in international law, but in undertaking such comparisons it is essential to have a firm understanding of the way that the unique dispute settlement procedures in UNCLOS work. We begin by outlining the primary features of the UNCLOS dispute settlement system.

1.2 *Dispute Settlement under the UN Convention on the Law of the Sea*

The adoption of UNCLOS in 1982 was the culmination of complex negotiations that created a 'package deal' across 320 articles and nine annexes.[8] Among its many achievements, the Convention delineates a suite of maritime zones, sets out the rights and duties of States therein, and establishes new institutions for the delimitation of the outer continental shelf and for the exploration and exploitation of the deep seabed.[9]

The Convention also struck new ground, "heralding in a new era in international law" by introducing "an innovative and far-reaching compulsory dispute settlement system".[10] The system is described as 'compulsory' because when a State becomes a party to UNCLOS, that State accepts the possibility of arbitration or adjudication pursuant to Part XV of the Convention without the need for a further act of consent and without the possibility of a reservation to opt out of the mandatory dispute settlement procedures. The compulsory nature of the dispute settlement system has been described by the Registrar of the

7 See further n. 32 and Chapter 2.4.

8 The 'package' language is used in text introducing UNCLOS. Source: <https://www.un.org/depts/los/convention_agreements/convention_historical_perspective.htm>. See also Koh (n. 5), at xxxiv (observing that "the provisions of the Convention are closely interrelated and form an integral package").

9 Namely, the Commission on the Limits of the Continental Shelf and the International Seabed Authority: UNCLOS, Annex II and Part XI, Section 4, respectively.

10 R. Rayfuse, 'The Future of Compulsory Dispute Settlement under the Law of the Sea Convention' (2005) 36(1) *Victoria University of Wellington Law Review* 683, 683.

International Court of Justice ('ICJ') as being "the success of UNCLOS" and essential to ensuring compliance with the Convention's provisions.[11]

When a dispute arises, under Section 1 of Part XV, parties must initially proceed to an exchange of views as to the means of resolving the dispute,[12] and may potentially be required to utilise dispute settlement mechanisms available under other agreements.[13] To this end, States are given great latitude to determine the most appropriate mechanism to resolve the dispute at hand, and may choose to settle the dispute "by any peaceful means of their own choice" at any time.[14]

Where the parties fail to settle their dispute under Section 1 of Part XV, they can refer the dispute to compulsory procedures entailing binding decisions in line with the choice of forum selected under Article 287 of UNCLOS.[15] Article 287 provides four choices of compulsory procedure. States may utilise a standing international tribunal created by Annex VI to the Convention, the International Tribunal for the Law of the Sea ('ITLOS'), which commenced operations in 1996. States may also refer disputes to the International Court of Justice; ad hoc arbitration in accordance with Annex VII of the Convention; or to special arbitration, which entails the use of subject-matter experts, under Annex VIII of UNCLOS.[16] Decisions rendered by these UNCLOS courts and tribunals are final and binding as between the parties.[17]

Some disputes are excluded from compulsory jurisdiction under Article 297 of UNCLOS, such as disputes concerning coastal State decisions over fishing in the exclusive economic zone ('EEZ').[18] Further, States may, by their own election, opt to exclude particular disputes, including maritime boundary

11 P. Gautier, 'Some Reflections on the "New Law of the Sea"' (2022) 99 *International Law Studies* 1051, 1062. Registrar Gautier served as Registrar of the International Tribunal for the Law of the Sea between September 2001 and July 2019.

12 UNCLOS, Art. 283.

13 Ibid., Arts. 281, 282.

14 Ibid., Art. 280. UNCLOS explicitly anticipates the possible use of conciliation, which produces a legally non-binding award. See UNCLOS, Art. 284 and Annex V.

15 The States party to the dispute must agree on the same forum for the settlement of the dispute, failing which, or absent an election from a State, the parties are to use Annex VII arbitration: ibid., Art. 287(3)–(5). States may also, notwithstanding their choices of forum, opt to submit their dispute to a particular UNCLOS court or tribunal by way of special agreement (or, in French, *compromis*). For instance, Article 24(1) of the Statute of the International Tribunal for the Law of the Sea permits States to institute proceedings by special agreement.

16 UNCLOS, Art. 287(1).

17 Ibid., Art. 296.

18 Ibid., Art. 297(3).

delimitation disputes and disputes concerning military activities.[19] There are limited instances where disputes over fishing in the EEZ or in relation to maritime boundary disputes may still be submitted to compulsory conciliation, but the conciliation process produces recommendations rather than binding decisions.[20] While some subjects are (or may be) excluded from compulsory procedures entailing binding decisions, the dispute settlement regime is nonetheless critical for guaranteeing the balance of rights and duties that exists among States across ocean space.

One of the unique features of the UNCLOS dispute settlement system is that it lacks a coordinating body tasked with overseeing compliance with decisions rendered by UNCLOS courts and tribunals. This fact distinguishes UNCLOS from some other multilateral conventions conferring jurisdiction on international courts and tribunals. For instance, the UN Charter provides that the Security Council may "make recommendations or decide upon measures" to give effect to ICJ judgments;[21] the Dispute Settlement Body of the World Trade Organization ('WTO') is empowered to "maintain surveillance of implementation of rulings and recommendations" rendered by WTO dispute settlement panels and appellate bodies;[22] the Committee of Ministers of the Council of Europe is required to "supervise the execution of the terms of friendly settlement" of decisions of the European Court of Human Rights, as well as the execution of judgments.[23] The Inter-American Court of Human Rights is tasked with monitoring post-judgment compliance and making "pertinent recommendations" arising out of that surveillance to the General Assembly of the Organization of American States.[24] While the jurisdiction of these bodies to enforce the decisions of their respective courts and tribunals may sometimes be theoretical rather than practical, their existence alone may serve as a political motivator to comply. In the case of UNCLOS dispute settlement procedures, which lack such a body, States are simply obligated to comply with decisions

19 Ibid., Art. 298.

20 See ibid., Art. 297(3)(b) and Art. 298(1)(a); Annex V, Section 2.

21 United Nations Charter, Art. 94(2).

22 Marrakesh Agreement Establishing the World Trade Organization, adopted 15 April 1994, entered into force 1 January 1995, 1867 UNTS 154, Art. 4(3); Understanding on Rules and Procedures Governing the Settlement of Disputes, Marrakesh Agreement Establishing the World Trade Organization, Annex 2, 1869 UNTS 501, Art. 2(1).

23 Convention for the Protection of Human Rights and Fundamental Freedoms (European Convention on Human Rights), adopted 4 November 1950, entered into force 3 September 1953, 212 UNTS 221, Art. 39(4) and Art. 46(2)–(5).

24 American Convention on Human Rights (Pact of San José), adopted 22 November 1969 entered into force 18 July 1978, 1144 UNTS 123, Art. 65.

rendered by UNCLOS courts and tribunals.[25] Whether the Convention's lack of a body tasked with surveilling the execution of the orders of UNCLOS courts and tribunals impacts the propensity of States to comply with those orders is a question to which we will return in Chapter 8.

Given that the UNCLOS dispute settlement regime has now been in operation for close to 30 years, it is timely to consider not only the significance of the judgments rendered for their contribution to the law of the sea,[26] but also the extent of compliance with, and outcomes emerging from, the decisions of the dispute settlement bodies constituted under Part XV of the Convention. One early study by Posner and Yoo, conducted during ITLOS' infancy, suggested that

> ITLOS will not be an effective international tribunal ... Because of the independence of the tribunal, states have little influence over how it resolves disputes. They cannot expect outcomes that are satisfactory to both parties, and thus they cannot expect widespread compliance. If compliance is likely to be weak, there is little point in using the Tribunal in the first place.[27]

It is now opportune to consider whether, with the benefit of time and an increasing number of cases heard by ITLOS and ad hoc arbitral tribunals, this early hypothesis holds true.

Although the number of cases decided under the dispute settlement procedures in Part XV of UNCLOS may seem like a modest amount,[28] it has been suggested that the very existence of compulsory jurisdiction has influenced

25 UNCLOS, Art. 296(1); Annex VI, Art. 33(1); Annex VII, Art. 11. The latter provision applies *mutatis mutandis* to Special Arbitration under Annex VIII, Art. 4.

26 For such studies, see A. Del Vecchio and R. Virzo (eds), *Interpretations of the United Nations Convention on the Law of the Sea by International Courts and Tribunals* (Springer, 2019); Ø. Jensen (ed), *The Development of the Law of the Sea Convention: The Role of International Courts and Tribunals* (Elgar, 2020); A. G. Oude Elferink, T. Henriksen and S. Veierud Busch (eds), *Maritime Delimitation: The Case Law – Is It Consistent and Predictable?* (Cambridge University Press, 2018); N. Klein and K. Parlett, *Judging the Law of the Sea: Judicial Interpretations of the UN Convention on the Law of the Sea* (Oxford University Press, 2022).

27 E. A. Posner and J. C. Yoo, 'Judicial Independence in International Tribunals' (2005) 93(1) *California Law Review* 1, 72. Note also the observations of Rayfuse (n. 10), made in the same year, that at the time it was "undoubtedly premature to definitively assess the contribution to international law" of UNCLOS dispute settlement system provisions: 684.

28 The World Trade Organisation's dispute settlement mechanism has been in existence since 1995 and in roughly the same amount of time has seen over 610 cases submitted to it. Source: <https://www.wto.org/english/tratop_e/dispu_e/dispu_e.htm>.

State decision making and negotiations for certain maritime disputes.[29] Out of almost 50 cases instituted under Part XV of UNCLOS, the majority has been heard by ITLOS, and the remainder by ad hoc arbitral tribunals established under Annex VII of UNCLOS. In all but one instance, the Annex VII arbitrations have proceeded under the auspices of the Permanent Court of Arbitration ('PCA').

While the ICJ is an option for States to resolve UNCLOS disputes,[30] and some States have listed the ICJ as their preferred forum,[31] its jurisdiction has not yet been invoked under Part XV of UNCLOS. The ICJ has, however, continued to adjudicate cases involving the law of the sea, particularly in relation to maritime boundary delimitation, on other bases of jurisdiction functionally separate to the jurisdiction given to it by UNCLOS.[32]

This study focusses on compliance in relation to the cases that have been presented for resolution under Part XV of UNCLOS, as well as some other outcomes resulting from the cases even where they do not constitute 'compliance', which is defined in Chapter 2, in relation to a specific judgment or order. This examination of cases resolved through the dispute settlement bodies constituted under UNCLOS allows not only a manageable scope for this study but also enables a spotlight on UNCLOS as a dispute settlement system, rather than on one judicial institution established in the Convention.[33] In the next two sections of this Chapter, we outline the cases that have been instituted under UNCLOS and indicate which cases are the subject of the study.

29 See S. McLaughlin Mitchell and A. P. Owsiak, 'Judicialization of the Sea: Bargaining in the Shadow of UNCLOS' (2021) 115 *American Journal of International Law* 579.

30 States may declare in advance their preferred forum for dispute settlement under UNCLOS Art. 287(1).

31 States that have selected the ICJ as their forum of preference include Denmark, Honduras, and Nicaragua: United Nations, 'United Nations Convention on the Law of the Sea: Declarations and Reservations', *United Nations Treaty Collection*, available at: <https://treaties.un.org/pages/ViewDetailsIII.aspx?src=TREATY&mtdsg_no=XXI-6&chapter=21&Temp=mtdsg3&clang=_en>.

32 See, e.g., *Land and Maritime Boundary* (*Cameroon v. Nigeria*), Judgment, *ICJ Reports* 2002; *Maritime Delimitation in the Black Sea* (*Romania v. Ukraine*), Judgment, *ICJ Reports* 2009. Most recently: *Alleged Violations of Sovereign Rights and Maritime Spaces in the Caribbean Sea* (*Nicaragua v. Colombia*), Judgment, 21 April 2022, General List No. 155.

33 As has been the focus in some other studies. See, e.g., Nienke Grossman, H. G. Cohen, A. Follesdal and G. Ulfstein (eds), *Legitimacy and International Courts* (Cambridge University Press, 2018); G. Born, 'A New Generation of International Adjudication' (2012) 61 *Duke Law Journal* 775; R. Mackenzie, C. P. R. Romano, Y. Shany and P. Sands (eds), *The Manual on International Courts and Tribunals* (2nd edn., Oxford University Press, 2010).

1.3 *Proceedings before ITLOS*

In considering the 32 cases before ITLOS, they can roughly be divided between prompt release procedures under Article 292 of the Convention, provisional measures decisions pursuant to Article 290(1) and (5), and contentious cases. Two cases were settled prior to decisions on merits, and one is pending. There have also been three requests for advisory opinions; one opinion was issued by the Seabed Disputes Chamber, another issued by ITLOS, and a request for an advisory opinion on climate change and international law is presently pending before the Tribunal. As advisory opinions do not produce binding decisions with which parties must comply,[34] they are outside the scope of this study. All ITLOS cases are set out below in Table 1, indicating the type of case and / or the basic outcome:

TABLE 1 List of ITLOS cases

Case number	Name	Type/Outcome
1	*M/V Saiga (Saint Vincent and the Grenadines v. Guinea)*[a]	Prompt release
2	*M/V Saiga* (*No. 2*) (*Saint Vincent and the Grenadines v. Guinea*)[b]	Provisional measures; decision on merits
3	*Southern Bluefin Tuna* (*New Zealand v. Japan*)[c]	Provisional measures

a *M/V Saiga* (*Saint Vincent and the Grenadines v. Guinea*), Prompt Release, Judgment of 4 December 1997, *ITLOS Reports* 1997 ('*Saiga*').

b *M/V Saiga* (*No. 2*) (*Saint Vincent and the Grenadines v. Guinea*), Provisional Measures, Order of 11 March 1998 ('*Saiga* (*No. 2*), Provisional Measures'), *ITLOS Reports* 1998; *M/V Saiga* (*No. 2*) (*Saint Vincent and the Grenadines v. Guinea*), Merits, Judgment of 1 July 1999, *ITLOS Reports* 1999 ('*Saiga* (*No. 2*), Merits').

c *Southern Bluefin Tuna Cases* (*New Zealand v. Japan; Australia v. Japan*), Provisional Measures, Order of 27 August 1999, *ITLOS Reports* 1999 ('*Southern Bluefin Tuna*, Provisional Measures').

34 ITLOS' power to provide an advisory opinion derives not from UNCLOS, but rather where "an international agreement related to the purposes of the Convention specifically provides for the submission to the Tribunal of a request for such an opinion": Rules of the International Tribunal for the Law of the Sea, Art. 138(1). ITLOS has held that these advisory opinions have "no binding force": *Request for an Advisory Opinion submitted by the Sub-Regional Fisheries Commission* (*SRFC*) (*Request for Advisory Opinion submitted to the Tribunal*), Advisory Opinion of 2 April 2015, *ITLOS Reports* 2015, 26 [76] ('*SRFC Advisory Opinion*'), citing *Interpretation of Peace Treaties with Bulgaria, Hungary and Romania*, Advisory Opinion (First Phase), *ICJ Reports* 1950, 71.

TABLE 1 List of ITLOS cases (*cont.*)

Case number	Name	Type/Outcome
4	*Southern Bluefin Tuna (Australia v. Japan)*[d]	Provisional measures
5	*Camouco (Panama v. France)*[e]	Prompt release
6	*Monte Confurco Case (Seychelles v. France)*[f]	Prompt release
7	*Conservation and Sustainable Exploitation of Swordfish Stocks in the South-Eastern Pacific Ocean (Chile/European Union)*[g]	Settled; proceedings discontinued
8	*Grand Prince (Belize v. France)*[h]	Prompt release
9	*Chaisiri Reefer 2 (Panama v. Yemen)*[i]	Prompt release. Settled; proceedings discontinued
10	*MOX Plant (Ireland v. United Kingdom)*[j]	Provisional measures
11	*Volga (Russian Federation v. Australia)*[k]	Prompt release
12	*Land Reclamation by Singapore in and around the Straits of Johor (Malaysia v. Singapore)*[l]	Provisional measures

d Ibid. Australia and New Zealand each instituted separate proceedings against Japan, which were later joined before the prescription of provisional measures due to the commonality of their subject matter and relief sought: *Southern Bluefin Tuna (New Zealand v. Japan; Australia v. Japan)*, Provisional Measures, Order 1999/4 of 16 August 1999, *ITLOS Reports* 1999, 274–275. We refer to the joined proceedings as the *Southern Bluefin Tuna* cases.

e *Camouco (Panama v. France)*, Prompt Release, Judgment of 7 February 2000, *ITLOS Reports* 2000 ('*Camouco*').

f *Monte Confurco (Seychelles v. France)*, Prompt Release, Judgment of 18 December 2000, *ITLOS Reports* 2000 ('*Monte Confurco*').

g *Conservation and Sustainable Exploitation of Swordfish Stocks in the South-Eastern Pacific Ocean (Chile/European Union)*, Termination of Proceedings, Order 2009/1 of 16 December 2009, *ITLOS Reports* 2009.

h *Grand Prince (Belize v. France)*, Prompt Release, Judgment of 20 April 2001, *ITLOS Reports* 2001 ('*Grand Prince*').

i *Chaisiri Reefer 2 (Panama v. Yemen)*, Prompt Release, Order 2001/4 of 13 July 2001 ('*Chaisiri Reefer 2*').

j *MOX Plant (Ireland v. United Kingdom)*, Provisional Measures, Order of 3 December 2001, *ITLOS Reports* 2001 ('*MOX Plant*, Provisional Measures').

k *Volga (Russian Federation v. Australia)*, Prompt Release, Judgment of 23 December 2002, *ITLOS Reports* 2002 ('*Volga*').

l *Land Reclamation by Singapore in and around the Straits of Johor (Malaysia v. Singapore)*, Provisional Measures, Order of 8 October 2003, *ITLOS Reports* 2003 ('*Land Reclamation*, Provisional Measures').

TABLE 1 List of ITLOS cases (*cont.*)

Case number	Name	Type/Outcome
13	*Juno Trader* (*Saint Vincent and the Grenadines v. Guinea-Bissau*)[m]	Prompt release
14	*Hoshinmaru* (*Japan v. Russian Federation*)[n]	Prompt release
15	*Tomimaru* (*Japan v. Russian Federation*)[o]	Prompt release
16	*Delimitation of the Maritime Boundary between Bangladesh and Myanmar in the Bay of Bengal* (*Bangladesh/Myanmar*)[p]	Decision on merits
17	*Responsibilities and Obligations of States Sponsoring Persons and Entities with Respect to Activities in the Area*[q]	Advisory opinion
18	*M/V Louisa* (*Saint Vincent and the Grenadines v. Spain*)[r]	Provisional measures; decision on lack of jurisdiction
19	*M/V Virginia G* (*Panama/Guinea-Bissau*)[s]	Decision on merits
20	*ARA Libertad* (*Argentina v. Ghana*)[t]	Provisional measures
21	*Request for an Advisory Opinion submitted by the Sub-Regional Fisheries Commission*[u]	Advisory opinion

m *Juno Trader* (*Saint Vincent and the Grenadines v. Guinea-Bissau*), Prompt Release, Judgment of 18 December 2004, *ITLOS Reports* 2004.

n *Hoshinmaru* (*Japan v. Russian Federation*), Prompt Release, Judgment of 6 August 2007, *ITLOS Reports* 2007 ('*Hoshinmaru*').

o *Tomimaru* (*Japan v. Russian Federation*), Prompt Release, Judgment of 6 August 2007, *ITLOS Reports* 2007 ('*Tomimaru*').

p *Delimitation of the Maritime Boundary between Bangladesh and Myanmar in the Bay of Bengal* (*Bangladesh/Myanmar*), Merits, Judgment of 14 March 2012, *ITLOS Reports* 2012 ('*Bay of Bengal Delimitation*').

q *Responsibilities and Obligations of States Sponsoring Persons and Entities with Respect to Activities in the Area* (*Request for Advisory Opinion submitted to the Seabed Disputes Chamber*), Advisory Opinion of 1 February 2011, *ITLOS Reports* 2011.

r *M/V Louisa* (*Saint Vincent and the Grenadines v. Spain*), Provisional Measures, Order of 23 December 2010, *ITLOS Reports* 2010 ('*Louisa*, Provisional Measures'); *M/V Louisa* (*Saint Vincent and the Grenadines v. Spain*), Merits, Judgment of 28 May 2013, *ITLOS Reports* 2013 ('*Louisa*, Merits').

s *M/V Virginia G* (*Panama/Guinea-Bissau*), Merits, Judgment of 14 April 2014, *ITLOS Reports* 2014 ('*Virginia G*').

t *ARA Libertad* (*Argentina v. Ghana*), Provisional Measures, Order of 15 December 2012, *ITLOS Reports* 2012 ('*ARA Libertad*, Provisional Measures').

u *SRFC Advisory Opinion*.

TABLE 1 List of ITLOS cases (*cont.*)

Case number	Name	Type/Outcome
22	*Arctic Sunrise (Netherlands v. Russian Federation)*[v]	Provisional measures
23	*Delimitation of the Maritime Boundary between Ghana and Côte d'Ivoire in the Atlantic Ocean (Ghana/Côte d'Ivoire)*[w]	Provisional measures; decision on merits
24	*Enrica Lexie (Italy v. India)*[x]	Provisional measures
25	*M/V Norstar (Panama v. Italy)*[y]	Preliminary objections; decision on merits
26	*Detention of Three Ukrainian Naval Vessels (Ukraine v. Russian Federation)*[z]	Provisional measures
27	*M/T San Padre Pio (Switzerland v. Nigeria)*[aa]	Provisional measures
28	*Delimitation of the Maritime Boundary between Mauritius and Maldives in the Indian Ocean (Mauritius/Maldives)*[ab]	Preliminary objections; decision on merits
29	*M/T San Padre Pio (No. 2) (Switzerland/Nigeria)*[ac]	Settled; proceedings discontinued

v *Arctic Sunrise (Netherlands v. Russian Federation)*, Provisional Measures, Order of 22 November 2013, *ITLOS Reports* 2013 ('*Arctic Sunrise*, Provisional Measures').

w *Delimitation of the Maritime Boundary between Ghana and Côte d'Ivoire in the Atlantic Ocean (Ghana/Côte d'Ivoire)*, Provisional Measures, Order of 25 April 2015, *ITLOS Reports* 2015 ('*Ghana/Côte d'Ivoire*, Provisional Measures); *Delimitation of the Maritime Boundary between Ghana and Côte d'Ivoire in the Atlantic Ocean (Ghana/Côte d'Ivoire)*, Merits, Judgment of 23 September 2017, *ITLOS Reports* 2017 ('*Ghana/Côte d'Ivoire*, Merits').

x *Enrica Lexie (Italy v. India)*, Provisional Measures, Order of 24 August 2015, *ITLOS Reports* 2015 ('*Enrica Lexie*, ITLOS Provisional Measures').

y *M/V Norstar (Panama v. Italy)*, Preliminary Objections, Judgment of 4 November 2016, *ITLOS Reports* 2016 ('*Norstar*, Provisional Measures'); *M/V Norstar (Panama v. Italy)*, Merits, Judgment of 10 April 2019, *ITLOS Reports* 2019 ('*Norstar*, Merits').

z *Detention of Three Ukrainian Naval Vessels (Ukraine v. Russian Federation)*, Provisional Measures, Order of 25 May 2019, *ITLOS Reports* 2019 ('*Three Ukrainian Naval Vessels*').

aa *M/T San Padre Pio (Switzerland v. Nigeria)*, Provisional Measures, Order of 6 July 2019, *ITLOS Reports* 2019 ('*San Padre Pio*').

ab *Delimitation of the Maritime Boundary between Mauritius and Maldives in the Indian Ocean (Mauritius/Maldives)*, Preliminary Objections, Judgment of 28 January 2021, ITLOS Case No. 28 ('*Mauritius/Maldives*'); *Delimitation of the Maritime Boundary between Mauritius and Maldives in the Indian Ocean (Mauritius/Maldives)*, Judgment of 28 April 2023, ITLOS Case No. 28 ('*Mauritius/Maldives*, Merits').

ac *M/T San Padre Pio (No. 2) (Switzerland/Nigeria)*, Merits, Order 2021/6 of 29 December 2021 ('*San Padre Pio (No. 2)*').

TABLE 1 List of ITLOS cases (*cont.*)

Case number	Name	Type/Outcome
30	*M/T Heroic Idun (Marshall Islands v. Equatorial Guinea)*[ad]	Prompt release; proceedings discontinued
31	*Request for an Advisory Opinion submitted by the Commission of Small Island States on Climate Change and International Law*[ae]	Pending
32	*M/T Heroic Idun* (*No.* 2) (*Marshall Islands/ Equatorial Guinea*)[af]	Pending

ad *Heroic Idun (Marshall Islands v. Equatorial Guinea)*, Prompt Release, Order 2022/3 of 15 November 2022.

ae *Request for an Advisory Opinion submitted by the Commission of Small Island States on Climate Change and International Law* (*Request for an Advisory Opinion submitted to the Tribunal*), ITLOS Case No. 31.

af *The M/T "Heroic Idun"* (*No.* 2) *Case* (Marshall Islands/Equatorial Guinea), Order of 27 April 2023.

1.4 *Proceedings before Annex VII Tribunals*

There have been 15 cases that proceeded as Annex VII arbitrations, with two of those cases pending at time of writing. Both pending cases concern disputes between Ukraine and the Russian Federation: a decision on jurisdiction has been issued in *Detention of Ukrainian Naval Vessels and Servicemen*, with the proceedings now moving to the merits phase. Further, a judgment is due on the merits in *Coastal State Rights in the Black Sea, Sea of Azov, and Kerch Strait*.

Among the remaining cases, four were terminated before decisions on jurisdiction or merits: *MOX Plant*, *Land Reclamation*, *ARA Libertad*, and *Atlanto-Scandian Herring*. The *Southern Bluefin Tuna* cases were dismissed for lack of jurisdiction. Of the remaining eight cases resolved through Annex VII arbitration, three primarily concerned maritime boundary delimitations: *Guyana v. Suriname*, *Barbados v. Trinidad and Tobago*, *Bay of Bengal Maritime Boundary Arbitration* (*Bangladesh v. India*). A further three cases addressed the detention of vessels and/or crew: *Arctic Sunrise*, *Duzgit Integrity* and *Enrica Lexie*. The *Chagos Marine Protected Area* ('*Chagos MPA*') and *South China Sea* arbitrations involved a range of distinct issues under UNCLOS; both those cases had an underlying territorial sovereignty dispute that could not be resolved through the proceedings instituted pursuant to Part XV of UNCLOS. Table 2 below lists the cases referred to Annex VII arbitration and indicates the status of the case.

TABLE 2 List of Annex VII arbitrations

Case	Name	Status
1	*Southern Bluefin Tuna (Australia v. Japan; New Zealand v. Japan)*[a]	Decision on lack of jurisdiction
2	*MOX Plant (Ireland v. United Kingdom)*[b]	Provisional measures; proceedings discontinued
3	*Land Reclamation by Singapore in and around the Straits of Johor (Malaysia v. Singapore)*[c]	Settled; award on agreed terms
4	*Guyana v. Suriname*[d]	Decision on merits; maritime boundary delimitation
5	*Barbados v. Trinidad and Tobago*[e]	Decision on merits; maritime boundary delimitation
6	*Bay of Bengal Maritime Boundary Arbitration (Bangladesh v. India)*[f]	Decision on merits; maritime boundary delimitation
7	*Chagos Marine Protected Area (Mauritius v. United Kingdom)*[g]	Decision on merits
8	*ARA Libertad (Argentina v. Ghana)*[h]	Settled; proceedings discontinued.

a *Southern Bluefin Tuna (New Zealand v. Japan; Australia v. Japan)*, Jurisdiction and Admissibility, Decision of 4 August 2000, 23 *RIAA* 1 ('*Southern Bluefin Tuna*, Jurisdiction and Admissibility').

b *MOX Plant (Ireland v. United Kingdom)*, Provisional Measures, Order No. 3 of 24 June 2003, PCA Case No. 2002–01 ('*MOX Plant*, Annex VII Provisional Measures'); *MOX Plant (Ireland v. United Kingdom)*, Termination of Proceedings, Order No. 6 of 6 June 2008, PCA Case No. 2002–01.

c *Land Reclamation by Singapore in and around the Straits of Johor (Malaysia v. Singapore)*, Merits, Award on Agreed Terms of 1 September 2005, 27 *RIAA* 133 ('*Land Reclamation*, Merits').

d *Guyana v. Suriname*, Merits, Award of 17 September 2007, 30 *RIAA* 1 ('*Guyana v. Suriname*').

e *Barbados v. Trinidad and Tobago*, Merits, Award of 11 April 2006, 27 *RIAA* 147 ('*Barbados v. Trinidad and Tobago*').

f *Bay of Bengal Maritime Boundary Arbitration (Bangladesh v. India)*, Merits, Award of 7 July 2014, PCA Case No. 2010–16 ('*Bay of Bengal Arbitration*').

g *Chagos Marine Protected Area Arbitration (Mauritius v. United Kingdom)*, Merits, Award of 18 March 2015, PCA Case No. 2011–03 ('*Chagos MPA*').

h *ARA Libertad (Argentina v. Ghana)*, Termination of Proceedings, Order of 11 November 2013, PCA Case No. 2013–11 ('*ARA Libertad*, Annex VII').

TABLE 2 List of Annex VII arbitrations (*cont.*)

Case	Name	Status
9	*South China Sea Arbitration* (*Philippines v. China*)[i]	Decision on jurisdiction and admissibility; decision on merits
10	*Atlanto-Scandian Herring* (*Denmark in respect of the Faroe Islands v. the European Union*)[j]	Settled; proceedings discontinued.
11	*Arctic Sunrise* (*Netherlands v. Russian Federation*)[k]	Decisions on jurisdiction, merits, and compensation
12	*Duzgit Integrity* (*Malta v. São Tomé and Príncipe*)[l]	Decisions on merits and compensation
13	*Enrica Lexie* (*Italy v. India*)[m]	Provisional measures; decision on merits
14	*Coastal State Rights in the Black Sea, Sea of Azov, and Kerch Strait* (*Ukraine v. Russian Federation*)[n]	Decision on jurisdiction; merits phase pending

i *South China Sea Arbitration* (*Philippines v. China*), Jurisdiction and Admissibility, Award of 29 October 2015 ('*South China Sea*, Jurisdiction and Admissibility'), PCA Case No. 2013–19; *South China Sea Arbitration* (*Philippines v. China*), Merits, Award of 12 July 2016, PCA Case No. 2013–19 ('*South China Sea*').

j *Atlanto-Scandian Herring* (*Denmark in respect of the Faroe Islands v. the European Union*), Termination Order of 23 September 2014, PCA Case No. 2013–30.

k *Arctic Sunrise* (*Netherlands v. Russian Federation*), Jurisdiction, Award of 26 November 2014, PCA Case No. 2014–02 ('*Arctic Sunrise*, Jurisdiction'); *Arctic Sunrise* (*Netherlands v. Russian Federation*), Merits, Award of 14 August 2015, PCA Case No. 2014–02 ('*Arctic Sunrise*, Merits'); *Arctic Sunrise* (*Netherlands v Russian Federation*), Compensation, Award of 10 July 2017, PCA Case No. 2014–02 ('*Arctic Sunrise*, Compensation').

l *Duzgit Integrity* (*Malta v. São Tomé and Príncipe*), Merits, Award of 5 September 2016, PCA Case No. 2014–07 ('*Duzgit Intergity*, Merits'); *Duzgit Integrity* (*Malta v. São Tomé and Príncipe*), Reparation, Award of 18 December 2019, PCA Case No. 2014–07 ('*Duzgit Integrity*, Compensation').

m *Enrica Lexie* (*Italy v. India*), Provisional Measures, Order of 29 April 2016, PCA Case No. 2015–28 ('*Enrica Lexie*, Provisional Measures'); *Enrica Lexie* (*Italy v. India*), Merits, Award of 21 May 2020, PCA Case No. 2015–28 ('*Enrica Lexie*, Merits').

n *Coastal State Rights in the Black Sea, Sea of Azov, and Kerch Strait* (*Ukraine v. Russian Federation*), Preliminary Objections, Award of 21 February 2020, PCA Case No. 2017–16 ('*Coastal State Rights*').

TABLE 2 List of Annex VII arbitrations (*cont.*)

Case	Name	Status
15	*Detention of Ukrainian Naval Vessels and Servicemen (Ukraine v. Russian Federation)*[o]	Decision on jurisdiction; merits phase pending

o *Detention of Ukrainian Naval Vessels and Servicemen (Ukraine v. Russian Federation)*, Preliminary Objections, Award of 27 June 2022, PCA Case No. 2019–28 ('*Detention of Ukrainian Naval Vessels and Servicemen*').

1.5 *Outline of Study*

This study assesses the judgments resulting from Part XV proceedings under UNCLOS in terms of compliance with those decisions. We have relied on publicly available information and have predominantly been limited to English-language and some French-language sources. We have sought to rely primarily on government statements, especially reports made to ITLOS or in the course of UNCLOS dispute settlement proceedings. In addition, newspaper accounts and some secondary sources have been utilised. Best endeavours have thus been used to ensure the accuracy of our findings, but we acknowledge possible limitations.

To frame the discussion that follows, Chapter 2 provides an explanation as to what is meant by compliance and what is perhaps an 'impact' or 'outcome' of the judgment albeit not a compliance issue. Chapter 3 examines the prompt release decisions of ITLOS, which have been issued further to the procedure set out in Article 292 of UNCLOS. Chapter 4 addresses compliance with provisional measures orders, primarily issued by ITLOS but also in several instances by Annex VII arbitral tribunals. Chapter 5 considers the maritime boundary delimitation cases decided by ITLOS, either sitting as a full court or in its special chambers, and before Annex VII arbitral tribunals. Both fora have also considered cases concerning the arrest and detention of vessels and their crew, which are examined for compliance in Chapter 6. Chapter 7 addresses compliance with the *Chagos MPA* and *South China Sea* arbitrations across the diverse issues and orders set out in those judgments.

In addition to cases before ITLOS and Annex VII arbitral tribunals, there has been one compulsory conciliation resulting from the operation of the optional exclusion of maritime boundary delimitation disputes from adjudication or arbitration under Article 298(1)(a) of UNCLOS, the *Timor Sea Conciliation* between Australia and Timor-Leste.[35] Chapter 5 addresses the outcomes from the *Timor Sea Conciliation* when assessing compliance with maritime boundary delimitation cases. Although the report of the Conciliation Commission sets out recommendations and does not issue a binding decision,[36] this section discusses what steps were taken by the parties further to the recommendations of the Commission.

The concluding Chapter assesses this compliance practice and contemplates this activity in light of the purposes of UNCLOS dispute settlement. Ultimately, any assessment of compliance needs to have a firm frame on the purpose of resolving disputes under UNCLOS. Conceived narrowly, the compliance record is not perfect but still evinces numerous successes. Contemplated more broadly, there should rightly be an appreciation of both the opportunities and limitations of settling disputes under Part XV of UNCLOS.

2 Understanding Compliance

2.1 *Introduction*

Louis Henkin famously asserted that "almost all nations observe almost all principles of international law and almost all of their obligations almost all of the time".[37] However, as Chayes and Chayes have noted, this assertion "is frequently repeated without anyone ... supplying any empirical evidence to support it".[38] This lack of empirical evidence is to be expected: assessing compliance with the decisions of international courts and tribunals is a task fraught with difficulty. A lack of publicly available information as to the actions taken by States in relation to judgments of international courts and tribunals complicates the task of determining if or how a State has complied. As Sir Robert Jennings observed, it is "ironic that the ... business [of international courts and tribunals] up to the delivery of judgment is lavish in detail, but it is not at all easy to find out what happened afterwards".[39] Even where such information is

35 *Conciliation between the Democratic Republic of Timor-Leste and the Commonwealth of Australia*, Report and Recommendations of the Compulsory Conciliation Commission, 9 May 2018, PCA Case No. 2016–10 ('*Timor Sea Conciliation*').

36 Consistent with the requirements under UNCLOS, Annex V, Section 2.

37 L. Henkin, *How Nations Behave* (Columbia University Press, 1979), 47.

38 A. Chayes and A. Chayes, 'On Compliance' (1993) 47(2) *International Organization* 175, 177.

39 R. Jennings, 'Presentation', in C. Peck and R. S. K. Lee (eds), *Increasing the Effectiveness of the International Court of Justice: Proceedings of the ICJ/UNITAR Colloquium to Celebrate the 50th Anniversary of the Court* (Kluwer, 1997), 81. See also S. Rosenne, *The Law and Practice of the International Court 1920–1996*, vol. 1, (5th edn., Brill, 2016), 202 (noting that

publicly available, the actions of States do not necessarily lend themselves to empirical study.[40] As complicated, multi-faceted and inherently political entities, States may say one thing but do another; determining which expressions to give weight to in assessing compliance is not always evident.

In addition, decisions of international courts and tribunals may be nuanced and even ambiguous, raising questions as to how compliance can be achieved, let alone measured. Further, there are many factors outside the control of international courts and tribunals that may impact compliance.[41] These may include the broader geopolitical environment in which the States party to the dispute operate, domestic political factors, and both the willingness and capacity of the State to comply with the orders issued. To this end, it is apt to observe that "the issuance of the decision does not tell the whole story of a judicial proceeding".[42]

It is with an awareness of these limitations and methodological difficulties that we proceed with assessing compliance with the decisions of UNCLOS dispute resolution bodies. At the outset, two preliminary questions beg further examination. First, to what extent does compliance matter and why is it worthy of academic focus? Second, what is compliance and how can it be measured? In this Chapter, each is discussed in turn.

2.2 *Why Compliance Matters*

Debates as to the necessity of compliance and as to how and why States comply with international law are well-rehearsed and form part of the foundation of the discipline.[43] It is not our intention to wade into these debates in this

---

"in general, a striking feature of the literature dealing with judicial settlement of international disputes is its comparative disinterest in the post-adjudication stage").

40 Chayes and Chayes (n. 38), 177 ("A moment's reflection shows that it would not be easy to devise a statistical protocol that would generate such evidence. For example, how would Iraq's unbroken respect for the borders of Turkey, Jordan and Saudi Arabia count in the reckoning against the invasions of Iran and Kuwait?").

41 See, e.g., K. J. Alter, 'Do International Courts Enhance Compliance with International Law?' (2003) 25 *Review of Asian and Pacific Studies* 51, 63–72.

42 C. Giorgetti, 'What Happens after a Judgment is Given? Judgment Compliance and the Performance of International Courts and Tribunals' in Theresa Squatrito, et al. (eds), *The Performance of International Courts and Tribunals* (Cambridge University Press, 2018) 324, 324.

43 See, e.g, H. H. Koh, 'Why Do Nations Obey International Law?' (1997) 106(8) *Yale Law Journal* 2599; A. T. Guzman, 'A Compliance-Based Theory of International Law' (2002) 90 *California Law Review* 1825; B. Simmons, 'International Law and State Behavior: Commitment and Compliance in International Monetary Affairs' (2000) 94 *American Political Science Review* 819; Chayes and Chayes (n. 2); E. A. Posner and J. C. Yoo, 'Judicial Independence in International Tribunals' (2005) 93(1) *California Law Review* 1, 20–21.

study. However, it would be remiss not to briefly evaluate the utility of such a study into compliance and other outcomes in UNCLOS dispute settlement and to indicate how compliance-based studies can assist in understanding the UNCLOS dispute settlement system more generally.

On the view of some classical realists and positivists,[44] international law is without value in the absence of compliance or enforcement.[45] To this end, subjecting the decisions of international courts and tribunals to study through the framework of compliance is necessary to both understand international law and to legitimise its existence. The same may be said to be true of the law of the sea and Part XV of UNCLOS. As Guzman has argued:

> [C]ompliance is one of the most central questions in international law … Without a theory of compliance, we cannot examine the role of treaties, customary international law, or other agreements. Nor can we consider how to improve the functioning of the international legal system, or develop a workable theory of international legal and regulatory cooperation.[46]

Other scholars disagree. For instance, Howse and Teitel have argued that a focus on compliance in international law scholarship

> obfuscates the character of international legal normativity, tending to ignore the centrality of interpretation to the generation of legal meaning … Looking at the aspirations of international law through the lens of rule compliance leads to inadequate scrutiny and understanding of the diverse complex purposes and projects that multiple actors impose and transpose on international legality, and especially a tendency to oversimplify if not distort the relation of international law to politics.[47]

---

44 We say 'some' as even some of the most influential positivists reject that view. See, e.g., H. L. A. Hart, *The Concept of Law* (Oxford University Press, 1961) 217 (observing that "[t]o argue that international law is not binding because of its lack of organized sanctions is tacitly to accept the analysis of obligation contained in the theory that law is essentially a matter of orders backed by threats").

45 The *locus classicus* for this view being H. J. Morgenthau, *Politics Among Nations* (A. A. Knopf, 1948). See also discussion in R. Howse and R. Teitel, 'Beyond Compliance: Rethinking Why International Law Really Matters' (2010) 1(2) *Global Policy* 127, 127–130.

46 Guzman (n. 43), 1873. For other approvals of the value of compliance-based studies, see Simmons (n. 45), at 91 (arguing that "research into the question of compliance … represents a substantial advance in the study of international law").

47 Howse and Teitel (n. 9), 128. See also K. Raustiala, 'Compliance and Effectiveness in International Regulatory Cooperation' (2000) 3 *Case Western Reserve Journal of*

Certainly, both views have merit. Guzman's comment reflects a view that compliance is inherent and fundamental in the operation of any legal system. Yet, whether a State undertakes certain action because of a judgment is not the only measure of the impact or influence of that judgment. Judgments of international courts and tribunals go beyond the dispute as between the parties and may have varied effects for actors in the international system.[48] These impacts include the creation of benchmarks for private decision-making, the transformation of policies into legal norms, and new approaches to the interpretation of both domestic and international law.[49] As Huneeus has observed:

> Rulings enunciate and clarify rules; they give civil society groups discursive tools with which to pursue their goals; they may influence how other judges and political actors frame an issue; and they may influence bargaining among actors 'in the shadow of the law' – all regardless of compliance.[50]

Compliance does not alone determine the influence of international institutions,[51] nor is it necessarily indicative of progress or success of the particular institution.[52] Indeed, strict and total compliance may never have been

International Law 387, 388 (arguing that "prevailing analytic focus on compliance is often misplaced and even counterproductive"), 397 ("evidence of compliance without more is largely meaningless ..."). Raustiala instead advocates for a better understanding of *effectiveness*; B. Kingsbury, 'The Concept of Compliance as a Function of Competing Conceptions of International Law' (1998) 19 *Michigan Journal of International Law* 345.

48 See N. Klein and K. Parlett, *Judging the Law of the Sea: Judicial Contributions to the UN Convention on the Law of the Sea* (Oxford University Press, 2022), 31–33.

49 See generally Howse and Teitel (n. 45), 130–133; T. Ginsburg, 'International Judicial Lawmaking' (University of Illinois College of Law, Law and Economics Working Paper No. 26), 14 (noting that "[i]f enough states change their strategy in response to the judicial decision, it can become a new equilibrium of customary international law, even if the particular party to the dispute does not comply").

50 A. Huneeus, 'Compliance with Judgments and Decisions' in C. P. Romano, K. J. Alter and Y. Shany (eds), *The Oxford Handbook of International Adjudication* (Oxford University Press, 2014) 437, 440; L. L. Martin, 'Against Compliance' in J. L. Dunoff and M. A. Pollack (eds), *Interdisciplinary Perspectives on International Law and International Relations* (Cambridge University Press, 2012), 608 ("A more productive turn would be to move away from studies of compliance").

51 K. J. Alter, 'The International Court of Justice in Comparison: Understanding the Court's Limited Influence' (2021) 21 *Melbourne Journal of International Law* 676, 688. Alter instead prefers a measure of effectiveness in assessing international courts.

52 As Guzman has noted:
"a high rate of compliance with tribunal rulings does not necessarily imply that the tribunal is encouraging compliance with the underlying legal obligation. A tribunal could get a

the goal of the States party to the agreement in question.[53] In the context of UNCLOS dispute settlement, where a judgment has articulated a particular interpretation of an UNCLOS provision, it may be queried whether the parties' subsequent conduct conforms to that interpretation. Moreover, do other States alter their behaviour or decisions in light of an elucidated interpretation of UNCLOS? Determining the extent of these other results is difficult to demonstrate as an empirical matter,[54] though is as significant as understanding whether there was compliance with the judgment in question.

It is not our intention in this study to conflate questions of *compliance* with the *effectiveness* of the UNCLOS dispute settlement system.[55] In many cases, an international court or tribunal can be said to be effective notwithstanding

---

> high rate of compliance, for example, by ruling in favor of the defendant in every case, or perhaps by ruling in favor of the more powerful party, regardless of the underlying merits, but this obviously serves no useful purpose. Slightly more realistically, a tribunal could ignore the relevant legal questions and simply seek to mimic the result that the parties would achieve through politics. This would lead to a high rate of compliance but would not support the relevant legal rule."

A. T. Guzman, 'International Tribunals: A Rational Choice Analysis' (2008) 157 *University of Pennsylvania Law Review* 171, 187.

53 Ibid., 189, observing that:

> it is not the case that parties to an international agreement always want to maximise compliance. If they did, they would always enter into agreements with robust dispute resolution, including some form of sanctioning mechanism. States sometimes prefer to stop short of the strongest possible enforcement scheme.

54 Huneeus (n. 50), 440.

55 The distinction (or lack thereof) between compliance and effectiveness has been subject to great debate. See, e.g., L. R. Helfer and A. Slaughter, 'Toward a Theory of Effective Supranational Adjudication' (1997) 107 *Yale Law Journal* 273, 278, defining effective adjudication in terms of a court's basic ability "to compel or cajole compliance with its judgments". Further, "In the supranational context, effective adjudication depends on a supranational tribunal's ability to secure such compliance by convincing domestic government institutions, directly and through pressure from private litigants, to use their power on its behalf".

But note that Helfer and Slaughter later expressed a different opinion in L. R. Helfer and A-M. Slaughter, 'Why States Create International Tribunals: A Response to Professors Posner and Yoo' (2005) 93 *California Law Review* 899, 918 ('Why States Create International Tribunals'). ICJ President Joan E. Donoghue suggests a more nuanced approach, describing compliance with ICJ judgments as a 'partial answer' to questions of effectiveness, but an unsatisfactory one in and of itself: J. E. Donoghue, 'The Effectiveness of the International Court of Justice' (2014) 108 *Proceedings of the American Society of International Law Annual Conference* 114, 114. See also Guzman (n. 43), 187; Raustiala (n. 45), 391–394 (divorcing effectiveness and compliance); Martin (n. 50), 591; L. R. Helfer, 'The Effectiveness of International Adjudicators' in C. P. Romano, K. J. Alter and Y. Shany (eds), *The Oxford Handbook of International Adjudication* (Oxford University Press, 2014) 464, 468 (arguing that the "conflation of compliance and effectiveness" may be "problematic").

the fact that the decision in question may not have been fully complied with as between the parties to the dispute.[56] For instance, the judgment may result in policy reforms by other States subject to the international court or tribunal's jurisdiction,[57] perhaps leading to the crystallisation of new rules of customary international law[58] or some observable change in behaviour by the State in question. Such outcomes are noteworthy notwithstanding, or even in spite of, a lack of compliance. Similarly, an international court or tribunal may be *ineffective* even where its judgments are complied with where those judgments merely reflect existing State practice, or where they "mirror the outcomes that States would have obtained through negotiation and politics".[59] Indeed, as Shany has noted, "a low-aiming court, issuing minimalist remedies, may generate a high level of compliance but have little impact on the state of the world".[60] As a result, it is apt to acknowledge, as Neyer and Wolf argue, that "[p]erfect compliance, imperfect implementation and zero effectiveness ... are not necessarily mutually exclusive".[61] It is for this reason that this study not only focusses on compliance, but also considers some other outcomes that arise from UNCLOS dispute settlement.

Notwithstanding the above, an emphasis on compliance is still warranted. It is evident that compliance does bear practical effect; the relevant debate is over the extent of that effect. All courts and judges seek compliance.[62] If an international court or tribunal's judgments are consistently not complied with, "other states will eventually conclude that the tribunal is biased or defective and refuse to use it themselves", as there is little use in referring a dispute to an international court or tribunal that is unable to secure acceptable levels of compliance with its judgments.[63] Further, a lack of compliance with

56 See, e.g., Helfer (n. 19), 470ff. (Helfer described this concept as *erga omnes* effectiveness).

57 Ibid.

58 Raustiala (n. 45), 394.

59 Helfer (n. 55), 469; Helfer and Slaughter, 'Why States Create International Tribunals' (n. 55), 941 (explaining that, in bilateral interstate disputes, international courts "may operate as an extension of nonlegal, diplomatic methods of ... compliance inducement"). See also Raustiala (n. 45), 397–99.

60 Y. Shany, 'Assessing the Effectiveness of International Courts: A Goal-Based Approach' (2012) 106 *American Journal of International Law* 225, 227.

61 J. Neyer and D. Wolf, 'The Analysis of Compliance with International Rules: Definitions, Variables and Methodology' in M. Zürn and C. Joerges (eds), *Law and Governance in Postnational Europe* (Cambridge University Press, 2005) 40, 41–42.

62 K. J. Alter, 'Agents or Trustees? International Courts in their Political Context' (2008) 14(1) *European Journal of International Relations* 33, 46, citing M. Shapiro, *Courts: A Comparative Political Analysis* (University of Chicago Press, 1981), 5–8.

63 Posner and Yoo (n. 43), 21, 72. See also B. N. Patel, 'Recommendations on the Enhancement of the Role and Effectiveness of the International Court of Justice and State Practice: The

an international court or tribunal's judgments is likely to "impair the dignity of [the international court or tribunal] and raise doubts as to [its] judicial role".[64] Compliance is also said to determine the significance of the tribunal in question as a political actor.[65] On the macro scale, a lack of compliance with the judgments of courts and tribunals constituted under UNCLOS may in turn undermine the legitimacy of the Convention, as well as international law generally.[66] Consequently, a focus on compliance is still warranted, though caution should be exercised so as not to regard compliance as the sole or determinative indicum of effectiveness of the UNCLOS dispute settlement system.

2.3 *Defining and Measuring Compliance*

As a general matter, compliance is concerned with matching behaviour to a particular rule.[67] Some commentators consider that compliance is not simply a matching exercise, but rather requires the presence of a causal link such that the behaviour occurs *because* of the existence of the rule.[68] Compliance may be most readily discerned when the rule causes a change in behaviour;[69] such as where a State found to be in long-term violation of its treaty

---

Gap between Recommendation and Practice (1971–2006)' (2007) 11 *Singapore Yearbook of International Law* 99, 122 (noting that a record of compliance makes it more likely that States will be motivated to come to an international court or tribunal to resolve the dispute in question).

64 *Armed Activities on the Territory of the Congo* (*Democratic Republic of the Congo v. Uganda*), Provisional Measures, Order of 1 July 2000, *ICJ Reports* 2000, 132 [6] (Declaration of Judge Shigeru Oda).

65 Helfer and Slaughter, 'Toward a Theory of Effective Supranational Adjudication' (n. 55), 283.

66 See, e.g., T. M. Franck, *The Power of Legitimacy Among Nations* (Oxford University Press, 1990), 29–33.

67 See, e.g., O. R. Young, *Compliance and Public Authority* (John Hopkins University Press, 1979), 3 ("Compliance can be said to occur when the actual behavior of a given subject conforms to prescribed behavior"); Raustiala (n. 45), 391 (arguing that "[c]ompliance generally refers to a state of conformity or identity between an actor's behavior and a specified rule"). But see J. von Stein, 'The Engines of Compliance' in J. L. Dunoff and M. A. Pollack (eds), *Interdisciplinary Perspectives on International Law and International Relations: The State of the Art* (Cambridge University Press, 2012) 477, 493 (noting criticisms and observing more generally that the view one has as to compliance depends on one's theory of law).

68 Huneeus (n. 50), 438–439; D. Hawkins and W. Jacoby, 'Partial Compliance: A Comparison of the European and Inter-American Courts of Human Rights' (2010) 6(1) *Journal of International Law and International Relations* 35, 39 (arguing that "[t]o say that an actor complies with the rule is not to imply that the rule causes the behaviour", and proposing a criteria of "effectiveness").

69 This approach was followed by Llamzon in his study of ICJ decisions. See A. P. Llamzon, 'Jurisdiction and Compliance in Recent Decisions of the International Court of Justice' (2007) 18(5) *European Journal of International Law* 815, 823.

obligations changes its practices following a judgment of an international court or tribunal.[70] Yet, in many cases, proving the causal link may not always be evident.[71]

In the context of judicial compliance, Shany defined judgment compliance as "a causal relationship between the contents of judicial decisions and state practice, leading to a convergence of the two."[72] In his assessment, which is utilised in this study, an examination is required as to whether State practice has changed to align, purposely, with the judgment of a court or tribunal constituted under UNCLOS. The shift in State behaviour or specific State action that is prompted by an international court or tribunal's judgment allows for an assessment of 'compliance'. However, as acknowledged in the previous section, compliance is not the only benchmark for assessing international courts and tribunals.

As opposed to compliance, there may be defiance in the face of a judgment whereby a judgment is firmly rejected, possibly denounced as invalid, and there is an explicit refusal to comply.[73] Such non-compliance should not be confused with mere disapproval, nor should it be inferred from the negative reaction of a State to a judgment without more. Non-compliance "requires more than initial disapproval; it requires a complete, unceasing refutation of the judgment from which the defiant party has not recanted."[74] This reaction was ostensibly

70 As Hawkins and Jacoby (n. 68) observe at 39–40:

> When a country persists in behaviour long enough for an international court to rule against that country's practices, and the country subsequently changes its practices, we assume that the court's ruling helped to trigger the change in behavior, even if other factors may also have been important ... Compliance in these circumstances is very unlikely to be the result of chance ... any resulting behavioural changes after an adverse court ruling can suggest court effectiveness.

71 Though note that there is argument as to whether proving such a causal link is even possible. For instance, Raustiala (n. 45) argues at 397–398 that "[e]valuating and improving compliance requires data about state behavior plus a theory and analysis of the causality of compliance, coupled with a counterfactual analysis ... the likely course of events if the ... particular institution had not existed. In sum, to speak of compliance is to be agnostic about causality".

See also Martin (n. 14), 591–2 ("compliance is a legal concept that is unusually ill-suited to the central social-scientific pursuit: the identification and measurement of causal effects"), 606 ("compliance and causal effect are independent concepts that do not necessarily covary").

72 Shany (n. 60), 261. Other scholars state the definition differently. See, e.g., Llamzon (n. 69), who argued that compliance "should consist of the acceptance of the judgment as final *and* reasonable performance in good faith of any binding obligation": at 822.

73 Llamzon (n. 69), 823.

74 H. L. Jones, 'Why Comply? An Analysis of Trends in Compliance with Judgments of the International Court of Justice since *Nicaragua*' (2012) 12(1) *Chicago-Kent Journal of International and Comparative Law* 57, 59. See also Chayes and Chayes (n. 38), 187 (in

manifested in China's response to the *South China Sea* arbitration.[75] The value of non-compliance is debated; "non-compliance can be part of a successful strategy", such as where that non-compliance galvanises domestic action that results in a change in the State's behaviour.[76]

Falling between full compliance and defiance are instances where a State has made some effort to comply with the judgment but been unsuccessful in full implementation despite bona fide effort.[77] Such instances may arise where actual compliance is, for reasons external to the State's control, not possible or desirable, such as where the *dispositif* is ambiguous,[78] or where the State lacks the capacity to fulfill the undertakings therein.[79] This idea of good faith compliance may further indicate that when a State has acted in a way that undermines implicit assumptions or expectations with a court or tribunal's order or judgment then there has been a failure at full compliance. For example, a vessel may be returned as was required following dispute settlement

---

the context of compliance with international instruments, asserting that "[i]f the [S]tate's decision whether or not to comply with a treaty is the result of a calculation of costs and benefits, as the realists assert, the implication is that noncompliance is the premeditated and deliberate violation of a treaty obligation"), 204 (asserting that noncompliance is "a deviant rather than an expected behaviour ... endemic rather than deliberate").

75 As recounted in B. Hayton, 'Denounce but Comply: China's Response to the South China Sea Arbitration Ruling' (2017) 18(2) *Georgetown Journal of International Affairs* 104; F. Zhang, 'Assessing China's Response to the South China Sea Arbitration' (2017) 71(4) *Australian Journal of International Affairs* 440; P. Jakhar, 'Whatever Happened to the South China Sea Ruling?' 12 July 2021, *The Interpreter*, available at: <https://www.lowyinstitute.org/the-interpreter/whatever-happened-south-china-sea-ruling>. The extent of defiance is explored in Chapter 7.

76 See, e.g., M. A. Levy, 'European Acid Rain: The Power of Tote-Board Diplomacy' in P. M. Haas, et al. (eds), *Institutions for the Earth: Sources of Effective Environmental Protection* (MIT Press, 1993) 75, 77.

77 Jones (n. 74), 59–60.

78 Chayes and Chayes (n. 38) note, in some cases, "even conscientious legal advice may not avoid issues of compliance": at 190. See also R-C. Liwanga and C. Turner, 'Demystifying the Legitimacy of International Tribunals: Case Study of the International Court of Justice and its Decisions on Armed Activities in the Congo' (2021) 35(3) *Emory International Law Review* 413, 435–436 (discussing this point in relation to *Armed Activities on the Territory of the Congo* at the ICJ).

79 In which case, a question arises as to whether compliance occurs where the State does all that is necessary legislatively and administratively to attempt compliance, or whether compliance requires that the intended result actually manifest. As Chayes and Chayes (n. 38) note at 194:

"the construction of a domestic regulatory apparatus is not a simple or mechanical task. It entails choices and requires scientific and technical judgment, bureaucratic capability, and fiscal resources. Even developed Western [S]tates have not been able to construct such systems with confidence they will achieve the desired objective."

proceedings, but stripped of equipment or damaged while in possession of the respondent State. At most, the latter situation could be considered as 'nominal compliance'.

There may additionally be situations of what might be termed 'part compliance', where a State has responded to some of the requirements of the judgment but not others. Part compliance should not be conceived of as a transitional state toward full compliance, but rather as an independent end point on a continuum of compliance.[80] To this end, non-compliance is "a matter of increment and degree";[81] it should not be conceived of as binary but rather as a "complex phenomenon where states commonly engage in varying types of partial compliance".[82] While anything less than full compliance puts a State in breach of its obligations under international law, States often tolerate part compliance. A State's decision to accept part compliance is likely to depend on a range of factors including the nature of the behaviour involved, the wrong alleged and the specific facts of the case (including the parties to it, their histories, and their level of relative power in the international system).[83]

Measuring compliance may be straightforward in some instances: a judgment determines that a ship must be released, and the ship is released; or that compensation or a bond must be paid, and the amount of money required is paid. In these instances, the ship may not have been released nor the monies paid *but for* the order of the international court or tribunal, which satisfies Shany's causal link approach. The analysis in this study indicates that these sorts of results do occur in UNCLOS dispute settlement. However, in some instances, information as to whether compensation has been paid may not be readily available.[84]

There are also instances where compliance is difficult to measure, which especially emerges in situations of part compliance. As Simmons notes, "compliance is rarely a transparent, binary choice. Actors' behavior is often intentionally ambiguous, dilatory, or confusing, and frequently takes place

80 Hawkins and Jacoby (n. 68), 36, 79ff (discussing 'low motion compliance' in the latter).

81 Llamzon (n. 69), 823.

82 Hawkins and Jacoby (n. 68), 40; Guzman (n. 52), 188–189 ("Notice that a tribunal's ability to encourage compliance with underlying legal rules is not a simple binary measure ... Effectiveness, then, is inevitably a relative measure"), 216 ("The defendant can offer partial compliance, and unless the complainant objects, the defendant will be perceived to be in compliance").

83 See Chayes and Chayes (n. 38), 201ff.

84 This difficulty emerged most frequently in relation to cases involving the detention of vessels and crew. See discussion in Chapter 6.

under conditions in which verification of compliance is difficult".[85] States may profusely reject a judgment but still take positive steps to implement some of the orders. Questions arise as to whether such steps can be considered as compliance with a judgment, particularly where the State asserts that the steps taken were the result of some other process, such as diplomatic negotiation. States may also, in some instances, lack the capacity to comply with the order of an international court or tribunal, even where they would like to, such as where the level of compensation ordered is too high or where internal political processes make full compliance difficult.

Separately, the task of assessing compliance is not made easier by the nature of judging. Judgments are not always exact, and orders may be framed in broad, rather than prescriptive, terms; for instance, orders for States to 'cooperate' to a particular end. In such circumstances, the necessary steps to achieve compliance may be open to varied interpretations, complicating assessment of the extent to which a State has complied with the judgment in question. Part compliance is thus the more likely result – or perhaps some form of good faith or otherwise nominal compliance. International courts and tribunals are unlikely to be able to assist in clarifying the steps required for a State to be fully compliant; they are generally not concerned with such clarifications or with assessing post-judgment compliance.[86] In both regards, the issue is one of causation.

2.4 *Conclusion*

In examining compliance with decisions emanating from courts or tribunals constituted for UNCLOS dispute settlement, we hope to contribute in some small way to discussions about the extent to which compliance matters and what impacts, if any, compliance (or a lack thereof) may have on the integrity of international dispute settlement. The examination of compliance following the issuance of judgments as a result of Part XV proceedings, as well as reflections on other outcomes of UNCLOS, may assist in discussions of 'effectiveness' or 'performance' of the different tribunals operating under UNCLOS.

The UNCLOS dispute settlement system is not often included in international dispute settlement studies, or only ITLOS is addressed without any

85 B. A. Simmons, 'Compliance with International Agreements' (1998) 1 *Annual Review of Political Science* 75, 79, citing Young (n. 31).

86 See, e.g., *Haya de la Torre (Colombia/Peru)*, Judgment, *ICJ Reports* 1951, 79. Though note that some international courts and tribunals do issue compliance reports, most notably the Inter-American Court of Human Rights and European Court of Human Rights (through the annual reports of the Committee of Ministers). See further Chapter 1.2.

account of the other dispute settlement fora available under UNCLOS.[87] Such omission, while notable, is explicable: in addition to difficulties with measuring and defining compliance, the number of cases concerning the interpretation and application of the Convention conducted outside the auspices of one standing institution like ITLOS makes collating and gleaning insights from such cases a more complex endeavour. In our view, accounting for the frequency of compliance in UNCLOS dispute settlement in varied fora may have a practical benefit for States weighing up advantages and disadvantages to proceeding to litigation to settle their law of the sea disputes. Importantly, this study seeks to fill a gap in understanding a fuller picture of dispute settlement under UNCLOS.

3 Prompt Release Proceedings

3.1 *Introduction to Prompt Release in UNCLOS Dispute Settlement*

Prompt release cases involve a distinct dispute settlement process under UNCLOS. In accordance with Article 292, a flag State may challenge the detention of its vessel and a failure to adhere to requirements to promptly release that vessel upon payment of a reasonable bond. When presented with an application for the prompt release of a vessel, the role of the international court or tribunal to which the application has been submitted is to assess the reasonableness of the bond or other financial security that has been set by the detaining State for the release of the vessel and, if necessary, revise it; or, where no bond has been set, set a reasonable bond itself.[88] The international court or tribunal is required to assess the application with expedition and in

87 See, e.g., T. Squatrito, O. R. Young, A. Follesdal and G. Ulfstein (eds), *The Performance of International Courts and Tribunals* (Cambridge University Press, 2018); I. de la Rasilla and J. Viñuales (eds), *Experiments in International Adjudication* (Cambridge University Press, 2018); D. Peat, *Comparative Reasoning in International Courts and Tribunals* (Cambridge University Press, 2019); Y. Shany, *Assessing the Effectiveness of International Courts* (Oxford University Press, 2014). Some of the general textbooks on international dispute settlement do include chapters on the law of the sea. See, e.g., J. G. Merrills, *International Dispute Settlement* (6th edn., Cambridge University Press, 2017); Y. Tanaka, *The Peaceful Settlement of International Disputes* (Cambridge University Press, 2018). ITLOS is examined in N. Grossman, H. G. Cohen, A. Follesdal and G. Ulfstein (eds), *Legitimacy and International Courts* (Cambridge University Press, 2018); G. B. Born, 'A New Generation of International Adjudication' (2012) 61 *Duke Law Journal* 775; R. Mackenzie, C. P. Romano, Y. Shany and P. Sands (eds), *The Manual on International Courts and Tribunals* (2nd edn., Oxford University Press, 2010).

88 UNCLOS, Art. 292.

a confined fashion; the international court or tribunal must "deal only with the question of release, without prejudice to the merits of any case before the appropriate domestic forum against the vessel, its owner or its crew".[89] Once the bond or other financial security set or otherwise declared to be reasonable by the international court or tribunal has been posted, the detaining State is required to comply with the decision of the international court or tribunal and release the vessel "promptly".[90]

The parties may submit the prompt release application to any court or tribunal subject to the agreement of the parties, but the time frames involved (given the inherent urgency of such proceedings) mean that ITLOS is effectively the default forum.[91] Indeed, only ITLOS has heard cases under Article 292 of the Convention. Proceedings under Article 292 may be instituted "only by or on behalf of" the flag State.[92] This provision allows for the possibility of the owner of the detained vessel instituting proceedings with the authority of the flag State and in the name of the flag State, in effect constituting a private prosecution undertaken in the name of the flag State.[93] The attachment of international procedural rights to what is, in effect, a private claim results in a procedure "atypical in the international judicial panorama";[94] broadly analogous to (but not to be confused with) diplomatic protection.[95]

Article 292 proceedings are available in relation to arrests of vessels in enforcement of a coastal State's fisheries laws in its EEZ pursuant to Article 73(4) of the Convention, and the investigation and arrest of vessels in enforcement of a coastal State's pollution laws in its EEZ under Articles 220 and 226. With the exception of *Heroic Idun*, which concerned the detention of a very large

89 Ibid., Art. 292(3).

90 Ibid., Art. 292(4).

91 Ibid., Art. 292(1). If the parties fail to agree on which court or tribunal to submit the prompt release within 10 days of the arrest taking place, then the parties are deemed to have accepted to submit the dispute "to a court or tribunal accepted by the detaining State under Article 287 or to the International Tribunal for the Law of the Sea, unless the parties otherwise agree": Art. 292(1).

92 Ibid., Art. 292(2).

93 As Judge Treves noted in *Grand Prince*: "In submitting an application for release, the flag State espouses a private claim of persons linked to it by the nationality of the ship". *Grand Prince*, [63] (Separate Opinion of Judge Treves). See also S. Trevisanut, 'Twenty Years of Prompt Release of Vessels: Admissibility, Jurisdiction, and Recent Trends' (2017) 48(3–4) *Ocean Development & International Law* 300, 303 (observing that "[p]rivate parties also play an important role in the postadjudication phase since the bond or other financial security fixed by the Tribunal will likely be paid either by the shipowner or by [their] insurance company").

94 Trevisanut (n. 93), 303.

95 Ibid., 302.

crude carrier, all the prompt release proceedings before ITLOS have concerned fishing vessels arrested under Article 73 of the Convention. Article 73(1) provides coastal States with the power to board and inspect vessels, to arrest them and their crew, and to institute judicial proceedings to ensure compliance with the laws and regulations adopted by the coastal State in relation to the exploration, exploitation, conservation and management of the living resources of the EEZ. Arrested vessels and crew are to be released upon the posting of a reasonable bond pursuant to Article 73(2).

In cases where a vessel and its crew have been arrested in exercise of an enforcement power not covered by Article 292, it may still be possible for the flag State to secure the release of the vessel and its crew by seeking the prescription of provisional measures. This approach was adopted, not without criticism,[96] in three cases where the detention of the vessel and its crew was not undertaken pursuant to coastal State powers contained within Articles 73, 220 or 226.[97] These cases are discussed in detail in Chapter 4.

Out of 32 cases before ITLOS, ten have been prompt release cases.[98] Most of the early ITLOS decisions concerned prompt release, with a substantial gap between the most recent prompt release proceeding, *Heroic Idun* (resolved in November 2022), and its immediate predecessors, *Tomimaru* and *Hoshinmaru* (resolved in August 2007). Three of those prompt release proceedings were either settled,[99] or dismissed for jurisdiction or admissibility issues.[100] The most recent case, *Heroic Idun*, was terminated unilaterally by the flag State before any substantive steps could be made by ITLOS on the prompt release application. Given that no judgment against which compliance can be measured was rendered in that case, it is not discussed within this Chapter. Among the remaining six cases, five of the vessels were released,[101] while one was scrapped when the requisite bond payment was not forthcoming.[102]

The results of each of these cases is considered in this Chapter, though it should be acknowledged that in some cases, information is ambiguous or not readily available, and there are gaps in understanding what in fact occurred.

---

96 See, e.g., the view that this approach "amounts to a back-door prompt release remedy": *Arctic Sunrise*, Provisional Measures, 265–266 [7(b)] (Separate Opinion of Judge Jesus).

97 *Arctic Sunrise*, Provisional Measures; *ARA Libertad*, Provisional Measures; *Three Ukrainian Naval Vessels*.

98 *Saiga*, Prompt Release; *Camouco*; *Monte Confurco*; *Grand Prince*; *Chaisiri Reefer*; *Volga*; *Juno Trader*; *Hoshinmaru*; *Tomimaru*.

99 *Chaisiri Reefer 2*.

100 *Grand Prince*, *Tomimaru*.

101 *Saiga*, Prompt Release; *Camouco*; *Monte Confurco*; *Juno Trader*; *Hoshinmaru*.

102 *Volga*.

As Churchill has observed, "[i]t is not always easy to discover what happens to a vessel after the ITLOS has given its judgment in a prompt-release case".[103]

3.2 *Saiga*

Saiga was the first case before ITLOS. The case started as a prompt release application under Article 292 of UNCLOS. The events leading to the arrest of the vessel spurred a substantive proceeding before ITLOS, which was filed by the flag State, Saint Vincent and the Grenadines, against Guinea in November 1997.[104] In summary, the M/V Saiga was a bunkering vessel, which provided gasoil to fishing vessels in the EEZ of Guinea. Guinea arrested the vessel in October 1997, alleging that it was engaged in smuggling in violation of its Customs Code.[105] In the process of the law enforcement action, Guinean officials injured at least two crew members because of the force used.[106]

In the prompt release proceedings relating to the M/V Saiga, ITLOS determined that there was a sufficiently plausible allegation that enforcement of Guinean fisheries laws in the EEZ under Article 73(2) of UNCLOS was at issue.[107] Although Saint Vincent and the Grenadines had not posted any bond prior to the institution of the proceedings, ITLOS considered that it was not at fault for failing to do so in light of Guinea's failure to notify Saint Vincent and the Grenadines of the arrest of the vessel and its crew, as required under Article 73(4) of UNCLOS.[108] The Tribunal ordered Guinea to promptly release the M/V Saiga and its crew from detention upon posting of a reasonable bond or security, which was determined by ITLOS to be a sum of US$400,000, plus the value of the gasoil discharged from the vessel.[109]

Saint Vincent and the Grenadines alleged that Guinea had failed to comply with the order for prompt release after the bank guarantee was posted at the merits stage of the case.[110] Saint Vincent and the Grenadines argued that Guinea had failed to release the vessel and crew promptly because there had been a delay of 80 days before the vessel was released.[111] The Tribunal rejected Saint Vincent and the Grenadines' allegation of non-compliance, noting that

103 R. Churchill, 'Dispute Settlement under the UN Convention on the Law of the Sea: Survey for 2004' (2006) 21(1) *International Journal of Marine and Coastal Law* 1, 11.

104 The merits decision (*Saiga (No. 2)*, Merits) is discussed in Chapter 6.

105 *Saiga* [36].

106 Ibid., [30].

107 Ibid., [59].

108 Ibid., [78].

109 Ibid., [86].

110 *Saiga (No. 2)*, Merits [163].

111 Ibid., [164].

the delay was not entirely Guinea's fault.[112] The Tribunal indicated, however, that an 80-day gap between order and action "cannot be considered as prompt release".[113] During the prompt release proceedings, ITLOS had commented on the importance of a prompt release, observing:

> The requirement of promptness has a value in itself and may prevail when the posting of the bond has not been possible, has been rejected or is not provided for in the coastal State's laws or when it is alleged that the required bond is unreasonable.[114]

The bond was, however, paid and the vessel and crew released. Therefore, the central purpose of Article 292 proceedings was largely fulfilled, though recalling that '*prompt*' release is necessary to satisfy full compliance. It is nonetheless notable that this one aspect of possible non-compliance was not enough for ITLOS to proceed in the merits phase to assess whether its order had been violated. The lack of promptness was seemingly not sufficient to constitute an internationally wrongful act in its own right. Perhaps the effort of good faith compliance influenced the judicial finding on this point.

3.3 *Camouco*

The *Camouco* case is an example of compliance, albeit again delayed, with ITLOS orders. At the time of the Article 292 proceedings, the Camouco was flagged to Panama and licensed to fish on the high seas. France had arrested the vessel for unlawful fishing of Patagonian toothfish in the EEZ of France's Crozet Islands in the southern Indian Ocean.[115] The French Navy escorted the vessel to Réunion, where the master was charged and placed under court supervision whereas the remaining crew, apart from four members needed to maintain the vessel, were allowed to leave.[116] The French courts originally set a bond of 20 million French francs,[117] an amount that was confirmed by a French court of first instance in Saint-Paul, Réunion in December 1999.[118] The vessel's

112 Ibid., [165].
113 Ibid.
114 *Saiga* [77].
115 *Camouco* [29].
116 Ibid., [34].
117 Ibid., [52].
118 Ibid., [36]; Decision No 052/AM/99 of the *Tribunal d'Instance de Saint Paul* of 14 December 1999.

owners lodged a notice of appeal in late December, which was under consideration at the time ITLOS issued its judgment.[119]

In considering the prompt release application, the Tribunal noted the posting of a bond or other financial security is not a precondition for the submission of an application for prompt release by a flag State.[120] In this instance, ITLOS determined that the bond amount set by the Réunion courts was not reasonable, taking into account

> the gravity of the alleged offences, the penalties imposed or imposable under the laws of the detaining State, the value of the detained vessel and of the cargo seized, the amount of the bond imposed by the detaining State and its form.[121]

ITLOS issued judgment on 7 February 2000, ordering that France promptly release the Panamanian vessel and its master upon payment of a reasonable bond, which it determined to be in the amount of 8 million French francs, in the form of a bank guarantee.[122]

Consistent with the Tribunal's order, Panama produced a bank guarantee on 24 February 2000, which was produced to the French Maritime Administration on 1 March 2000.[123] The Court of Appeal of Saint Denis issued judgment on 21 February 2000. The Court revised the value of the bond payable from 20 million French francs to 8 million French francs, considering that the order of ITLOS as to the value of the bond was binding upon France.[124] Once the French Maritime Administration was in possession of a bank guarantee to that amount, the Court ordered the immediate release of the Camouco on 21 March 2000.[125] This decision was consistent with France's obligations under Article 292 of UNCLOS, which forms part of France's domestic law.[126] The vessel was released on 22 March 2000, with Panama advising the Tribunal that the

119 *Camouco* [36]; *Merce Pesca Company v. The French State*, Judgment of the Court of Appeal of Saint Denis of 21 March 2000, Judgment No 267/2000. Translated version available in ITLOS, 'Selected Communications from Parties on Matters of Implementation of Judgments and Orders' (2000) 4 *Yearbook of the International Tribunal for the Law of the Sea* 147, 155–158.

120 *Camouco* [62], [64].

121 Ibid., [67].

122 Ibid., [78].

123 Letter to the ITLOS Registry from the Agent of Panama dated 10 March 2000, excerpted in ITLOS (n. 119), 150; *Merce Pesca Company v The French State*.

124 *Merce Pesca Company v. The French State*.

125 Ibid.

126 Given that France is a monist State.

ship's master had been returned his passport and that the Camouco had been 'liberated' and was in a Mauritian shipyard for repair works.[127] The Camouco was reflagged and renamed several times after this case, before being broken up in 2013.[128]

From this experience, it is clear that there was a small, but significant, time lag of some three weeks between the production of the bond and the release of vessel, rendering France non-compliant with the ITLOS order, even if only for a brief period. This delay is easily explainable and perhaps not unreasonable, even if not legally defensible given the criterion of promptness: it was not until the Court of Appeal of Saint Denis revised down the value of the bond payable to align with the amount set by ITLOS that the guarantee produced by Panama met the value prescribed by French law. While the operation of internal law or the legal and political arms of the State do not excuse a State from complying with its obligations under international law,[129] including those obligations to comply promptly and fully with the Tribunal's orders,[130] it at least appears that the Camouco was more promptly released than the M/V Saiga, and good faith compliance may be discerned.

3.4 *Monte Confurco*

On 27 November 2000, the Seychelles instituted prompt release proceedings against France in relation to the arrest of one of its vessels, the Monte Confurco. The Monte Confurco was only licensed to fish on the high seas. France arrested the Monte Confurco in the EEZ of the Kerguelen Islands in the French Southern and Antarctic Territories on 8 November 2000 for undertaking illegal toothfish fishing without France's prior authorisation.[131] A bond for the release of the Monte Confurco and its master was set by Réunion courts at over 56 million French francs.[132] The master of the ship was charged and placed under court supervision,[133] but denied fishing was conducted within the French EEZ.[134]

---

127 Letter to the ITLOS Registry from the Agent of Panama dated 10 March 2000, excerpted in ITLOS (n. 119), 150.

128 Source: <https://iuu-vessels.org/Vessel/GetVessel/714580fc-0d2c-4613-976f-4bd7d71a7dbd>.

129 International Law Commission, *Report of the International Law Commission on the Work of Its Fifty-Third Session*, UN GAOR, 56th sess., Supp. No. 10, UN Doc. A/56/10 (2001) ('*Articles on Responsibility of States for Internationally Wrongful Acts*'), Art. 32.

130 UNCLOS, Art. 296(1).

131 *Monte Confurco* [29]–[30].

132 Ibid., [39].

133 Ibid., [36].

134 Ibid., [50].

ITLOS issued a judgment on 18 December 2000, ordering France to promptly release the vessel upon payment of a reasonable bond of 18 million French francs.[135] The Tribunal observed that there were differences as to the valuation of the vessel,[136] and on the substantive question as to whether all the fish seized from the Monte Confurco had been harvested within France's EEZ.[137] The Seychelles seemingly complained to the Tribunal concerning proceedings with respect to the vessel and the master before French courts at the end of December 2000,[138] and in January 2001.[139] Emulating the path taken in *Camouco*, the French court subsequently revoked the original order and set a bond totalling 18 million French francs in line with the order of ITLOS.[140]

The promptness of the release was again at issue in relation to compliance with the ITLOS order. Nonetheless, the Monte Confurco was seemingly released following the adjustment of the bond, and information publicly available suggests that it is still in operation.[141]

3.5 *Volga*

The *Volga* case provides a different example of State responses in relation to prompt release orders. On 7 February 2002, Australian naval vessel HMAS Canberra arrested the Volga for unlawfully fishing in Australia's Antarctic waters within the EEZ of its Heard and McDonald Islands.[142] The Volga was escorted to Western Australia.[143] Under Australian law, ownership of the vessel, along with the 131 tonnes of Patagonian toothfish (and bait) as well as all nets, traps and equipment on board, were automatically forfeited to the

135 Ibid., [95]. The amount was comprised of the monetary equivalent of the value of the catch seized by French authorities, as well as an additional sum in the form of a bank guarantee: at [93].

136 Ibid., [84].

137 Ibid., [88].

138 ITLOS, *Annual Report of the International Tribunal for the Law of the Sea for 2000*, ITLOS Doc. SPLOS/63 (2001), 10.

139 ITLOS, *Annual Report of the International Tribunal for the Law of the Sea for 2001*, ITLOS Doc. SPLOS/74 (2002), 10.

140 ITLOS, 'Selected Communications from Parties on Matters of Implementation of Judgments and Orders', (2001) 5 *Yearbook of the International Tribunal for the Law of the Sea* 156.

141 The vessel apparently remains flagged to the Seychelles and is in operation, further to searches under its IMO number.

142 *Volga* [34]–[35].

143 Ibid., [35].

State.[144] Russia instituted proceedings under UNCLOS on 29 November 2002, seeking the release of the vessel and its crew.

Prior to the institution of Article 292 proceedings, Australia advised counsel for the owner of the vessel that it would release the Volga upon not only the payment of a financial bond set under Australian law of some AU$3.3 million, but also the fulfilment of certain conditions, which included the provision of information about the beneficial ownership of the Volga and the fitting of the Volga with a vessel monitoring system.[145] The owners refused to pay the bond requested or to meet the other conditions sought by Australia, and instead offered AU$500,000 as security.[146]

ITLOS ordered the prompt release of the vessel on 23 December 2002 and determined that only a financial bond was payable for the release of the vessel and its crew; the additional conditions set by Australia were in excess of coastal State competence under Article 73.[147] The Tribunal revised the financial bond, instead setting it at AU$1.9 million,[148] being roughly equivalent to the value of the vessel, fuel, lubricants and fishing equipment.[149] Ultimately, neither the shipowners nor Russia paid the bond.[150]

In a series of proceedings before Australian courts, the owner challenged the lawfulness of the arrest and the forfeiture but all legal actions were unsuccessful.[151] The final application for special leave to appeal to the High

144 *Fisheries Management Act 1991* (Cth), s. 106A (the relevant offence activating s. 160A being s. 100). Albeit subject to the possibility of a challenge before Australian courts within two months: s. 106G–2. The power to seize the vessel and items on board is given by s. 84(1)(ga) of that Act.

145 *Volga* [53].

146 Ibid., [54].

147 Ibid., [77].

148 Ibid., [90].

149 Ibid., [73], [90].

150 See discussion in M. W. D. White, *Australian Offshore Laws* (Federation Press, 2009), 204; Md. S. Karim, 'Conflicts over Protection of Marine Living Resources: The Volga Case Revisited,' (2011) 3 *Goettingen Journal of International Law* 101, 126. See also Rural and Regional Affairs and Transport Legislation Committee, Parliament of Australia, *Answers to Questions on Notice: Additional Estimates February 2015 (Agriculture)*, available at: <https://www.aph.gov.au/~/media/Committees/rrat_ctte/estimates/add_1415/ag/Answers/AFMAQoN9-13.pdf>. But note media reports, which appear to be in error, to the contrary: 'Illegal Fishers Face Bill' 26 November 2003, *Sydney Morning Herald*, available at: <https://www.smh.com.au/national/illegal-fishers-face-chase-bill-20031126-gdhuwh.html>.

151 See *Olbers v. Commonwealth of Australia (No. 4)* [2004] FCA 229 (12 March 2004); *Olbers Co Ltd v. Commonwealth of Australia* [2004] FCAFC 262 (16 September 2004). See discussion in R. Baird, 'Coastal State Fisheries Management: A Review of Australian Enforcement

Court of Australia was denied on 22 April 2005.[152] Such application did not mention the ITLOS order (although questions were raised – but not answered – as to the conformity of the relevant Australian law with international law). Given that the bond had not been paid, the Volga and the AU$1.9 million value of its catch were forfeited to Australia following the conclusion of the legal proceedings. Under Australian law,[153] the vessel was scrapped 30 days thereafter at a Western Australian shipyard.[154]

In relation to the Volga's crew, the fishing master, fishing pilot, and first officer of the Volga, each of whom were of Spanish nationality, were all detained and charged with the offence of using a foreign boat for fishing in the Australian Fisheries Zone.[155] Later, a further charge was laid against the fishing master. The ship's master, who died in hospital in Western Australia, was not charged. In 2003, following a series of cases in the Supreme Court of Western Australia, bail for release of the crew was set at a cash bond of AU$75,000 each.[156] At the time of the Article 292 proceedings before ITLOS, the crew members had departed Australia for Spain following the imposition of bail undertakings and were awaiting trial.[157] Russia submitted in the Article 292 proceedings that the amounts of bail set were unreasonable.[158] ITLOS, however, did not consider it necessary to deal with this submission given that the crew members had been released.[159] In 2004, the three Spanish crew members returned to Australia for their trial, pleaded guilty, and were fined AU$10,000 each, with the fishing master fined an additional AU$20,000.[160]

Ultimately, compliance with the ITLOS order was not entirely tested in light of the vessel owner's failure to pay the bond. It is notable that the ITLOS order does not mandate bond payment but only the release of the vessel on the

Action in the Heard and McDonald Islands Australian Fishing Zone' (2004) 9(1) *Deakin Law Review* 91.

152 *Olbers Co Ltd v. Commonwealth of Australia* [2005] HCATrans 228 (22 April 2005).

153 *Fisheries Management Act 1991* (Cth), Div. 6.

154 Parliament of Australia (n. 150); White (n. 150), 204.

155 Pursuant to *Fisheries Management Act 1991* (Cth) s. 100(2).

156 Bail had initially been set by the judge at first instance at AU$75,000 each. On appeal, that amount was varied to AU$225,000 each: *Director of Public Prosecutions (Cth) v. Lijo* [2002] WASC 154 (14 June 2002) (per Wheeler J). On further appeal, the amount set by the judge at first instance was by and large restored: *Lijo v. Director of Public Prosecutions* [2003] WASCA 4 (16 December 2002). See discussion in *Volga* [41]–[44].

157 See discussion in White (n. 150), 201.

158 *Volga* [48].

159 *Volga* [74].

160 The maximum fine for each offence was $275,000. See discussion in White (n. 150). See also Baird (n. 151).

assumption of a bond payment being rendered. Australia was thus within its rights to scrap the Volga in accordance with the requirements of its domestic law when the vessel's owners failed to pay any amount (whether that set by ITLOS or by the Australian government) to secure the release of the vessel.

It is a matter of speculation as to how Australia would have acted in the event the bond prescribed by the Tribunal was paid. Owing to its dualist tradition, the decisions of international courts and tribunals are not formally binding on Australian courts,[161] and, unlike the French courts in *Camouco*, Australian courts may not have revised the value of the bond set by the Australian government to meet the amount ordered by ITLOS in its prompt release judgment. Had the Volga's owners paid the entirety of the AU$1.9 million bond as anticipated in ITLOS' order, it would have been for the political arms of the Australian government to decide whether to release the vessel notwithstanding its capacity to insist upon the payment of the full AU$3 million bond payable under Australian domestic law.

While this discussion is largely hypothetical, it exposes core differences in compliance with UNCLOS dispute settlement in monist and dualist systems. Courts in monist systems may, in many cases, force compliance with ITLOS orders (and, indeed, the orders of other competent international courts and tribunals) thereby making the decision as to whether to comply a legal rather than political one. However, courts in dualist systems are, absent domestic legislation to the contrary,[162] potentially less likely to enforce an international court order, thereby subjecting compliance decisions to varied political considerations.

3.6 *Juno Trader*

Saint Vincent and the Grenadines instituted Article 292 proceedings against Guinea-Bissau in November 2004 in relation to the Juno Trader, a reefer vessel trans-shipping frozen fish. The Juno Trader, along with its crew, was arrested in the EEZ of Guinea-Bissau on 26 September 2004. At the time, the Juno Trader was transiting the EEZ of Guinea-Bissau en route to Ghana.[163] It was alleged that the Juno Trader had been anchored parallel to a fishing vessel

161 For discussion of the operation of international law in Australian law, see A. Devereux and S. McCosker, 'International Law and Australian Law', in D. R. Rothwell and E. Crawford (eds), *International Law in Australia* (3rd edn., Thomson Reuters, 2017), 23–46.

162 Such as those concerning the recognition and enforcement of foreign judgments and arbitral awards. See, e.g., *International Arbitration Act 1974* (Cth); *Foreign Judgments Act 1991* (Cth).

163 *Juno Trader* [35].

engaged in illegal fishing in the EEZ of Guinea-Bissau, and fled when it spotted a Bissau-Guinean naval vessel.[164] The local authorities imposed fines on both the master and the vessel, with only part of the fine for the vessel being paid (the fine levied totalling €184,168) whereas the full fine for the master was paid.[165] The failure to pay the full fine amount resulted in the vessel reverting to the ownership of Guinea-Bissau.[166] At the time of the Article 292 proceedings, six crew members had remained in Guinea-Bissau due to the State's confiscation of their passports.[167] However, Guinea-Bissau undertook during the course of the proceedings to allow those crew members to leave without condition.[168] This undertaking was reflected in the Tribunal's order.[169]

ITLOS determined that the transfer of ownership from the shipowner to the State under Bissau-Guinean law did not preclude the ship maintaining its nationality under the flag of Saint Vincent and the Grenadines.[170] The confiscation thus did not impact on the admissibility of the application nor the Tribunal's jurisdiction.[171] After finding that Guinea-Bissau was in violation of the requirements of Article 73(2), the Tribunal ordered the release of the Juno Trader upon the posting of a bank guarantee of €300,000.[172]

On 1 February 2005, the Tribunal was notified that difficulties had been encountered by the Juno Trader's owner concerning the terms and posting of the bank guarantee with the authorities of Guinea-Bissau. Subsequently, a confidential agreement was reached between representatives of Guinea-Bissau and the owners of the Juno Trader, resulting in the Juno Trader being released and leaving Guinea-Bissau on 27 March 2005.[173] It is not known if the bond or indeed any bond was in fact paid,[174] or whether the release "was as a result of the bond being posted or as a consequence of a further ruling by a court in

164 Ibid., [38].
165 Ibid., [50]–[51].
166 Ibid., [53].
167 Ibid., [78]–[79].
168 Ibid., [79].
169 For discussion of crew detentions, see V. P. Bantz, 'View from Hamburg: The Juno Trader Case or How to Make Sense of the Coastal State's Rights in the Light of Its Duty of Prompt Release' (2005) 24 *University of Queensland Law Journal* 415, 433–436.
170 *Juno Trader* [63].
171 Ibid., [63]–[68].
172 Ibid., [98].
173 ITLOS, *Annual Report of the International Tribunal for the Law of the Sea for 2005*, ITLOS Doc. SPLOS/136 (2006), 10.
174 T. Treves, 'The International Tribunal for the Law of the Sea' (2004) 14 *Italian Yearbook of International Law* 289, 302 (noting Guinea Bissau did not initially agree to the terms of the bank guarantee but the vessel was released by agreement).

Guinea-Bissau or a decision by an administrative body".[175] However, the fact that an agreement was reached between the parties and that the Juno Trader was released could still be counted as at least good faith compliance with the ITLOS order. Further, such settlement reflects the power given to parties to settle disputes between them at any time through pacific means, notwithstanding initial recourse to third-party adjudication.[176]

3.7 *Hoshinmaru*

The last substantive prompt release decision to consider is the *Hoshinmaru* case. On 6 July 2007, Japan instituted proceedings seeking the release of its vessel, the 88th Hoshinmaru, and its crew from Russia. The Hoshinmaru was arrested on 1 June 2007 after a Russian patrol boat spotted the vessel fishing in the Russian EEZ.[177] It was then discovered that sockeye salmon had been concealed under other catch, in excess of the authorized harvest amount. As a result, the vessel and its master were charged with misrepresenting fisheries data.[178] The vessel was escorted to a Russian port to face judicial proceedings.[179] Japan requested that the Hoshinmaru and its crew be released upon payment of a reasonable bond. Following the imposition of a bond of some 25 million roubles,[180] Japan instituted Article 292 proceedings.

ITLOS ordered the prompt release of the vessel and its crew on 6 August 2007, lowering the bond to ten million roubles.[181] In finding the bond set by Russia to be unreasonable, the Tribunal considered that the failure to report the catch was not the gravest violation of fisheries laws to have occurred.[182] The bond set by ITLOS was paid on 15 August 2007 and the vessel and crew released the next day.[183] An exemplary instance of compliance with the ITLOS judgment.

3.8 *Conclusion*

The track record of compliance with prompt release orders of ITLOS is excellent in relation to the release of the vessels concerned. In all cases bar one, the vessel subject to the prompt release proceedings was released. In the only

175 Churchill (n. 103), 11.
176 UNCLOS, Art. 280.
177 *Hoshinmaru* [29].
178 Ibid., [30].
179 Ibid., [34].
180 Ibid., [50].
181 Ibid., [51].
182 Ibid., [91]–[93].
183 ITLOS, *Annual Report of the International Tribunal for the Law of the Sea for 2007*, ITLOS Doc. SPLOS/174 (2008), 11.

exception, the vessel owner failed to pay any bond, negating what may be considered the reciprocal obligation to release the vessel promptly. The ITLOS proceedings have thus played a pivotal role in ensuring compliance with Article 73 of UNCLOS and have provided a counter-balance in favour of navigational rights in the face of vigorous coastal State authority being exercised in the EEZ.[184]

The *Volga* was a distinct result where no bond payment was ever forthcoming following the Article 292 proceedings. In the *Volga*, the failure to pay the bond meant that determining whether compliance occurred is unnecessary unless one is of the view that ITLOS' order setting the bond to be paid carried with it a concomitant obligation for Russia to comply with ITLOS' order by ensuring the bond was paid. Whereas paying a bond was not a condition precedent for an application before ITLOS,[185] a bond is required to secure the release of a vessel in ITLOS proceedings under Article 292. The ITLOS orders for prompt release have not set out the payment of the bond as a distinct or separate order for the applicant in the *dispositif*, but the order is directed at the respondent State to release the vessel upon payment of the bond. A respondent State may thus still be compliant when ITLOS sets a bond for the vessel's release and that new bond amount is not paid by the applicant.

Yet whether vessels were *promptly* released indicates a more difficult assessment for demonstrating compliance. Apart from the *Hoshinmaru* order, there were delays or subsequent challenges in securing the vessel's release once ITLOS had established a new bond amount. An analysis of State practice in relation to prompt release proceedings thus demonstrates some nuance as to how compliance is defined and framed. In the *Camouco* and *Saiga* cases, France and Guinea (respectively) released the vessels in question in compliance with the ITLOS orders, but not necessarily in a prompt fashion. Given that the very purpose of a prompt release proceeding is to secure the release of the vessel in question in an expeditious fashion, any unreasonable delay in releasing the vessel following the ITLOS order may be cast as non-compliance with an ITLOS order. The release of the vessel with a short, albeit reasonable, delay may still be construed as good faith compliance, or potentially part compliance where the full amount was paid and the vessel released with only a short delay.

184 Whether the Tribunal has weighed too far in favour of flag State interests is a point of contention. See discussion in N. Klein and K. Parlett, *Judging the Law of the Sea: Judicial Contributions to the UN Convention on the Law of the Sea* (Oxford University Press, 2022), 325–328.

185 See above nn. 108–109 and accompanying text.

The one instance where compliance was judicially challenged arose in relation to the M/V Saiga. In *Saiga (No. 2)*, which concerned the merits of the dispute rather than prompt release, ITLOS determined that its order was not breached by an 80-day delay.[186] In that instance, while it was said release after 80 days was not *prompt*, Guinea was not at fault as the delay was due to circumstances outside of its control. Allowing for some element of reasonableness in what may be considered prompt allows for the characterisation of good faith or part compliance. A different factual setting that indicates some recalcitrance on behalf of the flag State may give rise to a contrary determination. Arguably, France should not be considered at fault for allowing its national courts to follow the required process in adjusting a bond set given that prompt release applications under UNCLOS proceed without prejudice to domestic proceedings.[187] While a State cannot rely on its internal law to excuse an international law violation,[188] the operation of national legal systems could be taken into consideration in assessing the promptness of release.

It is thus apparent that what is 'prompt' may admit some flexibility, requiring a fact-based, subjective inquiry importing an element of reasonableness. If a vessel is released there is at least part compliance. Allowing flexibility is appropriate given that Article 292 proceedings are without prejudice to the merits of domestic proceedings and the detaining State's authorities maintain competence in relation to the release of vessel and its crew.[189] These circumstances may warrant a determination of at least good faith compliance with the order resulting from Article 292 proceedings. The most relevant indicator of compliance is whether or not the vessel was released following the bond payment. What might be 'prompt' will seemingly vary.

4 Provisional Measures

4.1 *Introduction to Provisional Measures Orders*

Under Article 290 of UNCLOS, a party that has submitted a dispute to a court or tribunal constituted under Part XV may seek provisional measures "to preserve the respective rights of the parties to the dispute or to prevent serious harm to the marine environment, pending the final decision".[190] Such measures

186 See above nn. 111–113 and accompanying text.
187 UNCLOS, Art. 292(3).
188 *Articles on Responsibility of States for Internationally Wrongful Acts* (n. 129), Art. 32.
189 UNCLOS, Art. 292(3).
190 UNCLOS, Art. 290(1).

prescribed pursuant to UNCLOS are binding.[191] Provisional measures seek either to protect a right that is the subject of litigation, or to prevent the aggravation of the dispute and preserve the *status quo ante* between the parties until a decision on the merits can be rendered.[192] Such measures cease to operate once the relevant international court or tribunal issues its judgment on the merits.[193]

Two bases of jurisdiction exist for the prescription of provisional measures under Part XV of UNCLOS. First, an UNCLOS court or tribunal may prescribe provisional measures in relation to a dispute submitted to it pursuant to Article 290(1) if it is satisfied both that it has *prima facie* jurisdiction[194] and that the situation is sufficiently urgent to warrant the prescription of such measures.[195] The procedure relating to the prescription of provisional measures before ITLOS is outlined in its Rules,[196] whereas Annex VII tribunals are empowered by Article 5 of Annex VII to promulgate their own rules of procedure, which extends to rules concerning the prescription of provisional measures.[197]

Second, under Article 290(5), if States are referring a dispute to Annex VII arbitration, it is possible to seek provisional measures from ITLOS pending the constitution of the arbitral tribunal if the urgency of the situation so warrants and if ITLOS considers that the Annex VII tribunal would have *prima facie* jurisdiction. The urgency in this instance refers to the time available before an arbitral tribunal is constituted and able to issue provisional measures itself, rather than urgency pending a final decision on the merits.[198]

191 UNCLOS, Art. 290(6).

192 C. Miles, *Provisional Measures before International Courts and Tribunals* (Cambridge University Press, 2017), 174.

193 See *Southern Bluefin Tuna*, Jurisdiction and Admissibility [66]. See also, e.g., *Arbitral Award of 31 July 1989 (Guinea-Bissau v. Senegal)*, Provisional Measures, *ICJ Reports* 1990, 69 [24]; UNCLOS, Art. 290(2)–(5).

194 UNCLOS, Art. 290(1); *Saiga (No. 2)*, Provisional Measures, 37 [29] ("before prescribing provisional measures the Tribunal need not finally satisfy itself that it has jurisdiction on the merits and yet it may not prescribe such measures unless the provisions invoked by the applicant appear *prima facie* to afford a basis on which the jurisdiction of the tribunal might be founded"). See generally Miles (n. 192), 155ff.

195 While not a formal requirement of UNCLOS, Art. 290(1), the requirement of urgency is well-accepted as a necessary element of the prescription of provisional measures. See, e.g., *Enrica Lexie*, Provisional Measures, [84]–[85]; *Louisa*, Provisional Measures, 76 [17] (Separate Opinion of Judge Paik); cf *Southern Bluefin Tuna*, Provisional Measures, 330 [3] (Dissenting Opinion of Judge Vukas).

196 Rules of the International Tribunal for the Law of the Sea, Arts. 89–95.

197 That is, to the extent that such rules are not inconsistent with UNCLOS: Miles (n. 192), 105–106.

198 *Southern Bluefin Tuna*, Provisional Measures, 316 [2] (Separate Opinion of Judge Treves).

Under either Article 290(1) or (5), an UNCLOS court or tribunal called upon to prescribe provisional measures will make a preliminary assessment as to the existence of *prima facie* jurisdiction, as well as determine the admissibility of the request and consider if the relief sought is warranted under the circumstances. Regard will also be given to the risk of irreparable harm, whether the State seeking provisional measures has a plausible claim to such rights,[199] and whether there is a link between the rights claimed in the principal proceedings and the provisional measures sought.[200] The measures can then later be revoked or altered by the tribunal hearing the merits of the dispute.[201] Measures different to those requested by a party to the dispute may be prescribed by tribunals acting *proprio motu*,[202] so long as a party to the dispute has sought the prescription of provisional measures and all parties have had an opportunity to be heard.[203]

As to compliance, concerns have been raised in relation to the ability of UNCLOS courts and tribunals to enforce provisional measures. As Tanaka has observed in the context of provisional measures prescribed by ITLOS, "an evident weakness of provisional measures is that they have no enforceability. An issue thus arises as to how it is possible to secure effective compliance with these measures".[204] One key marker of compliance, or lack thereof, is visible in the judicial supervision role undertaken by UNCLOS courts and tribunals in relation to the implementation of provisional measures prescribed by them. As indicated in Chapter 1, the lack of a supervisory body aimed at securing post-judgment compliance following the UNCLOS court or tribunal becoming *functus* may have a negative effect on the propensity of States to comply.[205]

---

199 *Ghana/Côte d'Ivoire*, Provisional Measures [58].

200 See *Ghana/Côte d'Ivoire*, Provisional Measures [63]. See generally M. Lando, 'Provisional Measures and the Link Requirement' (2020) 19 *The Law and Practice of International Courts and Tribunals* 177.

201 See *Southern Bluefin Tuna*, Provisional Measures, 19 [65].

202 Or, of its own motion: Rules of the International Tribunal for the Law of the Sea, Art. 89(5). To this end, UNCLOS courts and tribunals do not need to prescribe provisional measures in the exact form sought by the parties.

203 UNCLOS, Art. 290(3). It is in this respect that there is a substantial difference between the powers of ITLOS and the ICJ with respect to the prescription of provisional measures. ITLOS may only proceed to consider the question of whether to prescribe provisional measures upon the request of a party (though may prescribe measures different to that sought by the parties). The ICJ, on the other hand, may prescribe provisional measures *proprio motu* without a request by a State party to the dispute: Rules of the International Court of Justice, Art. 75(1).

204 Y. Tanaka, 'Provisional Measures Prescribed by ITLOS and Marine Environmental Protection' (2014) 108 *Proceedings of the Annual Meeting of the American Society of International Law* 365, 365.

205 See Chapter 1.2. For further discussion, see Chapter 8.

Nonetheless, UNCLOS courts and tribunals are competent to, in the absence of a supervisory body, exercise judicial supervision over the implementation of the provisional measures they have prescribed. Article 95 of ITLOS' Rules provides that each party to the dispute "shall inform the Tribunal as soon as possible as to its compliance with any provisional measures the Tribunal has prescribed",[206] and gives ITLOS the power to "request further information from the parties on any matter connected with the implementation of any provisional measures it has prescribed".[207] Moreover, compliance with provisional measures order may be assessed in the merits stage of the case, as is discussed in this Chapter.

Of the 11 requests for the prescription of provisional measures assessed by ITLOS, three were submitted pursuant to Article 290(1),[208] and a further eight pursuant to Article 290(5).[209] Two requests for provisional measures have been submitted to Annex VII tribunals in accordance with Article 290(1).[210] In five cases,[211] the tribunals ordered provisional measures in the form sought by the party making the request. In three cases,[212] the tribunals rejected the provisional measures sought by the State party making the request but exercised their power to prescribe provisional measures *proprio motu*. In a further two

---

206 Rules of the International Tribunal for the Law of the Sea, Art. 95(1).

207 Rules of the International Tribunal for the Law of the Sea, Art. 95(2).

208 *Saiga (No. 2)*, Provisional Measures; *Louisa*, Provisional Measures; *Ghana/Côte d'Ivoire*, Provisional Measures. Note that the request for the prescription of provisional measures made by Saint Vincent and the Grenadines in *Saiga (No. 2)*, Provisional Measures was originally submitted pursuant to Article 290(5). However, following the States coming to a special agreement to submit the dispute to ITLOS for hearing on the merits, ITLOS ordered that the request for provisional measures be treated as "having been duly submitted to the Tribunal under article [290(1)] …": *M/V Saiga (No. 2) (Saint Vincent and the Grenadines v. Guinea)*, Provisional Measures, Order of 20 February 1998, *ITLOS Reports* 1998, 12. See below Chapter 4.2.

209 *Southern Bluefin Tuna*, Provisional Measures; *MOX Plant*, Provisional Measures; *Land Reclamation*, Provisional Measures; *ARA Libertad*, Provisional Measures; *Arctic Sunrise*, Provisional Measures; *Enrica Lexie*, ITLOS Provisional Measures; *Three Ukrainian Naval Vessels*; *San Padre Pio*. Note that the dispute in *San Padre Pio* was later transferred for a hearing on the merits before ITLOS, as opposed to an Annex VII tribunal: *San Padre Pio (No. 2)*, 'Special Agreement and Notification of 17 December 2019 and the Minutes of Consultation, annexed thereto', 17 December 2019. Given that the request for the prescription for provisional measures was submitted and decided pursuant to Article 290(5), we categorise *San Padre Pio* as an Article 290(5) case.

210 *MOX Plant*, Annex VII Provisional Measures; *Enrica Lexie*, Annex VII Provisional Measures.

211 *Southern Bluefin Tuna*, Provisional Measures, *ARA Libertad*, *Arctic Sunrise*, *Three Ukrainian Naval Vessels* and *San Padre Pio*.

212 *Saiga (No. 2)*; *MOX Plant*; *Land Reclamation*, Provisional Measures.

cases,[213] provisional measures were prescribed in a form substantially similar to those sought by the State party making the request but on a more limited basis than those measures originally sought. Ultimately, provisional measures of some sort have been prescribed in all cases in which a request was made, bar one.[214] While compliance has largely been forthcoming, minor difficulties or complications in compliance can be seen in the majority of cases examined in this Chapter. In three cases,[215] questions have been raised as to whether that compliance was in good faith or the extent to which a causal link exists between the relevant order and the result. This Chapter outlines the initial provisional measures order and examines compliance with the order issued for each of the cases.

4.2 *Saiga (No. 2)*

Saiga (No. 2) was the first time that ITLOS was seised to prescribe provisional measures. It will be recalled from the discussion of the prompt release proceedings in Chapter 3 that the antecedent dispute concerned the detention of a vessel flagged to Saint Vincent and the Grenadines by Guinean authorities.[216] In December 1997, ITLOS ordered that the vessel be released upon payment of a reasonable bond or security.[217] This dispute, *Saiga (No. 2)*, concerned the lawfulness of Guinea's arrest of the M/V Saiga. In January 1998, Saint Vincent and the Grenadines requested the prescription of provisional measures pending the constitution of an Annex VII tribunal pursuant to Article 290(5) of the Convention.[218] In February 1998, the parties agreed to submit the dispute to the jurisdiction of ITLOS rather than to Annex VII arbitration.[219] As such, ITLOS ordered that the request for provisional measures be considered as submitted to ITLOS pursuant to its Article 290(1) jurisdiction, as opposed to its Article 290(5) jurisdiction.[220]

213 *Enrica Lexie*, Annex VII Provisional Measures; *Ghana/Côte d'Ivoire*, Provisional Measures.

214 Louisa, *Provisional Measures*. In that case, ITLOS accepted assurances from the arresting State, Spain, that it was carefully maintaining the vessel. As such, the requirement of urgency was not made out. Notably, ITLOS did not find it necessary to prescribe even minimal provisional measures aimed at reiterating the parties' obligations not to aggravate or extend the dispute, as it has done in other cases where the provisional measures sought by the applicant State were either rejected or were seen to warrant modification.

215 *Arctic Sunrise*, Provisional Measures; *Three Ukrainian Naval Vessels*; *San Padre Pio*.

216 *Saiga*. See Chapter 3.2.

217 *Saiga* [86].

218 *Saiga No 2*, Merits, 13–14 [1].

219 Ibid., 14–17 [4].

220 *M/V Saiga (No. 2) (Saint Vincent and the Grenadines v. Guinea)*, Provisional Measures, Order of 20 February 1998, *ITLOS Reports* 1998, 12.

The provisional measures requested by Saint Vincent and the Grenadines sought the release of the M/V Saiga and its crew, the suspension and prohibition of enforcement of Guinean court judgments concerning the Saiga, for Guinea to cease and desist from applying its customs laws in its EEZ and to respect the freedom of navigation therein, and for Guinea to cease and desist from undertaking hot pursuit of vessels flagged to Saint Vincent and the Grenadines except in conformity with the Convention.[221]

Considering that it had *prima facie* jurisdiction over the merits of the dispute,[222] and that the prescription of provisional measures was necessary to preserve the rights of Saint Vincent and the Grenadines pending a decision on the merits,[223] ITLOS ordered that Guinea "refrain from taking or enforcing any judicial or administrative measure against the M/V Saiga, its Master and the other members of the crew, its owners or operators".[224] ITLOS otherwise declined to prescribe the other provisional measures requested by Saint Vincent and the Grenadines.

However, in line with its powers under Article 89(5) of its Rules, ITLOS prescribed additional provisional measures different to those requested by Saint Vincent and the Grenadines. To this end, ITLOS *recommended* (as opposed to formally *ordered*) the parties to "find an arrangement to be applied pending the final decision", with a view to not aggravating or further extending the substantive dispute before the Tribunal.[225] The parties were ordered to submit reports as to compliance pursuant to Article 95(1) of the Rules.[226] As such, the only substantive order against which compliance can be assessed is whether Guinea ceased to enforce the judgments of the Tribunal at First Instance and Court of Appeal, including by releasing the master and the M/V Saiga from detention.

However, this question essentially became moot because the master and crew of the M/V Saiga were released by Guinea on 28 February 1998, nearly two weeks *before* ITLOS prescribed provisional measures.[227] As such, no question of compliance with ITLOS' provisional measures arises. In relation to the

221 *Saiga (No. 2)*, Provisional Measures [23].
222 Ibid., [30].
223 Ibid., [41].
224 Ibid., 39–40 [52(1)].
225 Ibid., 40 [52(2)].
226 Ibid., 40 [52(3)]. A further order was made reserving the costs of the proceeding but is outside the scope of this Chapter.
227 ITLOS, 'Minutes of Public Sittings held from 8 March to 20 March 1999' (1999) 3 *Pleadings, Minutes of Public Sittings and Documents* 493, 755 (Statement of Mr. Howe, Counsel of St Vincent and the Grenadines).

Tribunal's recommendation that the parties enter into a temporary arrangement pending the resolution of the merits, Saint Vincent and the Grenadines proposed that its vessels be prohibited from engaging in bunkering activities in Guinea's territorial sea and contiguous zone.[228] Guinea seemingly did not respond to this proposal. Further, while Saint Vincent and the Grenadines submitted its report on its compliance with the provisional measures prescribed on 29 April 1998,[229] no report was apparently lodged by Guinea.

In sum, while Guinea's execution of a deed of release over the M/V Saiga had the effect of ensuring compliance with the provisional measure prescribed by ITLOS, it must be observed that there was no causation in that the order of ITLOS did not prompt this event. Speculatively, the initiation of UNCLOS dispute settlement proceedings may have influenced Guinea's decision-making in the treatment of the M/V Saiga and its crew. The apparent failure of Guinea to submit reports on compliance, as prescribed in the order, indicates non-compliance. Guinea's failure to engage with the proposal submitted by Saint Vincent and the Grenadines in accordance with ITLOS' order further raises questions as to Guinea's commitment to the peaceful settlement of disputes. However, as a recommendation, Guinea could not be held internationally responsible for failing to come to a temporary arrangement.

4.3 *Southern Bluefin Tuna Cases*

The *Southern Bluefin Tuna* cases[230] concerned complaints by Australia and New Zealand that Japan had breached its obligations under UNCLOS in relation to the conservation and management of southern bluefin tuna stock.[231] Australia and New Zealand claimed that Japan was violating provisions of the Convention concerning fishing on the high seas because of Japan's experimental fishing program. This research program necessitated Japan harvesting

228 Letter from Bozo A Dabinovic (Agent of St Vincent and the Grenadines) to Hartmut von Brevern (Agent for Guinea) dated 7 April 1998 in ITLOS, 'Report under Article 95, Paragraph 1, of the Rules of the Tribunal Submitted by Saint Vincent and the Grenadines' (1998) 2 *Pleadings, Minutes of Public Sittings and Documents* 255, 256–257.

229 Ibid., 255. Reports submitted in relation to orders made under Article 95(1) of ITLOS' Rules are published in the *Pleadings, Minutes of Public Sittings and Documents*. While a report from Saint Vincent and the Grenadines appears in volume 2 of that collection, no such report appears from Guinea either in volume 2 or in a later volume.

230 Australia and New Zealand instituted separate proceedings on substantially identical terms against Japan in August 1998. Each of the applicant States submitted a request for the prescription of provisional measures in July 1999; the provisional measures orders were issued in August 1999.

231 *Southern Bluefin Tuna*, Provisional Measures, 285–288 [28] [29].

southern bluefin tuna in excess of its national allocation determined within the Commission for the Conservation of Southern Bluefin Tuna ('CCSBT'). Australia and New Zealand each requested provisional measures pursuant to Article 290(5) of the Convention in identical terms, most notably seeking that Japan be ordered to cease its unilateral experimental fishing for southern bluefin tuna and that its catch for southern bluefin tuna be restricted to the acceptable level agreed in the CCSBT.[232]

The Tribunal's order found that it had *prima facie* jurisdiction over the dispute and prescribed six provisional measures:[233] first, that no party to the dispute take any steps that may aggravate or extend the dispute; second, that no party to the dispute take any steps that may prejudice any decision on the merits that the Annex VII tribunal may make; third, that all parties to the dispute ensure their annual catches of southern bluefin tuna do not exceed the levels last agreed; fourth, that each party refrain from conducting experimental fishing programs involving southern bluefin tuna in excess of their annual allocation or otherwise without consent; fifth, that all parties resume negotiations "without delay with a view to reaching agreement on measures for the conservation and management of southern bluefin tuna" and, last, that all parties make further efforts to reach agreement as to optimum utilization and conservation with other States involved in the fishing of southern bluefin tuna.[234] In August 2000, the Annex VII tribunal found that it lacked jurisdiction to rule on the merits of the dispute and, accordingly, revoked ITLOS' provisional measures;[235] the parties later settled their dispute within the CCSBT.[236]

The provisional measures prescribed in the *Southern Bluefin Tuna* cases are notable, both in the number of provisional measures prescribed and because each measure imposed a direct obligation on the States party to the dispute. Dealing with the first two provisional measures in tandem, Australia, New Zealand and Japan all took the view that none of them had taken substantive or intentional steps to aggravate the dispute or otherwise frustrate any future arbitral award.[237] The views of the parties in response to these orders are

232 Ibid., 288–289 [30]–[32].

233 Ibid., 295 [62].

234 Ibid., 297–300 [90](1).

235 *Southern Bluefin Tuna*, Jurisdiction and Admissibility [67].

236 For discussion, see B. Mansfield, 'Letter to the Editor' (2001) 95 *American Journal of International Law* 624.

237 Australia and New Zealand reported that neither State had taken any such steps: 'Joint Report by Australia and New Zealand on Compliance with the Provisional Measures Ordered by the International Tribunal for the Law of the Sea in the *Southern Bluefin Tuna Cases*' in ITLOS, 'Communications from Parties on Matters of Implementation of the Tribunal's Orders' (1999) 4 *Pleadings, Minutes of Public Sittings and Documents* 602,

necessarily subjective given the inherent ambiguity entailed in orders not to aggravate a dispute or prejudice legal proceedings. Yet as no State challenged the position of the other State on this question, compliance may be assumed given the subjective nature of the standard involved.

As to the third and fourth provisional measures, Australia and New Zealand reported that they would not exceed their allocations for the taking of southern bluefin tuna in the 1999 fishing year.[238] However, two issues arose. First, the parties disagreed as to the correct interpretation of the Tribunal's provisional measure. Australia and New Zealand were of the opinion that Japan must immediately cease the taking of southern bluefin tuna once it reached its allocation, whereas Japan was of the opinion that it could continue taking southern bluefin tuna and debit any additional amount taken above its 1999 allocation from its 2000 allocation.[239] Notwithstanding this difference of interpretation, the parties were all in agreement that Japan must abide by the total allowable catch set by the CCSBT.[240] Indeed, Japan, while maintaining that ITLOS' provisional measure in relation to total allowable catch was *ultra vires* and not legally binding, pledged to abide by it on a "without prejudice basis" and "as a demonstration of Japan's good faith".[241] To this end, Japan announced that it would reduce its commercial catch for the 1999 season in compliance with the ITLOS order.[242] As such, the Tribunal's order was said to be "fully complied with".[243] Critically, for the purposes of the fourth provisional measure, Japan conceded that its experimental catch would be counted against its annual national allocation,[244] thereby ensuring compliance with that order. For their part, Australia and New Zealand had never operated such a program and so were also in compliance.[245]

Second, in March 2000, New Zealand informed the Tribunal and the other parties to the dispute that it had violated the Tribunal's third provisional

603 ('Australia and New Zealand Joint Report'). Japan submitted that it had continued to cooperate in good faith with Australia and New Zealand and would continue to act in accordance with ITLOS' provisional measures: 610–611.

238 Ibid., 603.

239 Ibid., 603–605. For Japan's view, see ibid., 612–613.

240 Ibid., 606.

241 Ibid., 611.

242 A. Serdy, *The Other Australia/Japan Living Resources Dispute: Inferences on the Merits of the Southern Bluefin Tuna Arbitration in Light of the Whaling Case* (Brill, 2017), 43.

243 D. Anderson, 'The Role of ITLOS as a Means of Dispute Settlement under UNCLOS' in D. Anderson (ed), *Modern Law of the Sea: Selected Essays* (Martinus Nijhoff, 2008), 547, 555.

244 Australia and New Zealand Joint Report (n. 237), 606 [14].

245 Ibid.

measure by exceeding its total allowable catch by 37 tonnes.[246] New Zealand claimed that this "regrettable, albeit unintentional, overcatch" was due to "a significant amount of non-reporting and mis-reporting of catch", along with proven inadequacies in its fisheries monitoring systems.[247] New Zealand proposed to reduce its catch limit for the 1999/2000 season to adjust for the overfishing in the 1998/1999 season.[248] For its part, Australia expressed regret at New Zealand's violation of ITLOS' order, but welcomed "the prompt remedial action taken by New Zealand".[249] It is difficult to reconcile Australia and New Zealand's strident criticism of Japan's attempts to implement ITLOS' provisional measure by 'pooling' its catch for the 1998/1999 and 1999/2000 seasons, with their later endorsement of the exact same approach when New Zealand found itself in breach of ITLOS' order. These contrary views exposed by the Tribunal's efforts in judicial supervision highlight how States may have different approaches as to how to comply with the orders of an UNCLOS court or tribunal. Further this experience indicates why UNCLOS courts and tribunals must take care to phrase orders with as little ambiguity as possible so as not to provide States with the scope to import their own varied interpretations as to how compliance is to be executed, which may differ in substantial respect from that intended by the court or tribunal in question. If UNCLOS courts or tribunals wish to provide States with the leeway to decide how to implement their orders, then that intention should be made explicit.

As to the fifth and sixth provisional measures, neither Australia nor New Zealand sought to impugn Japan's record on entering into negotiations for the conservation and management of southern bluefin tuna either as between the parties to the dispute or among the broader community of States. In fact, the States welcomed Japan's "determination ... to engage in renewed cooperation directed at the conservation and management of [southern bluefin tuna] stocks within the framework of the 1993 Convention ...".[250] For its part, Japan noted that the parties had conducted negotiations on conservation and management of southern bluefin tuna, and indicated its intention to reach agreement with non-parties to the CCSBT to ensure conservation of southern bluefin tuna stock.[251] In the absence of any complaint from a party to the dispute, it appears that the fifth and sixth provisional measures were complied with.

246 Australia and New Zealand Joint Report (n. 237), 623.
247 Ibid.
248 Ibid., 624.
249 Ibid., 625.
250 Ibid., 608.
251 Ibid., 613–614.

In sum, all but one of ITLOS' provisional measures appear to have been fully complied with. Compliance issues were encountered with ITLOS' third provisional measure, which required the States not to exceed their total allowable catch of southern bluefin tuna. In that regard, Japan took an approach to calculating total allowable catch that Australia and New Zealand had opposed. That disagreement, however, evaporated when New Zealand, as a matter of fact, violated ITLOS' third provisional measure by exceeding its total allowable catch and was compelled to adopt the Japanese interpretation of the Tribunal's order. Given that New Zealand's breach appeared to be as a result of poor administration and management as opposed to intentional non-compliance, and that Japan's approach was eventually adopted by New Zealand with the agreement of Australia, it would appear that the States undertook good faith compliance with the Tribunal's third provisional measure. Moreover, the post-judgment actions indicate that the prescription of provisional measures and efforts made in furtherance of those provisional measures – particularly requirements for the States to undertake further negotiations and discussions – may have facilitated the ultimate resolution of the dispute.[252] From this experience, it is evident that the prescription of provisional measures under UNCLOS and good faith efforts made pursuant to those measures can lead to outcomes separate to the question of compliance and play a facilitative role in the settlement of disputes.[253]

Finally, and separate to the question of compliance, the provisional measures orders in the *Southern Bluefin Tuna* cases have further resulted in important developments in the substantive law of UNCLOS, which are worth noting as a broader outcome of UNCLOS dispute settlement. First, the Tribunal stated that the conservation and management of living resources is part of the protection and preservation of the marine environment.[254] This statement made sense in the context of the order given that Article 290(1) of the

252 As Proelss noted:

> [T]he Annex VII arbitral tribunal, although deciding that it lacked jurisdiction, and that it had consequently to revoke the provisional measures prescribed by ITLOS, revoked the provisional measures *ex nunc* and not *ex tunc* and stated they had been well taken. It is well known that their implementation was conducive to the settlement of the dispute between the parties.

A. Proelss, *The United Nations Convention on the Law of the Sea: A Commentary* (C. H. Beck Hart Nomos, 2017), 1874, citing Mansfield (n. 236); B. Mansfield, 'The Southern Bluefin Tuna Arbitration, Comments on Professor Barbara Kwiatkowska's Article' (2000) 16 *International Journal of Marine and Coastal Law* 361.

253 An outcome also discernible in *Land Reclamation*, Provisional Measures, which is discussed further below, Chapter 4.5.

254 *Southern Bluefin Tuna*, Provisional Measures, 295 [70].

Convention explicitly draws attention to the need to prevent serious harm to the marine environment.[255] Yet the statement has subsequently allowed ITLOS and Annex VII tribunals to consider the impact on fisheries when determining cases related to the protection of the marine environment.[256] Second, the Tribunal referred to the need for States to exercise prudence and caution in the face of uncertainty of the conservation status of southern bluefin tuna.[257] While avoiding the precise term of 'precautionary approach' or 'precautionary principle', the decision reflected the effects of this principle.[258]

4.4 *MOX Plant*

ITLOS was next asked to prescribe provisional measures in the *MOX Plant* dispute between Ireland and the United Kingdom. The primary dispute, instituted in October 2001, concerned a decision by the United Kingdom to grant approval for the operation of a fuel reprocessing plant – set to produce mixed oxide fuel ('MOX') from plutonium and uranium oxides – on its northwest coast bordering the Irish Sea, which Ireland contended would have a significant impact on its marine environment and water quality, and on human health.[259]

Pending the constitution of an Annex VII arbitral tribunal, Ireland sought provisional measures from ITLOS, pursuant to Article 290(5), to suspend the United Kingdom's approval of the plant and to prevent any radioactive substances connected with or to the plant from entering Irish waters. ITLOS found that it had *prima facie* jurisdiction,[260] but declined to prescribe the provisional measures requested on the basis that the measures sought were not required as a matter of urgency.[261] The level of urgency required to be made out was such that an action prejudicial to the rights of the parties was unlikely to be taken

255 While the prescription of provisional measures in the *Southern Bluefin Tun* cases was undertaken pursuant to Article 290(5), ITLOS nonetheless drew attention to the text of Article 290(1) with respect to the prevention of harm to the marine environment: *Southern Bluefin Tuna*, Provisional Measures, 295 [67].

256 See, e.g., *South China Sea*, [956]. See further N. Klein and K. Parlett, *Judging the UN Convention on the Law of the Sea* (Oxford University Press, 2022), 349.

257 *Southern Bluefin Tuna*, Provisional Measures [77].

258 A. Boyle, 'The Environmental Jurisprudence of the International Tribunal for the Law of the Sea' (2007) 22(3) *International Journal of Marine and Coastal Law* 369, 373, 376.

259 For a summary of the facts and proceedings, see R. R. Churchill, 'MOX Plant Arbitration and Cases' in A. Peters (ed), *Max Planck Encyclopedia of Public International Law* (Oxford University Press, June 2018). See *MOX Plant*, Provisional Measures, 'Request for Provisional Measures and Statement of Case' [12].

260 *MOX Plant*, Provisional Measures, 107 [62].

261 Ibid., 110 [81].

before the constitution of the Annex VII tribunal.[262] The United Kingdom had made assurances to ITLOS that there would be no movement of MOX by sea, nor any export of MOX, until October 2002.[263] Accordingly, the provisional measures sought could not have been urgent.

Nonetheless, the Tribunal, acting *proprio motu*,[264] prescribed provisional measures requiring the parties to exchange information regarding the possible consequences for the Irish Sea as a result of the commissioning of the plant, to monitor the risks and effects of the plant on the Irish Sea, and to devise measures to prevent pollution of the marine environment that may arise from the operation of the plant.[265] Turning briefly to outcomes other than compliance, commentators have indicated that this further development of the precautionary principle in provisional measures proceedings concerning elements of international environmental law may be *MOX Plant*'s enduring legacy.[266] Further, questions have arisen as to how ITLOS could, after finding that the criterion of urgency was not made out, nonetheless prescribe provisional measures to any effect.[267]

As to whether compliance took place, in the later proceedings on the merits Ireland acknowledged that "there had been some improvement in the processes of co-operation and the provision of information" since the provisional

262 Ibid., 108 [64].

263 Ibid., 109 [79].

264 Rules of the International Tribunal for the Law of the Sea, Art. 89(5) allows the Tribunal to "prescribe measures different in whole or in part from those requested and indicate the parties which are to take or to comply with each measure". Notwithstanding this power, some commentators debate the jurisdictional basis invoked by the Tribunal to make the orders in question. See, e.g., C. Brown, 'Provisional Measures before the ITLOS: The Mox Plant Case' (2002) 17(2) *International Journal of Marine and Coastal Law* 267, 281ff; G. Jing, 'An Analysis of the Jurisdiction over Provisional Measures of the ITLOS' [2007] *China Oceans Law Review* 413, 422–423.

265 *MOX Plant*, Provisional Measures, 110–111 [89].

266 See, e.g., M. J. C. Foster, 'The *Mox Plant* Case: Provisional Measures in the International Tribunal for the Law of the Sea' (2003) 16 *Leiden Journal of International Law* 611, 619; Brown (n. 264), 267–68. Brown relevantly notes that the prescription of provisional measures by the Tribunal *proprio motu* "contradicted [the Tribunal's] previous finding of an absence of urgency", arguing that it is not a course of action ITLOS should have taken: at 268.

267 Brown (n. 264), 181ff. This point was picked up in many of the declarations and separate opinions. See, e.g., *MOX Plant*, Provisional Measures, 139 [7]–[8] (Separate Opinion of Judge Treves) (noting the "lack of urgency"); 143 [2] (Separate Opinion of Judge ad hoc Székely) (calling this an "inherent contradiction"). See also the Separate Opinions of Judge Anderson and Judge Mensah. This difference may, however, be of no moment given the parties are under obligations both per UNCLOS and customary international law to cooperate: see Brown (n. 264), 283.

measures order, but that there were some "continuing difficulties".[268] In any case, the parties met soon after the provisional measures order from ITLOS with an aim to improving processes for communication and monitoring on the matters relevant to the provisional measures.[269]

The framing of the orders – being merely an order to cooperate and exchange information – makes it difficult to determine whether compliance occurred as it involves a threshold question for which there is no clear guidance. The United Kingdom indicated it was in compliance with ITLOS' order to cooperate, whereas Ireland reserved its position.[270] Determination of compliance necessarily requires a value judgment as to the ideal level of cooperation; while the United Kingdom would likely submit that it undertook either actual or good faith compliance, Ireland is more likely to characterise the United Kingdom's actions as nominal compliance.

The Annex VII tribunal, once constituted, was also asked to prescribe further provisional measures in largely the same terms as that submitted to ITLOS.[271] This Tribunal also declined to prescribe the provisional measures requested on the basis that at the time there was no indication there would be further discharges from the MOX plant and, accordingly, Ireland could not establish an urgent and serious risk of irreparable harm.[272] Nonetheless, the Tribunal observed that ITLOS' provisional measures order remained in force absent a request from any party to the dispute that it be revoked or modified.[273]

Ultimately, the case was discontinued before the Annex VII tribunal in 2008,[274] as the European Court of Justice determined that Ireland was breaching European Union obligations in instituting proceedings against the United Kingdom under UNCLOS.[275] The MOX plant at Sellafield was closed in 2011 in the wake of the Fukushima nuclear disaster in Japan.[276] Nonetheless, the Irish

268 *MOX Plant*, Annex VII Provisional Measures [65].

269 *MOX Plant*, Annex VII Provisional Measures, Reply of Ireland, 7 March 2003 [7.7], [7.64]–[7.72].

270 ITLOS, 'Selected Communications from Parties on Matters of Implementation of Judgments and Orders' (2002) 6 *Yearbook of the International Tribunal for the Law of the Sea* 137, 138.

271 *MOX Plant*, Annex VII Provisional Measures, [32]–[33].

272 Ibid., [61]–[62].

273 Ibid., [66].

274 *MOX Plant* (*Ireland v. United Kingdom*), Termination of Proceedings, Order No. 6 of 6 June 2008, PCA Case No. 2002–01.

275 Judgment of the European Court of Justice (ECJ) in Case C-459/03 *Commission of the European Communities v. Ireland* (2006).

276 Fiona Harvey, 'Sellafield Mox nuclear fuel plant to close' 11 August 2011, *The Guardian*, available at <https://www.theguardian.com/environment/2011/aug/03/sellafield-mox-plant-close>.

Sea has been described as among the most radioactively contaminated seas in the world.[277]

4.5 *Land Reclamation*

In *Land Reclamation*, Malaysia instituted proceedings against Singapore alleging that Singapore's land reclamation activities constituted breaches of its obligations under UNCLOS and seeking the delimitation of the territorial waters between the two States.[278] Malaysia particularly took issue with Singapore for the "initiation and continuation of its land reclamation activities without due notification and full consultation with Malaysia".[279] As a result, Malaysia alleged that Singapore was in violation of obligations under UNCLOS relating to the protection and preservation of the marine environment.[280]

Malaysia sought provisional measures from ITLOS prior to the constitution of the Annex VII tribunal pursuant to Article 290(5), requiring Singapore to suspend any and all land reclamation activities in the vicinity of the maritime boundary claimed by the two States, and other measures regarding negotiations and showing due regard for the rights of each State.[281] While asserting that the Annex VII tribunal would have *prima facie* jurisdiction over the dispute[282] and that the request for provisional measures was admissible,[283] ITLOS considered that the request did not reveal a situation of urgency or a risk of irreversible damage to Malaysia's rights pending the constitution of the Annex VII tribunal.[284] Accordingly, the Tribunal rejected Malaysia's request for provisional measures.[285] Nonetheless, ITLOS placed on record undertakings by Singapore to share information and its purported readiness to enter into negotiations and give Malaysia notification of any construction that may affect its rights of passage.[286] In addition, the parties communicated during the course of the proceedings, resulting in a commitment from Singapore not to undertake certain land reclamation activities in 'Area D' at Pulau Tekong

277 See, e.g., T. Hall, '"... Carried by the Wind out to Sea" *Ireland and the Isle of Man v. Sellafield*: Anatomy of a Transboundary Pollution Dispute' (1994) 6(3) *Georgetown International Environmental Law Review* 639, 640; Brown (n. 264), 269.

278 *Land Reclamation*, Provisional Measures, 15 [22].

279 Ibid.

280 Ibid., 18 [31] (referring *inter alia* to UNCLOS Arts. 192, 194, 198, 200, 204, 205, 206 and 210).

281 Ibid., 16 [23].

282 Ibid., 21 [59].

283 Ibid., 21 [63].

284 Ibid., 22 [72].

285 Ibid., 22 [73].

286 Ibid., 23 [76]–[81].

that could cause irreversible action,[287] and proposing a joint scientific independent expert committee.

In light of the above, and in a substantially similar approach to *MOX Plant*,[288] ITLOS reiterated the parties' duty to cooperate pursuant to UNCLOS as well as their duty not to create an 'irremediable situation'.[289] Further, ITLOS reminded the parties of their duty not to aggravate or extend the dispute submitted to the Tribunal.[290] The Tribunal invoked Article 89(5) of its Rules to prescribe measures *proprio motu*.[291] To that end, ITLOS unanimously required the parties to: first, establish a joint group of independent experts to conduct a study on the effects of Singapore's land reclamation activities; second, exchange information on the risks and effects of Singapore's activities; and third, consult with a view to reaching prompt agreement on temporary measures to be taken with respect to 'Area D'.[292] These provisional measures, while differing from those originally sought by Malaysia, by and large reflected undertakings made by the parties in the course of the proceedings before ITLOS.

As to compliance, the parties jointly established the 'Group of Experts', which made a report to the parties in 2004. The recommendations of the Group were accepted by the parties in full and were said to "provide the basis for an amicable, full and final settlement of the said dispute".[293] To this end, the parties reached a joint agreement and discontinued the proceedings. Compliance with the provisional measures was therefore not only achieved but also resulted in the overall resolution of the proceedings; leading one commentator to reflect on the "significant role" ITLOS can play in "conflict management through its provisional measures jurisdiction".[294]

287 Ibid., 24–25 [85]–[87].

288 Churchill (n. 259); R. Churchill, 'The International Tribunal for the Law of the Sea: Survey for 2003' (2004) 19(4) *International Journal of Marine and Coastal Law* 369, 378–379.

289 *Land Reclamation*, Provisional Measures, 25 [90]–[92].

290 Ibid., 26 [102].

291 Ibid., 26 [101].

292 Ibid., 27 [106].

293 *Land Reclamation*, Merits [11].

294 Churchill (n. 288) 380. See also R. Churchill, 'Dispute Settlement under the UN Convention on the Law of the Sea: Survey for 2005' (2006) 21(4) *International Journal of Marine and Coastal Law* 377, 385; Z. Keyuan, 'International Tribunal for the Law of the Sea: Procedures, Practices, and Asian States' (2010) 41(2) *Ocean Development and International Law* 131, 136, 146–47; H. Tuerk, 'The Contribution of the International Tribunal for the Law of the Sea to International Law' (2007) 26(2) *Penn State International Law Review* 289, 304.

4.6 ARA *Libertad*

In ARA *Libertad*, Argentina instituted proceedings before an Annex VII tribunal against Ghana and sought provisional measures from ITLOS pursuant to Article 290(5). The primary dispute concerned the detention of an Argentine warship, the ARA Fragata Libertad, by Ghana. Argentina alleged that Ghana prevented the vessel from exercising its freedom of navigation, resulting in a violation of Argentine sovereign immunity.[295] The frigate was seized in port at the request of a US company seeking recovery of a judgment issued against Argentina.[296]

Argentina sought provisional measures allowing the ARA Libertad to leave Ghana.[297] ITLOS considered that the Annex VII tribunal would have *prima facie* jurisdiction over at least part of the dispute.[298] Attempts by Ghanaian authorities to board the vessel "demonstrate[d] the gravity of the situation and underline[d] the urgent need for measures pending the constitution of the Annex VII arbitral tribunal".[299] ITLOS thus unanimously prescribed provisional measures in the manner sought by Argentina on 15 December 2012.[300]

Four days after ITLOS' order, the Ghanian Attorney General requested the Supreme Court of Ghana to quash the interlocutory injunction that had allowed for the detention of the ARA Libertad under Ghanaian law.[301] The ARA Libertad departed soon after, "without resistance from the Ghanaian authorities".[302] In June 2013, the Supreme Court of Ghana rendered a judgment upholding the position at customary international law on the immunity of warships.[303] The parties then terminated the Annex VII arbitral proceedings.[304]

It is notable that the situation was comparable to the prompt release cases in that the executive branch of government could not necessarily interfere

---

295 ARA *Libertad*, Provisional Measures, 336–337 [26]. These claims implicated Article 32 of UNCLOS on immunity and navigational rights alleged under Articles 18(1)(b), 87(1)(a) and 90. Ibid.

296 An action taken to enforce a judgment of the US Supreme Court in *Republic of Argentina v. NML Capital, Ltd.* (2014) 573 US 134.

297 ARA *Libertad*, Provisional Measures, 338 [27].

298 Ibid., 344 [66]–[67]; cf 343–344 [61].

299 Ibid., 349 [99].

300 Ibid., 350 [108(1)].

301 ARA *Libertad* (*Argentina v. Ghana*), Agreement between Argentina and Ghana, 27 September 2013, PCA Case No. 2013–11, [1].

302 *The Republic v. High Court (Comm. Div.) Accra ex parte; Attorney General* (Supreme Court of Ghana, Case No. J5/10/2013, 20 June 2013) 16, reproduced in ITLOS, 'Documents' (2012) 18 *Pleadings, Minutes of Public Sittings and Documents* 359, 391–426.

303 Agreement between Argentina and Ghana (n. 301) [2]; ibid.

304 ARA *Libertad* (*Argentina v. Ghana*), Termination of Proceedings, Order of 11 November 2013, PCA Case No. 2013–11.

with domestic court proceedings. In ARA *Libertad*, several judges noted that the Ghanaian executive supported the release of the vessel but could not intercede in national judicial processes.[305] The ITLOS order thus enabled the executive to act where it was not otherwise able to do so. Not only was compliance achieved, but the resulting court decision clarified the Ghanaian law on sovereign immunity, thereby bringing Ghana into compliance with the position both in accordance with UNCLOS and under customary international law. To this end, it may be observed that provisional measures can be an "effective and timely procedure … to obtain the release of a vessel"[306] where prompt release proceedings are unavailable due to the scope of jurisdiction. The ARA Libertad continues to sail as a training ship of the Argentine navy at time of writing.[307] Argentina has also settled the outstanding claims against it that had prompted the seizure of the ship.[308]

4.7 *Arctic Sunrise*

In *Arctic Sunrise*, the Netherlands sought the release of a Greenpeace vessel flying its flag that had 30 crew members on board who were protesting at a Russian oil platform, *Prirazlomnaya*. Russian officials seized the Arctic Sunrise and arrested the so-called 'Arctic 30' on 19 September 2013.[309] The Arctic 30 were initially investigated for a violation of the Russian criminal code for piracy by an organised group,[310] but this charge was changed to one of hooliganism.[311] The Arctic Sunrise vessel was boarded and searched by Russian officials and seized as part of their investigations.[312] Despite diplomatic efforts to secure the release of the Dutch vessel and all crew members,[313] the Netherlands instituted proceedings under Part XV of UNCLOS.

---

305 ARA *Libertad*, Provisional Measures, 376–377 (Separate Opinion of Judges Wolfrum and Cot), 387 [31] (Separate Opinion of Judge Lucky), 358 [4] (Separate Opinion of Judge Rao), 353 [4] (Declaration of Judge Paik).

306 M. Cabrera Mirassou, 'ARA Libertad' in A. Peters (ed), *Max Planck Encyclopedia of Public International Law* (Oxford University Press, 2014) [23], cited in S. Trevisanut, 'Twenty Years of Prompt Release of Vessels: Admissibility, Jurisdiction, and Recent Trends' (2017) 48(3–4) *Ocean Development & International Law* 300, 306.

307 Source: <https://seawaves.com/?p=19191>.

308 A. Stevenson, 'How Argentina Settled a Billion-Dollar Debt Dispute With Hedge Funds' 25 April 2016, *The New York Times*, available at: <https://www.nytimes.com/2016/04/25/business/dealbook/how-argentina-settled-a-billion-dollar-debt-dispute-with-hedge-funds.html>.

309 *Arctic Sunrise*, Merits [3].

310 Ibid., [106].

311 Ibid., [123].

312 Ibid., [110], [112], [120].

313 These requests are outlined in ibid., [105], [108], [111], [114]–[115].

The Netherlands requested the release of the vessel and crew members pursuant to Article 290(5), and ITLOS issued an order to this effect on 22 November 2013.[314] Russia did not participate in these proceedings, but the crew were allowed to leave Russia following an amnesty decree on 18 December 2013.[315] The amnesty decree was issued to celebrate an anniversary of the Russian Constitution and in the lead up to the 2014 Winter Olympics; critics considered the decision a public relations exercise.[316] Greenpeace's vessel was subsequently released as well on 1 August 2014, albeit not as a direct response to the provisional measures order either.[317] In these circumstances, it is difficult to take the position that compliance was a concrete, causal result of the provisional measures order. The provisional measures order was perhaps a factor but given Russia's refusal to participate in the proceedings, it appears that other matters (also or alternatively) influenced Russia's decisions to release the Arctic 30 and the vessel.

In the merits phase of *Arctic Sunrise*, the Annex VII tribunal considered whether Russia was in compliance with the ITLOS order on provisional measures. The Tribunal noted that the Arctic 30 were released from detention within seven days of the Tribunal's prescription of provisional measures, which placed Russia in compliance with its order. However, it took 27 days from the time the Netherlands posted the bank guarantee to the Arctic 30 being able to leave Russia.[318] Ultimately, the Tribunal held that, notwithstanding the fact that Russia had 'released' the crew, this 27-day delay in facilitating the Arctic 30's departure from Russian jurisdiction "did not meet the promptness requirement" of the ITLOS order.[319]

This approach largely echoed the determination made in *Saiga (No. 2)*, in which ITLOS considered that an 80-day delay in compliance in prompt release proceedings did not meet requirements of promptness.[320] The finding of non-compliance in *Arctic Sunrise* is significant as it is one of the few explicit findings of breach of provisional measures made by an UNCLOS court or tribunal. However, as Miles notes, the Tribunal did not indicate "whether that

---

314 *Arctic Sunrise*, Provisional Measures.

315 *Arctic Sunrise*, Merits [3].

316 'Russia drops first Greenpeace Arctic 30 case' 24 December 2013, *BBC News*, available at: <https://www.bbc.com/news/world-europe-25504016>.

317 John Vidal, 'Arctic 30: Russia Releases Greenpeace Ship' 6 June 2014, *The Guardian*, available at: <https://www.theguardian.com/environment/2014/jun/06/arctic-30-sunrise-russia-to-release-greenpeace-ship>.

318 *Arctic Sunrise*, Merits [343].

319 Ibid., Merits [350].

320 *Saiga (No. 2)*, Merits [165]. See above Chapter 3.2.

breach would result in any additional penalty to Russia beyond the compensation already required for the detention of the vessel and those aboard".[321] As such, while a finding of breach was made, no practical consequences appear to have arisen therefrom.

Further, the Arctic Sunrise did not leave the Russian port at which it had been detained until eight months after the ITLOS order; the Tribunal considered that this delay violated the promptness requirement of the provisional measures order and, accordingly, rendered Russia non-compliant.[322] *Arctic Sunrise*, in conjunction with ITLOS' past jurisprudence in *Saiga (No. 2)*, provides an indication of the level of immediacy expected of States by ITLOS and Annex VII tribunals in complying with orders with an element of promptness or urgency, altering the yardstick by which compliance with such orders is measured vis-à-vis orders lacking such an element. Despite this experience, the Arctic Sunrise continues to be used by Greenpeace in its work protesting environmental degradation.[323]

4.8 *Ghana/Côte d'Ivoire*

The Tribunal was next asked to prescribe provisional measures in *Ghana/Côte d'Ivoire*. The dispute, the merits of which are discussed in greater detail in Chapter 5, concerned the delimitation of the maritime boundaries and outer continental shelf between the two States in a zone containing valuable hydrocarbon resources. Notably, the dispute is the first time a provisional measures request was heard and determined by a special chamber of ITLOS, composed of five judges.[324] Pursuant to Article 290(1), Côte d'Ivoire requested that the Special Chamber prescribe provisional measures to the effect of requiring Ghana to refrain from unilateral action in the disputed area, to cease all ongoing oil exploration and exploitation, including the granting of any new permits, in the disputed area, as well as to take all necessary steps to preserve the disputed area and to prevent it being used in a way detrimental to Côte d'Ivoire.[325]

The Special Chamber first considered that the *prima facie* jurisdiction requirement had been made out by the mere fact that the parties had submitted the dispute to ITLOS by special agreement, such agreement evidencing a

321 Miles (n. 192), 336.

322 *Arctic Sunrise*, Merits [350].

323 Greenpeace, 'About the Arctic Sunrise', available at: <https://www.greenpeace.org/usa/about/shiptour-old/about-the-arctic-sunrise/>.

324 Three permanent judges of ITLOS sat in the Special Chamber (Judges Bouguetaia, Wolfrum and Paik), along with Judges ad hoc Mensah and Abraham.

325 *Ghana/Côte d'Ivoire*, Provisional Measures, 148 [5].

concession that the Special Chamber had jurisdiction over the dispute.[326] The Special Chamber then found that the circumstances were sufficiently urgent and Côte d'Ivoire's claims sufficiently plausible to warrant the prescription of the provisional measures sought.[327] The Special Chamber did not, however, consider the suspension of Ghanaian oil exploration and exploitation in the disputed area to be an appropriate provisional measure in the circumstances. While noting the risk of serious harm to the marine environment that could be caused by oil exploration and exploitation in the disputed area,[328] and that such activities by Ghana would likely cause a risk of irreparable prejudice to the sovereign rights invoked by Côte d'Ivoire,[329] the Special Chamber considered that the wholesale suspension of such activities in the disputed area would cause Ghana significant financial loss and undue prejudice, in addition to potentially causing adverse environmental effects. As such, the Special Chamber refused to prescribe the provisional measure sought.[330] Instead, the Special Chamber exercised its power to prescribe provisional measures *proprio motu*, preventing Ghana from undertaking any new (as opposed to ongoing) drilling activities in the disputed area.[331] The other provisional measures prescribed were in substantially the same form as sought by Côte d'Ivoire, though with slight alterations to emphasise the parties' duty to cooperate to prevent the aggravation of the dispute and any harm to the marine environment for the pendency of the proceedings.[332]

In the primary proceedings, Côte d'Ivoire submitted that Ghana had failed to comply with two of the Special Chamber's provisional measures: first, that requiring Ghana to ensure no new drilling activities took place in the disputed area; and, second, to pursue cooperation and refrain from unilateral action in the disputed area that might aggravate the dispute.[333] As to the first alleged breach, the dispute between the parties was largely interpretive in nature. Côte d'Ivoire submitted that Ghana had artificially accelerated its drilling activities in the disputed area, and that this new crushing of rock constituted a breach

326 Ibid., 155 [37]–[38].
327 Ibid., 159 [62]–[63].
328 Ibid., 160 [68].
329 Ibid., 163 [89], [96].
330 Ibid., 164–165 [99]–[102].
331 Ibid., 165 [102].
332 Ibid., 166 [108(1)].
333 *Ghana/Côte d'Ivoire*, Merits, 172 [648]. Côte d'Ivoire originally also alleged violation of an additional provisional measure that required Ghana to carry out continuous monitoring activities in the disputed area to prevent harm to the marine environment, but did not maintain this argument at the final hearing: at 173 [649].

of the provisional measures order.[334] For its part, Ghana maintained that the Special Chamber's order only prevented drilling in new wells, with drilling activities able to continue to the extent desired by Ghana in wells existing as at the time of the provisional measures order.[335] The Special Chamber accepted Ghana's interpretation in its entirety and rejected Côte d'Ivoire claim that Ghana's drilling activities constituted a breach of the provisional measures order.[336]

As to the second alleged breach, Côte d'Ivoire complained that Ghana had repeatedly failed to provide it with information concerning activities in the disputed area, constituting a breach of its obligation to cooperate.[337] Ghana submitted that it had always responded to reasonable requests for information by Côte d'Ivoire.[338] The Special Chamber noted that while Ghana had responded to a number of Côte d'Ivoire's requests for information,[339] it only provided all relevant information after the President of the Special Chamber requested it to comply,[340] which Ghana promptly did. The Special Chamber considered that this gap between the request for information and compliance "cannot reasonably be considered to constitute a violation" of the provisional measures ordered by the Special Chamber and that Ghana had continued to cooperate with Côte d'Ivoire in line with the Special Chamber's order.[341] As a result, both of Côte d'Ivoire's claims as to the international responsibility of Ghana for non-compliance with the provisional measures orders were rejected.[342]

The final judgment in *Ghana/Côte d'Ivoire* is notable as it provides one of the few extended analyses of compliance by a State with orders of an UNCLOS court or tribunal to date.[343] Echoing the findings of the tribunals in *Saiga (No. 2)*, and the merits decision of *Arctic Sunrise*, the Special Chamber was of the view that a slight delay in compliance, even if rectification of that delay requires intervention by judicial officers, does not constitute a violation of the State's obligations to comply with orders of the relevant UNCLOS court or

334 Ibid., 169–170 [636]–[637].
335 Ibid., 169 [636], 170–171 [642]–[644].
336 Ibid., 173–174 [650]–[652].
337 Ibid., 170 [638]–[639].
338 Ibid., 172 [646].
339 Ibid., 174 [653]–[654].
340 Ibid., 174 [655].
341 Ibid., 174 [656]–[657].
342 Ibid., 175 [658].
343 Another such finding is anticipated in *Three Ukrainian Naval Vessels*. See further below, Chapter 4.10.

tribunal.[344] It may be possible to conclude from this line of jurisprudence that UNCLOS courts and tribunals are minded not to insist on strict and immediate compliance, and instead are prepared to allow States a certain amount of latitude and flexibility in complying with their orders. Admittedly, the violation of the obligation to cooperate complained of by Côte d'Ivoire was *de minimis* in nature, and it is likely that an UNCLOS court or tribunal may find differently where the violation alleged to be caused by the delay is more substantial in nature, or if the delay has the capacity to irreparably impact the rights of a party to the dispute. It is further notable that the Special Chamber was prepared to play an active role in requesting compliance with its orders, with such a facilitative role resulting in full compliance in this dispute.

4.9 *Enrica Lexie*

In the provisional measures phase of *Enrica Lexie*, Italy sought the release of two of its marines from Indian custody. The marines had been aboard an Italian-flagged oil tanker, the Enrica Lexie, and shot dead two Indian fishermen, who they thought to be pirates. India had arrested the marines and instituted criminal proceedings against them. Italy, however, objected to India's exercise of jurisdiction, arguing violations of UNCLOS as well as international law on the immunity of State officials.

Pursuant to Article 290(5), Italy sought provisional measures that would have required India to refrain from taking any judicial or administrative action against the marines, and to lift all restrictions on their liberty, including to allow both marines to return to Italy for the duration of the Annex VII proceedings. ITLOS declined to order that the marines be allowed to return to Italy, considering that to be an issue tied to the merits of the case such that it could only be properly adjudicated by the Annex VII tribunal.[345] ITLOS did order that Italy and India both suspend court proceedings and refrain from instituting new ones that may aggravate or extend the dispute before the Annex VII tribunal.[346] The Italian Public Prosecutor and the Supreme Court of India each stayed their respective investigations;[347] compliance was therefore exemplary.

The Annex VII tribunal later prescribed provisional measures further to Article 290(1), ordering the return of one of the marines, Sergeant Girone, to Italy for the pendency of the arbitral proceedings; Sergeant Girone was returned to Italy a month after the prescription of provisional measures

344 *Ghana/Côte d'Ivoire*, Merits, 174 [656]–[657].
345 *Enrica Lexie*, ITLOS Provisional Measures 204 [132].
346 Ibid., 205 [141].
347 *Enrica Lexie*, Annex VII Provisional Measures [11]; *Enrica Lexie*, Merits [13].

following an order by the Supreme Court of India.[348] The time lapse for compliance allowed for the implementation of the provisional measures order within India's judicial system. As Italy did not make any claim that India violated this order at the merits stage of the proceedings, it could be extrapolated that India was in full compliance with the order. This case proceeded to the merits and is discussed further in Chapter 6.

4.10 *Three Ukrainian Naval Vessels*

Three Ukrainian Naval Vessels concerned the detention of two Ukrainian warships, a naval auxiliary vessel,[349] and the 24 servicemen constituting their crew.[350] The vessels and servicemen were detained by Russia following their passage through the Kerch Strait; Russia claimed that innocent passage in the territorial sea leading to the Kerch Strait was suspended for foreign military vessels and the Ukrainian vessels had violated Russian law to that effect. The dispute took place in the broader context of contested sovereignty over the Kerch Strait and Black Sea; Russia has asserted full control over the Strait since its 2014 annexation of Crimea.[351]

Ukraine instituted proceedings under UNCLOS, claiming breaches of sovereign immunity alleged to arise under Articles 32, 58, 95 and 96 of the Convention.[352] Ukraine also sought provisional measures pending the constitution of an Annex VII arbitral tribunal pursuant to Article 290(5), namely the release of the three vessels and servicemen and the suspension of all proceedings against the servicemen. Russia did not appear in the provisional measures proceedings and ITLOS prescribed the provisional measures sought by Ukraine in May 2019.

In June 2019, Russia reported to ITLOS that it had "proposed specific procedural measures that, within the framework of Russian legislation, would allow [it] to release the servicemen from custody and hand over the vessels to Ukraine", indicating that Russia did not intend to implement the provisional measures in the form ordered or with the immediacy required.[353] At best, Russia's actions in this regard could be considered comparable to actions taken by Ghana and France in actioning the decision through national processes.

---

348 *Enrica Lexie*, Merits [30]–[33].

349 *Three Ukrainian Naval Vessels*, 291 [30].

350 Ibid., 289–290 [24].

351 See generally I. Marchuk, 'Powerful States and International Law: Changing Narratives and Power Struggles in International Courts' (2019) 26(1) *UC Davis Journal of International Law and Policy* 65, 79; N. Oral, 'Ukraine v the Russian Federation: Navigating Conflict over Sovereignty under UNCLOS' (2021) 97 *International Law Studies* 478.

352 *Three Ukrainian Naval Vessels*, 288 [22].

353 *Three Ukrainian Naval Vessels*, Report of the Russian Federation, 25 June 2019.

For its part, Ukraine did not consider the Russian proposals to be acceptable but inconsistent with the provisional orders made by ITLOS.[354] Ukraine seized a Russian tanker in the Black Sea in July 2019, which commentators indicated was likely an act of retaliation.[355] The servicemen were eventually released and returned to Ukraine in September 2019 as part of a prisoner swap.[356] While Ukraine achieved one of its principal goals in securing the release of the naval crew, it does not appear that this result occurred directly because of the ITLOS provisional measures order.

The vessels were not returned to Ukraine until November 2019; Ukraine claimed that the three naval vessels were returned in a sub-par condition, having been stripped of "dome lights, sockets, and toilet bowls" as well as some weaponry.[357] Russia refuted the claim. Certainly, Russia's delayed compliance had already placed it in breach of ITLOS' order; any interference or modification to the vessels would have implicitly placed Russia in further breach because good faith compliance would assume the property is returned in a comparable condition to when it was seized. In any case, while the measures sought by Ukraine were ultimately forthcoming, the releases were far from prompt and, given that promptness is a core component of the provisional measures order, it cannot be said that Russia was in full compliance with ITLOS' order. At most, there was nominal compliance with ITLOS' order. It has been noted that "if the ITLOS's order had been fully complied with, it would have gone a long way to settling the substance of the dispute before the Annex VII tribunal".[358]

The Annex VII tribunal constituted to hear the primary dispute, *Detention of Ukrainian Naval Vessels and Servicemen*, released its award on Russia's preliminary objections on 27 June 2022.[359] In contrast to the provisional measures proceedings before ITLOS, Russia submitted an appearance before the Annex VII tribunal. Subject to certain jurisdictional limitations, the Tribunal

354 *Three Ukrainian Naval Vessels*, Supplementary Report of Ukraine to the Registry, 26 June 2019.

355 Matthew Bodner, 'Ukraine Seizes Russian Tanker in Black Sea in Retaliation for 2018 Flotilla Clash' 26 July 2019, *Sydney Morning Herald*, available at: <https://www.smh.com.au/world/europe/ukraine-seizes-russian-tanker-in-black-sea-in-retaliation-for-2018-flotilla-clash-20190726-p52axd.html>.

356 'Ukraine and Russia Exchange Prisoners in Landmark Deal' 7 September 2019, *BBC News*, available at: <https://www.bbc.com/news/world-europe-49610107>.

357 'Ukraine Accuses Russia of Returning Ships "Stripped of Toilets"' 21 November 2019, *BBC News*, available at: <https://www.bbc.com/news/world-europe-50501241>.

358 R. Churchill, 'Dispute Settlement in the Law of the Sea: Survey for 2019' (2020) 35 *International Journal of Marine and Coastal Law* 621, 637.

359 While the award is dated 27 June 2022, it was not publicly released until 11 July 2022, so as to allow the parties to identify whether any components of the judgment constituted confidential information that should not be made publicly available.

found itself competent to adjudge the merits of the dispute, rejecting several of Russia's preliminary objections and deferring the determination of others to the merits phase.[360] Two of the preliminary objections lodged by Russia concern questions of compliance with ITLOS' provisional measures order and provide some insight into the parties' views as to the nature of compliance with that order.

First, Ukraine argued before the Tribunal that Russia had "violated Articles 290 and 296 of the Convention by failing to comply with the ITLOS provisional measures order".[361] Ukraine argued that Russia's four-month delay in releasing the servicemen and six-month delay in releasing the vessels subject to ITLOS' provisional measures order violated the inherent requirement of promptness and aggravated the dispute.[362] Further, the vessels were returned "in an unacceptable state of disrepair".[363] Russia made a preliminary objection to the Tribunal determining such a question, submitting that because, in its view, the Tribunal lacked jurisdiction to decide the dispute between the parties on the merits, it also lacked jurisdiction to adjudge questions of compliance with ITLOS' provisional measures order.[364] In the alternate, Russia argued that it had complied with the order by releasing the servicemen and vessels.[365] The Tribunal rejected Russia's preliminary objection on the basis that it had already found that it had jurisdiction over the main dispute between the parties,[366] opening the door to an assessment of compliance in the merits phase.

Second, Ukraine submitted that Russia acted in contravention of its obligations under Article 279 of the Convention, which requires parties to settle disputes by "peaceful means", as it "aggravated the dispute ... by extending the detention of Ukraine's servicemen and continuing to maintain the criminal cases against them after their release".[367] Russia objected to the Tribunal considering Ukraine's claim on the basis that Article 279 "contains no reference to aggravation of disputes",[368] and that, in any event, by meeting with Ukraine and negotiating the release of the servicemen and vessels, it had "attenuated

360 *Detention of Ukrainian Naval Vessels and Servicemen* [158].
361 Ibid., [158].
362 Ibid., [162].
363 Ibid.
364 Ibid., [159].
365 Ibid., [160].
366 Ibid., [167]–[168].
367 Ibid., [175].
368 Ibid., [171].

rather than aggravated the dispute".[369] The Tribunal dismissed Russia's preliminary objection, deferring the question of whether Article 279 prohibits the aggravation of disputes to the merits phase,[370] in light of the fact that the ITLOS provisional measures order required the parties not to take any action that might "aggravate or extend the dispute".[371] This order was, in the view of the Tribunal, enough to impose on the parties "a duty of non-aggravation",[372] with the question of compliance to be determined at the merits phase.

From this phase of proceedings, it is evident that Ukraine is of the view that Russia has, by its delay in releasing the vessels and servicemen and in returning the vessels in a state of disrepair, failed to comply with the ITLOS provisional measures order and/or the Convention in two material respects. Russia, on the other hand, is of the view that its actions, far from constituting non-compliance, demonstrate actual and good faith, rather than nominal, compliance with the ITLOS provisional measures order. It will be for the Tribunal to determine the interpretation of the facts and law it favours during the merits phase.

Without speculating too closely on hypotheticals, the Tribunal's approach to determining the extent to which compliance with provisional measures orders imposes a duty of promptness on parties, and whether such a duty is qualified by an element of reasonableness, will be of interest. The case also presents an ideal opportunity for the clarification of issues of causation in assessing compliance; the Tribunal may be able to reflect on whether compliance must result because of the provisional measures order or whether behaviour that correlates with the order (nominal compliance) is sufficient. A determination as to whether leaving the vessels in a state of disrepair rendered Russia non-compliant may also illuminate the nature of good faith compliance. Further, the Tribunal may clarify the extent to which parties to disputes concerning the application or interpretation of the Convention are under a duty not to aggravate the dispute absent an order from the Tribunal to the contrary should it interpret and apply Article 279 of the Convention in accordance with Ukraine's claim. Such clarification would certainly represent an opportunity to advance understandings of what it means for State parties to a dispute in reacting to provisional measures decisions, and indeed other judgments that are binding on the parties.

369 Ibid., [173].
370 Ibid., [185].
371 *Three Ukrainian Naval Vessels*, 312 [124(c)].
372 *Detention of Ukrainian Naval Vessels and Servicemen* [183]–[184].

Last, it is worth briefly noting that the question of compliance with any order on the merits issued by the Tribunal will be inextricably tied to the current geopolitical climate following the 2022 Russian invasion of Ukraine. Such circumstances demonstrate how compliance with decisions of international courts and tribunals may be motivated or vitiated by political circumstances outside the control of the tribunal and perhaps even the parties.

4.11 *San Padre Pio*

San Padre Pio concerned the arrest of a Swiss-flagged vessel, the San Padre Pio, along with its master and three of its crew by Nigeria. Nigeria claimed that the San Padre Pio had been engaged in bunkering in its EEZ in violation of Nigerian law. In May 2019, Switzerland instituted proceedings seeking the prescription of provisional measures pursuant to Article 290(5) in the form of the release of the San Padre Pio and its crew.[373] Switzerland claimed that Nigeria had violated the freedom of navigation of vessels in the EEZ through the interception, arrest and detention of the San Padre Pio, as well as violating Switzerland's exclusive flag State jurisdiction.[374]

In July 2019, ITLOS granted the provisional measures sought contingent on Switzerland posting a US$14 million bond. Further, ITLOS made an order requiring the parties not to take any action that may aggravate or extend the dispute submitted to the Annex VII tribunal.[375] Switzerland prepared a bank guarantee in November 2019,[376] though Nigeria did not accept its terms.[377] Nigerian court proceedings in relation to the incident remained on foot following the provisional measures order; Switzerland claimed that a decision of the Nigerian Court of Appeal meant that there were no grounds under Nigerian law for the continued detention of the crew and vessel, rendering the provisional measures ordered moot.[378] The Master and the crew were found not guilty by the Nigerian courts in November 2019 and were released promptly thereafter, having been detained for nearly two years.[379] The parties agreed to submit the primary dispute to ITLOS.[380] The parties concluded a memorandum of understanding and the San Padre Pio departed the Nigerian EEZ in

373 *San Padre Pio*, 381 [27].
374 Ibid., 380–381 [26].
375 Ibid., 410 [146].
376 *San Padre Pio*, Additional Report of the Swiss Confederation, 8 November 2019.
377 *San Padre Pio*, Additional Report of the Swiss Confederation, 5 November 2020.
378 Ibid.
379 *San Padre Pio* (*No. 2*), Memorial of Switzerland [0.14].
380 *San Padre Pio* (*No. 2*), Special Agreement and Notification.

December 2021 in accordance with that memorandum.[381] The ITLOS proceedings were then discontinued.[382]

Determining compliance is difficult in this instance and would require an investigation as to whether the bank guarantee drawn up by Switzerland was, in fact, unreasonable. Nigeria's resistance to negotiating more favourable terms may not be consistent with what may be considered good faith compliance.[383] While compliance was eventually forthcoming, questions arise as to whether both Nigeria and Switzerland acted in compliance with the ITLOS order at all material times. The actions taken may have potentially aggravated or extended the dispute but the fact that the dispute was settled may instead indicate that there was compliance with this order.

4.12 *Conclusion*

The outcomes of the provisional measures orders have generally been positive in that this stage of proceedings has led to the resolution of the dispute and discontinuance of the proceedings in several instances. In addition, the orders of the tribunals have facilitated cooperation between the parties and such enhancements of inter-State relations may not have been forthcoming in the absence of the UNCLOS proceedings. As such, it may be observed that even if the relevant tribunal's orders were not fully complied with, or were imperfectly complied with, the mere act of instituting proceedings may lead to greater diplomatic communication between the States, allowing for the resolution of the dispute outside of the UNCLOS compulsory dispute settlement system, as occurred in the *Southern Bluefin Tuna* cases and *Land Reclamation*.[384] Further, UNCLOS courts and tribunals have demonstrated that, where appropriate, they are willing to take a more active role in ascertaining compliance with their orders, as occurred with the provisional measures phase of *Ghana/Côte d'Ivoire*. This role is consistent with the ability of UNCLOS courts and tribunals to exercise judicial supervision over the execution of provisional measures and other orders made during the pendency of the proceedings. Finally, the applicant State has frequently obtained what was sought in the request for provisional measures, even if not reflecting immediate compliance with the tribunal's orders.

It should, however, be noted that the compliance record in provisional measures proceedings has entailed significant questions of non-compliance in

381 *San Padre Pio (No. 2)*, Order of 29 December 2021.
382 Ibid.
383 See Chapter 2.
384 See above Chapter 4.3, 4.5.

relation to three of these proceedings.[385] Three factors may assist in explaining this result. First, two of the three cases in which compliance concerns exist involve alleged breaches of provisional measure orders by Russia.[386] Both cases took place against much larger concerns involving Russian sovereignty and, in the case of *Three Ukrainian Naval Vessels*, the Russo-Ukrainian War. Such tensions may go some way to explaining the more complicated approach to compliance.

Second, whether a State has acted in compliance with provisional measures orders can be a more difficult benchmark than in relation to other orders because there is an inherent criterion of promptness needed for compliance with provisional measures orders to be properly given effect. This requirement arises because of the nature of provisional measures proceedings, in that they respond to an urgent need of a State. Hence, provisional measures orders require not only that the orders in question be complied with but, alike prompt release proceedings, that compliance is timely if not reasonably immediate. A failure to take timely action is therefore likely to render a State substantially non-compliant, even if some form of compliance is eventually forthcoming, as in *Three Ukrainian Naval Vessels* and *San Padre Pio*. The *Arctic Sunrise* tribunal's finding of non-compliance by Russia with the provisional measures order reflects consideration of the importance of timing. In such cases, while the States in question were eventually in compliance, that compliance was imperfect.

Finally, in several instances the provisional measures ordered appear to be ambiguous and the way in which they were complied with open to interpretation. In the provisional measures proceedings in *MOX Plant*, *Land Reclamation* and *Ghana/Côte d'Ivoire* – three of the five proceedings in which tribunals acted *proprio motu* to prescribe or vary provisional measures of their own accord – orders were made requiring the States party to the dispute to either cooperate and/or exchange information. Such loosely framed and aspirational orders import significant latitude in compliance and raise the question of the extent to which a party must comply in order for it to be deemed in compliance with the tribunal's order.[387] Certainly, if the approach of the *Ghana/Côte d'Ivoire* tribunal is indicative of a broader practice, it appears that tribunals are prepared to accept imperfect or even nominal compliance with such orders, perhaps out

385 *Arctic Sunrise*, Provisional Measures; *Three Ukrainian Naval Vessels*; *San Padre Pio*.

386 *Arctic Sunrise*, Provisional Measures (and the proceedings generally); *Three Ukrainian Naval Vessels*.

387 See further Chapter 2.3.

of recognition of the fact that attempting to determine compliance with orders that are general in nature is likely to be an elusive task.

5 Maritime Boundary Delimitation Cases

5.1 *Introduction to Maritime Boundary Disputes under* UNCLOS

UNCLOS expects States with overlapping maritime entitlements to reach agreement as to the maritime boundary delimiting their respective maritime zones. Article 15 of UNCLOS provides that the delimitation of the territorial sea between States is to be effected by the drawing of a line of equidistance between the two States "from the nearest points on the baselines" from each State's coasts, except in cases of "historic title or other special circumstances" or agreement by the States in question to the contrary,[388] to be considered on a case-by-case basis.[389] Articles 74(1) and 83(1) of UNCLOS set out how the EEZ and continental shelf, respectively, are to be delimited: "by agreement on the basis of international law ... in order to achieve an equitable solution".[390] These provisions, in effect, provide States with a wide discretion to delimit the boundaries between them.[391] Several hundred maritime boundaries have been delimited through negotiations.[392]

In cases where States cannot, within a 'reasonable period of time', come to agreement by negotiation as to how the EEZ and continental shelf maritime boundaries between them ought to be delimited, they must have recourse to the dispute resolution procedures provided by Part XV of the Convention.[393] Resolution by arbitration or adjudication does not necessarily follow, however. Some States have made declarations in accordance with Article 298(1) in Section 3 of Part XV, which allows for the optional exclusion of compulsory proceedings entailing binding decisions (that is, arbitration or adjudication) with respect to maritime boundary delimitations pursuant to Articles 15, 74

388 UNCLOS, Art. 15. Article 15 was preceded by Convention on the Territorial Sea and the Contiguous Zone, opened for signature 29 April 1958, entered into force 10 September 1964, 516 UNTS 205, Art. 12.

389 *Guyana v. Suriname* [303].

390 UNCLOS, Arts. 74(1), 83(1).

391 As noted in *North Sea Continental Shelf*, there is "no legal limit to the considerations which States may take account of": *North Sea Continental Shelf* (*Federal Republic of Germany/Netherlands*), Judgment, *ICJ Reports* 1969, 50 [93].

392 As evident in the collection of eight volumes currently edited by C. Lathrop, *International Maritime Boundaries* (Brill Nijhoff, 1993–2020).

393 UNCLOS, Arts. 74(2), 83(2).

and 83.[394] For instance, in 2002, Australia made a declaration to the effect that it "does not accept any of the [dispute resolution] procedures provided for in [UNCLOS]... concerning the interpretation or application of articles ... relating to sea boundary delimitations as well as those involving historic bays or titles".[395] Australia made such a declaration as, in its view, "maritime boundaries ... are best resolved by negotiation and not through resort to third party dispute settlement".[396]

Where a State has opted to exclude compulsory proceedings entailing binding decisions in relation to maritime boundary delimitation under Article 298, there remains a possibility that the dispute will be referred to compulsory conciliation if the conditions listed in Article 298(1)(a) are met. It was on this basis that the maritime delimitation dispute between Australia and Timor-Leste was settled by compulsory conciliation in accordance with UNCLOS rather than Annex VII arbitration; conciliation was the only option open to Timor-Leste as a result of Australia's declaration.[397] It follows that compulsory resolution of maritime delimitation disputes pursuant to UNCLOS will vary based on any declarations made by States party to the dispute. Such declarations do not, however, absolve a State of the obligation to settle the dispute by peaceful means.[398]

Despite the availability of this exception from adjudication or arbitration under UNCLOS, international courts and tribunals have been called upon to delimit the maritime boundaries between States in contentious proceedings. Commentators have asserted that more States are now turning to third-party dispute settlement procedures rather than direct negotiation to settle maritime boundaries.[399] Indeed, it has been observed that "[t]he delimitation of

394 While some of the declarations have obscure phrasing, there are at least 37 States that explicitly exclude compulsory dispute settlement under Article 298(1)(a) of the Convention. UN, 'Declarations and Reservations', available at: <https://treaties.un.org/Pages/ViewDetailsIII.aspx?src=TREATY&mtdsg_no=XXI-6&chapter=21&Temp=mtdsg3&clang=_en>.

395 Commonwealth of Australia, *Declaration under the United Nations Convention on the Law of the Sea concerning the Application to Australia of the Dispute Settlement Provisions of that Convention*, adopted and entered into force 21 March 2002.

396 Joint Standing Committee on Treaties, Parliament of the Commonwealth of Australia, *Report 47: Treaties Tabled on 18 and 25 June 2002* (2002), available at: <https://www.aph.gov.au/parliamentary_business/committees/house_of_representatives_committees?url=jsct/18_25_june_2002/report/chapter4.pdf> at [4.20].

397 See below Chapter 5.5.

398 UNCLOS, Art. 279.

399 A. G. Oude Elferink, T. Henriksen and S. V. Busch, 'The Judiciary and the Law of Maritime Delimitation' in A. G. Oude Elferink, T. Henriksen and S. V. Busch (eds), *Maritime Boundary Delimitation: The Case Law* (Oxford University Press, 2018), 27. As to the motivation for

the maritime boundaries is one of the areas of the law of the sea that has been most heavily litigated".[400] Of the 46 cases instituted under UNCLOS,[401] six cases have concerned maritime delimitation, representing 13 per cent of the caseload of the UNCLOS dispute settlement system. In comparison, 17 cases concerning maritime delimitation have been heard by the ICJ, representing nearly 11 per cent of the Court's case load, even though the ICJ has jurisdiction over any question of international law.[402] Some maritime boundary disputes have also been submitted to ad hoc arbitration outside the auspices of UNCLOS pursuant to heads of jurisdiction arising under other international instruments.[403] During the time in which UNCLOS has been in force, more maritime delimitation disputes have been litigated pursuant to other instruments (at least nine cases) than under the Convention (six cases).[404]

This Chapter addresses compliance with maritime boundary delimitation awards issued further to UNCLOS dispute settlement proceedings before ITLOS and Annex VII arbitral tribunals. Consideration is also given to the compulsory conciliation between Australia and Timor-Leste concerning the Timor Sea.[405]

5.2 *Compliance in Maritime Boundary Delimitation Cases*

Before considering specific instances of compliance (or lack thereof) with maritime boundary decisions of international courts and tribunals under UNCLOS, it is first convenient to make some general observations on compliance with judgments made in maritime boundary delimitation cases generally.

One perspective is that compliance with maritime boundary delimitations resolved by third-party dispute resolution may not be readily expected because of the high stakes associated with sovereignty disputes, particularly where

---

this, see generally S. Fietta and R. Cleverly, *A Practitioners' Guide to Maritime Boundary Delimitation* (Oxford University Press, 2016), 114–115.

400 Oude Elferink, Henriksen and Busch (n. 399), 3.

401 See Chapter 1.

402 Oude Elferink, Henriksen and Busch (n. 399), 3 (citing 15 cases as being resolved by the ICJ, correcting for an error in item B15) Two cases have been instituted since publication of that book: *Guatemala's Territorial, Insular and Maritime Claim (Guatemala v. Belize)*, General List No. 177; and *Land and Maritime Delimitation and Sovereignty over Islands (Gabon v. Equatorial Guinea)*, General List No. 179.

403 See, e.g., *In the matter of an Arbitration Pursuant to an Agreement to Arbitrate dated 3 October 1996 (Eritrea/Yemen)*, Award of the Arbitral Tribunal in the Second Stage of the Proceedings (Maritime Delimitation), 17 December 1999, 22 *RIAA* 335; *In the matter of an Arbitration under the Arbitration Agreement between the Government of the Republic of Croatia and the Government of the Republic of Slovenia signed on 4 November 2009*, Final Award, 29 June 2017, PCA Case No. 2012–04.

404 Oude Elferink, Henriksen and Busch (n. 399), 18.

405 *Timor Sea Conciliation.*

that dispute involves "resource-rich territory".[406] Such disputes are necessarily "charged with political passions and entirely trammelled by hindsight",[407] which may compromise compliance. Further, it has been observed that compliance with territorial delimitation cases may be complicated by domestic constitutions and legislation that assert sovereignty over specific territory subject to the dispute, which leads States to develop avoidance techniques to prevent full implementation of the judgment of the international court or tribunal.[408] A similar view may be applicable in relation to disputes over territorial sea boundaries where full sovereignty is at stake.

By contrast, another perspective is that compliance with decisions concerning the delimitation of maritime boundaries is likely to be more forthcoming than decisions concerning sovereignty over land. "Due to the centrality of marketable title to maritime areas, there is little value in continuing to claim maritime areas as to which one has been declared not to be the owner ... maritime spaces are hardly worth possessing without [marketable title]".[409] On this view, while not every delimitation of a maritime boundary necessarily resolves every dispute between the parties, we can generally expect adherence to internationally recognised maritime boundaries given their importance for

406 See, e.g., B. A. Simmons, 'Capacity, Commitment and Compliance: International Institutions and Territorial Disputes' (2002) 46(6) *Journal of Conflict Resolution* 829, 846–847.

407 A. Siegfreid, 'Preface' in J. Ancel, *Géographie Des Frontières* (Gallimard, 1938), vii, cited in J. R. V. Prescott, 'On the Resolution of Marine Boundary Conflicts' in J. P. Craven, J. Schneider and C. Stimson (eds), 'The International Implications of Extended Maritime Jurisdiction in the Pacific' (1987) 21 *Proceedings of the Law of the Sea Institute Conference* 33. Siegfreid opined that:

> The study of boundaries is dangerous ... because it is thoroughly charged with political passions and entirely encumbered by after-thoughts. The people are too interested in the issues when they speak of boundaries to speak with detachment: the failing is permanent!

408 See generally W. A. Ramírez, 'Resistance to Territorial and Maritime Delimitation Judgments of the International Court of Justice and Clashes with "Territory Clauses" in the Constitutions of Latin American States' (2022) 35 *Leiden Journal of International Law* 185.

409 L. Brilmayer and N. Klein, 'Land and Sea: Two Sovereignty Regimes in Search of a Common Denominator' (2001) 33 *New York University Journal of International Law and Politics* 704, 748, 750. Though note that Brilmayer and Klein warn at 750 that

> [t]he fact that a mandatory regime exists should not be taken as a cause for general optimism about the creation of international legal decision making processes in the future. Its success is limited to cases in which direct consumption of the particular property or asset in question is not possible.

See also N. Klein, 'Land and Sea: Resolving Contested Land and Disappearing Land Disputes under the UN Convention on the Law of the Sea' in C. Giorgetti and N. Klein (eds), *Resolving Conflicts in the Law: Essays in Honour of Lea Brilmayer* (Brill, 2019) 249, 250–251.

stability and for ocean governance more generally.[410] This stability, in turn, is necessary for the commercialisation of maritime areas with hydrocarbon or mineral deposits. Moreover, maritime boundary disputes frequently involve a compromise between the maximalist demands of each State. A compromise result may more easily allow for compliance.[411]

Two further factors may explain why, on this view, increased compliance with maritime delimitation judgments may be anticipated. First, as a matter of practicality, compliance with such judgments may be made easier by their highly technical nature; these judgments may eschew the issues of ambiguity and uncertainty present in other cases resolved pursuant to the UNCLOS dispute settlement system. Second, a number of political considerations may result in a State assigning a lesser weight to rights over maritime zones vis-à-vis sovereignty over land. These factors include that the State's rights in the EEZ and continental shelf, which fall short of sovereignty, do not have the same character as the intrinsic territory of the State; that such rights are relatively new in comparison to those over land; and that disputes over land territory are more easily politicised.[412]

Having clarified the competing theories of compliance with maritime delimitation judgments, in this Chapter we examine each maritime delimitation judgment rendered by UNCLOS courts and tribunals to test the competing hypotheses as to whether judgments concerning maritime boundary delimitations are more likely to engender higher rates of compliance than in other cases concerning the interpretation or application of the Convention. Such an assessment requires a consideration of how to measure compliance with maritime delimitation judgments. Given the complexity of these cases, it may take some time between the delivery of judgment and final settlement of maritime boundaries. States may implement the judgment by way of treaty and coordinate to that effect through the use of technical experts or a body such as a mixed boundary commission.[413] This practice may result in the modification

410 "One of the core principles of the international system is the need for stability and finality in boundary questions and much flows from this": M. N. Shaw, *International Law* (6th edn., Cambridge University Press, 2008), 522.

411 H. L. Jones, 'Why Comply? An Analysis of Trends in Compliance with Judgments of the International Court of Justice since *Nicaragua*' (2012) 12(1) *Chicago-Kent Journal of International and Comparative Law* 57, 76.

412 M. Lando, *Maritime Delimitation as a Judicial Process* (Cambridge University Press, 2019), 321.

413 See discussion of the Cameroon/Nigeria Mixed Commission, which facilitates the implementation of *Land and Maritime Boundary between Cameroon and Nigeria (Cameroon v. Nigeria; Equatorial Guinea intervening)*, Judgment, *ICJ Reports* 2002, in Fietta and Cleverly (n. 399), 155.

of the maritime boundary as delimited by the UNCLOS dispute settlement body where necessary to correct any technical or material errors. Such modification should not be regarded as rendering the States party to the dispute non-compliant but instead as perfecting the award as delivered.[414] In relation to cases concerning the delimitation of the outer continental shelf, States are still required to submit information to the Commission on the Limits of the Continental Shelf ('CLCS'), which will determine the entitlement of that State to the outer continental shelf as well as the limits of that maritime zone.[415] Such submissions may indicate the extent to which States have implemented or complied with the award.

5.3 *Maritime Boundary Cases at ITLOS*

Three maritime boundary delimitation cases have been resolved at ITLOS: one before the full bench of ITLOS and two before special chambers of ITLOS. The *Mauritius/Maldives* maritime boundary dispute was only very recently decided on the merits. While both States have endorsed the judgment and, as such, the early indicators of compliance are promising,[416] it is too soon to reach a definitive decision on compliance, especially as the question of the outer continental shelf remains to be resolved between the parties.[417]

---

414 Concerns as to technical accuracy have arisen in *Maritime Delimitation in the Indian Ocean (Somalia v. Kenya)*, Judgment, *ICJ Reports* 2021. See C. Schofield, P. Bekker and R. van de Poll, 'The World Court Fixes the Somalia-Kenya Maritime Boundary: Technical Considerations and Legal Consequences' (2021) 25(25) *American Society of International Law Insights* <https://www.asil.org/insights/volume/25/issue/25>.

415 UNCLOS, Art. 76(8); UNCLOS, Annex II.

416 The Mauritian Prime Minister is reported as "greet[ing] this as a 'historic judgment' that in a legally binding way re-confirmed Mauritian sovereignty over the Chagos islands. 'The whole world has an obligation to respect it' as well as ending a simmering boundary dispute with Maldives." Iqbal Ahmed Khan, 'Mauritius: Chagos Maritime Boundaries – Why the ITLOS decided to split the claims of Mauritius and Maldives', *L'Express*, (30 April 2023), available at: <https://allafrica.com/stories/202305010055.html>. The President of the Maldives described the decision as "a great win for the Maldives and the people of the Maldives". The President's Office, Republic of the Maldives, 'The President states that the ITLOS decision on the Chagos Archipelago issue is a great win for the Maldives', Press Release, Ref: 2023–138 (28 April 2023), available at: <https://presidency.gov.mv/Press/Article/28222>.

417 *Mauritius/Maldives*, Merits, [457]–[458].

5.3.1 Bay of Bengal Delimitation (Bangladesh/Myanmar)

ITLOS was first called upon to delimit the maritime boundary between Bangladesh and Myanmar pursuant to a special agreement (referred to as the *Bay of Bengal Delimitation*). The special agreement conferred jurisdiction on ITLOS to adjudicate a dispute over the delimitation of the territorial sea, EEZ and continental shelf between the two States in the Bay of Bengal.[418] Simultaneously, Bangladesh instituted proceedings on an identical basis against India; these proceedings were submitted to Annex VII arbitration in accordance with the Article 287 declarations of the two States (referred to as the *Bay of Bengal Arbitration*).[419] The latter arbitration is discussed in Chapter 5.4.3 below.

A maritime delimitation dispute had existed between Bangladesh and Myanmar since 1974;[420] prior to settlement of the dispute pursuant to UNCLOS, the two States had held some 14 rounds of negotiations without reaching agreement. As a result, the parties invoked the binding dispute resolution mechanisms of UNCLOS. The judgment of ITLOS, delivered in March 2012, was long and complex, and has been covered in great detail elsewhere.[421] For the purposes of this Part, it suffices to say that ITLOS proceeded to delimit not only the territorial sea, EEZ and continental shelf between the two States in the Bay of Bengal, but also the extended/outer continental shelf beyond 200 nautical miles, having found almost unanimously that it possessed the requisite jurisdiction to do so.[422] In so doing, ITLOS created what is known as a 'grey area',[423] a small, wedge-shaped area, which was said to arise as a "consequence of delimitation".[424]

418 *Bay of Bengal Delimitation*, 10–11 [1].

419 See below Chapter 5.4.3.

420 *Bay of Bengal Delimitation*, 21 [36].

421 See, e.g., D. H. Anderson, 'Delimitation of the Maritime Boundary in the Bay of Bengal (Bangladesh/Myanmar)' (2012) 106(4) *American Journal of International Law* 817–824; R. Churchill, 'The Bangladesh/Myanmar Case: Continuity and Novelty in the Law of Maritime Boundary Delimitation' (2012) 1(1) *Cambridge International Law Journal* 137; M. Kałduński and T. Wasilewski 'The International Tribunal for the law of the sea on maritime delimitation: the Bangladesh v. Myanmar case' (2014) 45(2) *Ocean Development & International Law* 123.

422 *Bay of Bengal Delimitation*, 97 [363]. Only Judge Ndiaye was in dissent on this point.

423 Defined as 'an area of limited size located beyond 200nm from the coast of Bangladesh but within 200nm from the coast of Myanmar, yet on the Bangladesh side of the delimitation line': ibid., 119 [463].

424 Ibid., 120 [472]. See also B. M. Magnússon, 'The Grey Areas in the Bay of Bengal' (2016) 56 *Indian Journal of International Law* 41 (describing the 'grey area' as a "necessary evil").

In the grey area, Bangladesh had an entitlement to an area of extended continental shelf that was within 200 miles of Myanmar's EEZ.[425] ITLOS thus determined that Myanmar had jurisdiction consistent with its rights and obligations under the Convention over the water column, but that Bangladesh was to have jurisdiction over the seabed and subsoil of the continental shelf.[426] ITLOS left it to the parties to determine how to cooperate within the grey area and to "determine the measures that they consider appropriate for this purpose".[427] In sum, Bangladesh was awarded 111,631 km^2 of the disputed area while Myanmar was awarded 171,832 km^2.

The judgment of ITLOS was accepted by both States. Bangladesh proclaimed that all its "strategic objectives were achieved" by the judgment.[428] Myanmar, stating that it accepted ITLOS' judgment, purported to put the judgment into effect by submitting an amended submission to the CLCS in July 2015.[429] Declaring acceptance of the judgment is, however, only one part of compliance; the actions that followed because of the judgment must also be considered.

Since the submission of Myanmar's amended submission to the CLCS, Bangladesh has complained that the amended claim does not conform to the requirements of the judgment in the *Bay of Bengal Delimitation* or the award in the *Bay of Bengal Arbitration*. In Bangladesh's view, the revised claim submitted by Myanmar overlaps with the continental shelf area awarded to Bangladesh by ITLOS.[430] The CLCS deferred establishment of a sub-commission to consider the submission; no further action has since been taken.[431] Bangladesh also submitted an amended claim to the CLCS in October 2020, wherein it purported to "give effect to the binding maritime boundary delimitations" established in both the *Bay of Bengal Arbitration* and *Bay of Bengal Delimitation*; further

425 *Bay of Bengal Delimitation*, 119 [463].

426 Ibid., 121 [474].

427 Ibid., 121 [476].

428 'Bangladesh Hails UN Ruling in Myanmar Border Dispute' 15 March 2012, *Reuters*, available at: <https://www.reuters.com/article/bangladesh-myanmar-maritime-idUKL5E8EE40F20120314?edition-redirect=uk>.

429 Myanmar, *Continental Shelf Submission* (July 2015), available at: <https://www.un.org/depts/los/clcs_new/submissions_files/mmr08/Myanmar_Amended_Ex_Summary.pdf>.

430 Permanent Mission of Bangladesh to the United Nations, *Letter to the Secretary-General*, 22 October 2015, available at: <https://www.un.org/depts/los/clcs_new/submissions_files/mmr08/2015_10_22_BGD_NV_UN.pdf>.

431 See generally S. V. Busch, *Establishing Continental Shelf Limits beyond 200 Nautical Miles by the Coastal State: A Right of Involvement for Other States?* (Brill, 2016), at 156. No recent action appears to have been taken, as noted on the CLCS website: <https://www.un.org/depts/los/clcs_new/submissions_files/submission_mmr.htm>.

stating that "the determination of the outer limits of the continental shelf can no longer be considered the subject of any unresolved dispute".[432]

The question of compliance is further complicated by the existence of the grey area. While the two States were not formally ordered to cooperate in the grey area, no such order was arguably necessary given that States are under an obligation to cooperate both under UNCLOS and pursuant to customary international law.[433] Prospects for cooperation seemed low at the outset. As Nguyen has noted, this eventuality may have been optimistic given that "the parties were unable to resolve their differences after many years of diplomatic effort".[434] No joint development agreement appears to have been entered into by the parties; in fact, Myanmar has complained that Bangladesh's revised submission to the CLCS "minimizes the grey area recognized by ITLOS".[435] This approach is consistent with the goal of maximising national interest inherent in realist theories of international relations, notwithstanding that, as one commentator has noted, "a cooperative approach appears to be a more optimal solution".[436]

Overall, while there has been compliance with ITLOS' judgment in that both States have accepted it, including the new maritime boundary pronounced therein, and, at least ostensibly, signalled a willingness to comply

432 Bangladesh, *Submission by the People's Republic of Bangladesh to the Commission on the Limits of the Continental Shelf* (2020), available at: <https://www.un.org/depts/los/clcs_new/submissions_files/bgd55_11/Executive%20summary_BGD_AMD.pdf>; Permanent Mission of Bangladesh to the United Nations, *Letter to the Secretary-General*, 6 May 2021, available at: <https://www.un.org/depts/los/clcs_new/submissions_files/bgd55_11/20210506BgdNvUn009.pdf>; Permanent Mission of Bangladesh to the United Nations, *Letter to the Secretary-General*, 13 September 2021, available at: <https://www.un.org/depts/los/clcs_new/submissions_files/bgd55_11/20210913BgdNvUn010.pdf>.

433 See UNGA Res. 2625(XXV) (24 October 1970), Declaration on Principles of International Law concerning Friendly Relations and Cooperation among States in Accordance with the Charter of the United Nations, UN Doc. A/RES/2625(XXV).

434 L. N. Nguyen, 'The UNCLOS Dispute Settlement System: What Role Can It Play in Resolving Maritime Disputes in Asia' (2018) 8(1) *Asian Journal of International Law* 91, 98.

435 Permanent Mission of Myanmar to the United Nations, *Letter to the Secretary-General*, 26 January 2021, available at: <https://www.un.org/Depts/los/clcs_new/submissions_files/bgd55_11/20210126MmrNvUn002.pdf>.

436 R. Mishra, 'The Grey Area in the Northern Bay of Bengal: A Note on a Functional Cooperative Solution' (2016) 47(1) *Ocean Development and International Law* 29, 37. See also M. Kałduński, 'A Commentary on Maritime Boundary Arbitration between Bangladesh and India Concerning the Bay of Bengal' (2015) 28(4) *Leiden Journal of International Law* 799, 845 (relevantly noting that whether or not compliance with the order to cooperate in the grey zone in both the *Bay of Bengal Arbitration* and *Bay of Bengal Delimitation* "will depend mainly on the goodwill of the states concerned, and how they will exercise their rights and duties in order to mutually benefit from the grey area").

with it, some unresolved issues persist. The prompt acceptance of the ITLOS judgment may be explained by the existence of oil and gas deposits within the Bay, which had previously threatened to cause conflict between the two States.[437] The previously-unresolved dispute between the two States and its potential to turn into real conflict likely suppressed commercial exploitation activities in the Bay. As a result, each State had and has a clear interest in acquiring the requisite commercial certainty and confidence to exploit the resources of the Bay of Bengal, which follow not only from an authoritative judgment of an international tribunal, but also in the active acceptance of and consequent compliance with that judgment. A failure to comply by either State would place exploitation activities in further jeopardy. Accordingly, as Nguyen notes, the judgment "provided a peaceful and workable solution to the conflict ... [and] helped put an end to a dispute that had impeded economic development ...".[438] The lack of conflict over maritime boundaries between the two States in the following years may further underline compliance. In sum, the clear acceptance by both States of the judgment is an ideal outcome and one that has minimised the potential for conflict in the region. This approach may also serve as an exemplar for other States seeking resolution of maritime boundary disputes.[439]

One further outcome that can be observed is the development by ITLOS of the law of the delimitation of the outer continental shelf. This case was the first instance wherein an international court or tribunal had delimited the outer continental shelf between two States;[440] the ICJ had previously declined to do

437 *Reuters* (n. 428).

438 Nguyen (n. 434), 97.

439 See also M. Kałduński and T. Wasilewski, 'The International Tribunal for the Law of the Sea on Maritime Delimitation: The *Bangladesh v Myanmar* Case' (2014) 45(2) *Ocean Development and International Law* 123, 154 (relevantly noting that "[t]he *Bangladesh v Myanmar* case may also serve as an example for other Asian states of how to settle their disputes").

440 For discussion on the approach of international courts and tribunals to this question, see, e.g., S. W. de Herdt, 'The Relationship between the Delimitation of the Continental Shelf beyond 200 nm and the Delineation of Its Outer Limits' (2020) 51(3) *Ocean Development and International Law* 263; Busch (n. 44); A. G. Oude Elferink, 'ITLOS's Approach to the Delimitation of the Continental Shelf beyond 200 Nautical Miles in the *Bangladesh/Myanmar* Case: Theoretical and Practical Difficulties' in R. Wolfrum, M. Seršić, and T. Šošić (eds), *Contemporary Developments in International Law: Essays in Honour of Budislav Vukas* (Brill Nijhoff, 2016) 230; L. Bernard and C. Schofield, 'Disputes concerning the Delimitation of the Continental Shelf beyond 200 Nautical Miles' in T. Heidar (ed), *New Knowledge and Changing Circumstances in the Law of the Sea* (Brill Nijhoff, 2020) 157; J. Gao, 'The Delimitation Method for the Continental Shelf beyond 200

so in *Territorial and Maritime Dispute* (*Nicaragua v. Colombia*).[441] The Annex VII tribunal followed this precedent in the *Bay of Bengal Arbitration*, finding "no grounds why it should refrain from exercising its jurisdiction".[442] The ICJ followed soon after in *Delimitation of the Continental Shelf between Nicaragua and Colombia*, a dispute submitted to it pursuant to the Pact of Bogotá.[443] Such an outcome reflects cross-pollination of the decisions of international courts and tribunals on questions relating to the law of the sea.[444]

5.3.2 Ghana/Côte d'Ivoire

The next occasion on which ITLOS determined questions relating to maritime boundary delimitation was in the dispute between Ghana and Côte d'Ivoire regarding their boundaries in the Atlantic Ocean. The dispute was transferred in December 2014 to a special chamber of ITLOS constituted by Judges Bouguetaia, Wolfrum and Paik, and judges *ad hoc* Mensah (appointed by Ghana) and Abraham (appointed by Côte d'Ivoire) by way of *compromis* pursuant to Article 15(2) of the ITLOS Statute.[445]

The two States sought *inter alia* the delimitation of the maritime boundary in areas of national jurisdiction between the two States in the Atlantic Ocean, including the outer continental shelf.[446] There had been frequent disputes and bilateral discussions between the two States since the 1980s as to their maritime borders. The discovery of significant hydrocarbon reserves in the disputed area and consequent submissions to the CLCS precipitated the institution of proceedings at ITLOS. Those hydrocarbon reserves had been subject to unilateral exploration and exploitation activities by Ghana in the absence of a provisional agreement between the two States.[447]

Nautical Miles: A Reflection on the Judicial and Arbitral Decisions' (2020) 51(2) *Ocean Development and International Law* 116.

441 *Territorial and Maritime Dispute* (*Nicaragua v. Colombia*), Judgment, *ICJ Reports* 2012.

442 *Bay of Bengal Arbitration* [76]. See below Chapter 5.4.3.

443 *Question of the Delimitation of the Continental Shelf between Nicaragua and Colombia beyond 200 nautical miles from the Nicaraguan Coast* (*Nicaragua v. Colombia*), Preliminary Objections, *ICJ Reports* 2016, [114].

444 See generally, C. Brown, *A Common Law of International Adjudication* (Oxford University Press, 2007); A. Miron, 'The *Acquis Judiciaire*, a Tool for Harmonization in a Decentralized System of Litigation?' in C. Giorgetti and M. Pollack (eds), *Beyond Fragmentation: Cross-Fertilization, Cooperation and Competition among International Courts and Tribunals* (Cambridge University Press, 2022), 128.

445 *Ghana/Côte d'Ivoire*, Merits, 13 [1].

446 Ibid., 13–14 [2].

447 In the provisional measures phase of the proceedings, the Special Chamber ordered that Ghana cease all new activities for the pendency of the merits phase: *Ghana/Côte d'Ivoire*, Provisional Measures [108(1)(a)]. For discussion, see Chapter 4.8.

In September 2017, the Special Chamber's judgment was handed down and its substantive discussion has been examined in commentary on the case.[448] For present purposes, it suffices to say that the Special Chamber delimited the maritime boundaries of the territorial sea, EEZ, continental shelf and outer continental shelf between the two States, providing control over the hydrocarbon-rich disputed area to Ghana.[449]

In the *dispositif* of the judgment, the Special Chamber decided on the coordinates to delimit the maritime boundaries between Ghana and Côte d'Ivoire.[450] Each State is required to comply with this decision in accordance with Article 296(1) of UNCLOS. Compliance can therefore be assessed by considering the reaction of Côte d'Ivoire to the judgment and the extent to which it has ceased to dispute or interfere with Ghana's rights over the formerly disputed area. Compliance has been exemplary. Upon the release of the Special Chamber's judgment, both States released a joint communiqué wherein they "express[ed] their special gratitude" to the Special Chamber and indicated that they each "accepted the decision in accordance with the Statute of ITLOS".[451]

Further, reciprocal diplomatic visits at the Head of State level were held with the intent of deepening ties between the two States, resulting in the signing of a Strategic Partnership Agreement covering a range of areas including defence, mining, transport, environment and economic relations.[452] The two States further pledged to "ensure the smooth implementation" of the Special Chamber's judgment, establishing the Joint Committee for the Implementation of the ITLOS Judgment to this effect.[453] That Joint Committee later ratified the coordinates provided for in the Special Chamber's judgment as the maritime boundary between the two States. Ghana and Côte d'Ivoire continue to

448 See, e.g., Y. van Logchem, 'The Rights and Obligations of States in Disputed Maritime Areas: What Lessons Can Be Learned from the Maritime Boundary Dispute between Ghana and Cote d'Ivoire' (2019) 52 *Vanderbilt Journal of Transnational Law* 121; M. McCreath and Z. Scanlon, 'The Dispute Concerning the Delimitation of the Maritime Boundary Between Ghana and Côte d'Ivoire: Implications for the Law of the Sea' (2019) 50(1) *Ocean Development & International Law* 1.

449 *Ghana/Côte d'Ivoire*, Merits, 145 [540].

450 *Ghana/Côte d'Ivoire*, Merits, 175 [660(3)].

451 See C. Mirasola, *Ghana/Côte d'Ivoire: A Case Summary for the Maritime Dispute Resolution Project*, available at: <https://static1.squarespace.com/static/55d21ffee4b0d22e803fdca1/t/5f4d05bc29cfe63ea87eb389/1598883268056/GhanavCotedIvoire.pdf>, Section IV.

452 'Ghana and Côte d'Ivoire Sign Strategic Partnership Agreement' 18 October 2017, *Ghana Business News*, available at: <https://www.ghanabusinessnews.com/2017/10/18/ghana-and-cote-divoire-sign-strategic-partnership-agreement/>.

453 Ibid.; 'Akufo-Addo Reciprocates Ivorian Gesture; Honours Ouattara' 17 October 2017, *Ghana News Page*, available at: <https://ghananewspage.com/akufo-addo-reciprocates-ivorian-gesture-honours-ouattara/>.

undertake negotiations as to joint exploration activities in recognition of the liquid nature of hydrocarbons, which straddle and migrate across the delimited boundaries.[454] The judgment was also promptly welcomed by Tullow Oil, a major player in Ghanaian offshore oil exploration, which indicated that the company planned to resume drilling with haste.[455] Those activities have since resumed under Ghanaian control.

In sum, not only has compliance with the Special Chamber's judgment been paradigmatic, but the dispute resolution process provided an important opportunity for the two States to ventilate their concerns. In so doing, Ghana and Côte d'Ivoire have deepened their relationship in areas far beyond maritime delimitation; an excellent outcome for both States and the international community.

As to other outcomes, the Special Chamber rejected Côte d'Ivoire's arguments that, even if Ghana were to succeed on the delimitation question, it violated international law or, alternatively, an obligation to negotiate in good faith under Article 83(1) and duties further to Article 83(3) not to jeopardize or hamper the conclusion of a final agreement between the States[456] by undertaking oil exploration activities in an area wherein the States had conflicting and overlapping maritime claims.[457] The practical import of such a breach of State responsibility would likely be relief in the form of a not insubstantial sum of reparations to Côte d'Ivoire. The finding that no such breach was occasioned is a consequential holding in the judgment, with commentators suggesting that it has developed a line of jurisprudence that unilateral actions in disputed maritime areas will not entail a State's responsibility or otherwise constitute a breach of international law where those actions are taken in good faith and in reliance on the belief that the disputed maritime zone in fact was within the State's national jurisdiction.[458] This determination will potentially hold relevance in future cases involving contested maritime and land territory.

454 'Ghana, Côte d'Ivoire Agree on Delimiting Maritime Boundary' 13 August 2018, *GhanaWeb*, available at: <https://www.ghanaweb.com/GhanaHomePage/business/Ghana-Cote-d-Ivoire-agree-on-delimiting-maritime-boundary-676235>.

455 'ITLOS Judgment' 23 September 2017, *Tullow Oil*, available at: <https://www.tullowoil.com/media/press-releases/itlos-judgment/>.

456 *Ghana/Côte d'Ivoire*, Merits, 168–169 [633].

457 Ibid., 158 [589]–[591].

458 See, e.g., C. Yiallourides and E. R. Donnelly, 'Part II: Analysis of Dispute Concerning Delimitation of the Maritime Boundary between Ghana and Côte d'Ivoire in the Atlantic Ocean' 20 October 2017, *EJIL: Talk!*, available at: <https://www.ejiltalk.org/part-ii-analysis-of-dispute-concerning-delimitation-of-the-maritime-boundary-between-ghana-and-cote-divoire-in-the-atlantic-ocean/>. See also N. Klein, 'Resolving Disputes

5.4 *Maritime Boundary Cases before Annex VII Arbitral Tribunals*

There have been three maritime boundary delimitation cases resolved by Annex VII arbitral tribunals: *Barbados v. Trinidad and Tobago; Guyana v. Suriname*; and the *Bay of Bengal Arbitration*.

5.4.1 Barbados v. Trinidad and Tobago

The first time that maritime boundaries were delimited between two States pursuant to Part XV dispute resolution was in *Barbados v. Trinidad and Tobago*.[459] In February 2004, Barbados instituted Annex VII arbitral proceedings against Trinidad and Tobago concerning the delimitation of the EEZs and continental shelves between the two States. An Annex VII tribunal was convened, a hearing took place in October 2005, and a unanimous award was handed down in April 2006.

For some three decades preceding the institution of arbitral proceedings, the States had held diplomatic meetings and negotiations with a view to delimiting their maritime boundaries and establishing rights to the fisheries and hydrocarbon resources therein.[460] Matters were complicated when Trinidad and Tobago delimited its maritime boundaries with Venezuela by treaty, purporting to give it control over a maritime area claimed by Barbados. The overlapping maritime claims of the two States had caused some conflict, including the arrest of Barbadian fishers, who claimed historic artisanal fishing rights, on the grounds of illegal fishing in the EEZ.[461] Eventually, arbitral proceedings were instituted after negotiations broke down, with Barbados arguing that the Prime Minister of Trinidad and Tobago had called the negotiations "intractable".[462]

The Tribunal first found that it had jurisdiction over the dispute between the parties, including jurisdiction to delimit the continental shelf beyond 200 nm.[463] It then proceeded to delimit a single maritime boundary "without

---

under UNCLOS when the Coastal and User States are Disputed' in N. Hong and G. Houlden (eds), *Maritime Order and the Law in East Asia* (Routledge, 2018) 253.

459 It should, however, be noted that this was not the first time that proceedings had been instituted. The institution of proceedings in *Guyana v. Suriname* predated that of *Barbados v. Trinidad and Tobago*, but the award in the latter was issued first.

460 *Barbados v. Trinidad and Tobago* [46].

461 Ibid., [50], [55].

462 See Fietta and Cleverly (n. 399), 422.

463 It will be recalled that that the *Bay of Bengal Delimitation* was the first time that an international court or tribunal delimited the continental shelf beyond 200nm: see above Chapter 5.3.1. The Annex VII tribunal in *Barbados v Trinidad* did not actually delimit the outer continental shelf, it merely (though importantly) found that it possessed the requisite jurisdiction to do so.

prejudice to the question of the separate legal existence of the EEZ and the continental shelf".[464] However, in consideration of the fact that an outcome of the delimitation would be that some 600 traditional Barbadian artisanal fishers would be deprived of their livelihoods,[465] the Tribunal further placed the States under a duty to agree upon measures to ensure the conservation and development of flying fish stocks and to come to an agreement to ensure access of Barbadian fishers to the EEZ of Trinidad and Tobago.[466]

Immediately following the issue of the Award, each State claimed victory – described by one newspaper as "public relations tactics"[467] – commending the new maritime boundary. Each State also spoke favourably about concluding an agreement regarding fisheries access and conservation in line with the Tribunal's order.[468] The US Department of State recognised the boundaries as delimited by the Tribunal in accordance with the acceptance of the award by both States.[469] Further, both States explicitly noted that the EEZ and continental shelf boundaries between them had been conclusively determined by the Annex VII tribunal in their subsequent submissions to the CLCS.[470]

464 Ibid., [298].

465 Though, note, this fact was not taken to be a special circumstance warranting adjustment of the line of equidistance: ibid., [269].

466 *Barbados v. Trinidad and Tobago* [382], [384]–[385]. Note that the Tribunal could not have conclusively adjudicated on foreign access to fisheries within a State's EEZ as such claims are excluded from the UNCLOS compulsory dispute settlement regime pursuant to Article 297(3). See discussion in B. H. Oxman, 'The *Barbados/Trinidad & Tobago* Arbitration – The Law of Maritime Delimitation: Back to the Future', available at: <https://media.law.miami.edu/faculty-administration/pdf/bernard-oxman/oxman-barbados-trinidad-arbitration.pdf>, 11–13. See also discussion in L. Bernard, 'The Effect of Historic Fishing Rights in Maritime Boundaries Delimitation' (Law of the Sea Institute Conference, Seoul, May 2012), available at: <https://www.law.berkeley.edu/files/Bernard-final.pdf>.

467 P. Knight, '"Everyone Lost" in T&T-Barbados Fishing Boundary Dispute' June 2006, *Caribbean Today*, available at: <https://ufdcimages.uflib.ufl.edu/UF/00/09/92/85/00006/00006-2006_Page_08.txt>.

468 See B. Kwiatkowska, '*Barbados/Trinidad and Tobago*. Award on Jurisdiction and Merits' (2007) 101 *American Journal of International Law* 156, at fn 22. See also ibid.

469 Bureau of Oceans and International Environmental and Scientific Affairs, United States Department of State, *Limits in the Seas No. 131 – Trinidad and Tobago: Archipelagic and Other Maritime Claims and Boundaries* (31 January 2014), available at: <https://www.state.gov/wp-content/uploads/2020/01/LIS-131.pdf>, 5.

470 Republic of Trinidad and Tobago, *Submission to the Commission on the Limits of the Continental Shelf pursuant to Article 76, Paragraph 8 of the United Nations Convention on the Law of the Sea* (12 May 2009), available at: <https://www.un.org/depts/los/clcs_new/submissions_files/tto49_09/tto2009executive_summary.pdf>, 14; Government of Barbados, *Continental Shelf Submission: Executive Summary* (2008), available at: <https://www.un.org/depts/los/clcs_new/submissions_files/brb08/brb08_executive_summary.pdf>, 4.

However, difficulties have subsequently emerged in relation to the consistency of Trinidad and Tobago's claim to an outer continental shelf.[471]

It was the hope of Barbados that the Award would ease tensions between the two States.[472] Commentators shared this hope, relevantly noting that the dispute, having purportedly been resolved to the satisfaction of both States, "should promote resource development by, and friendly relations between, the two Caribbean island states, as well as provide encouragement for the peaceful settlement of other boundary disputes in this strategically important region".[473] The potential for the resolution of this dispute to serve as an exemplar for other States in the region indicates a further outcome of UNCLOS dispute settlement emanating beyond the immediate result of the dispute as between the two State parties.

As to the duty imposed on the parties with regard to traditional artisanal fishing, Barbados had claimed a right of access to a flying fish fishery in the EEZ of Trinidad and Tobago.[474] The Tribunal declined to exercise jurisdiction over this claim because of the exclusion of EEZ fisheries disputes in Article 297(3) of UNCLOS, but did note the commitments made by the agents during the arbitral proceedings to pursue negotiations on this matter in good faith. The Tribunal nonetheless set out in the *dispositif* that:

> Trinidad and Tobago and Barbados are under a duty to agree upon the measures necessary to co-ordinate and ensure the conservation and development of flyingfish stocks, and to negotiate in good faith and conclude an agreement that will accord fisherfolk of Barbados access to fisheries within the Exclusive Economic Zone of Trinidad and Tobago, subject to the limitations and conditions of that agreement and to the

471 See, e.g., Statement by the Chairperson of the Commission on the Limits of the Continental Shelf on the progress of work in the Commission, CLCS/66, 30 April 2010, <https://documents-dds-ny.un.org/doc/UNDOC/GEN/N10/337/97/PDF/N1033797.pdf?OpenElement>, [74]. Trinidad and Tobago submitted an amended submission, replacing its earlier submission, in 2023. Republic of Trinidad and Tobago, *Submission to the Commission on the Limits of the Continental Shelf pursuant to Article 76, Paragraph 8 of the United Nations Convention on the Law of the Sea (Amended)* (17 April 2023), available at: <https://www.un.org/depts/los/clcs_new/submissions_files/submission_tto_49_2009.htm#:~:text=On%2014%20April%202023%2C%20Trinidad,which%20the%20breadth%20of%20the>.

472 Indeed, as the Deputy Prime Minister of Barbados noted in a parliamentary speech following the issue of the award, 'Good fences make good neighbours', available at <https://wikileaks.org/plusd/cables/06BRIDGETOWN911_a.html>.

473 Kwiatkowska (n. 468), 156.

474 *Barbados v. Trinidad and Tobago*, [273], [283]–[292].

> right and duty of Trinidad and Tobago to conserve and manage the living resources of waters within its jurisdiction.[475]

In 2011, the Barbadian Minister for Foreign Affairs alleged that Trinidad and Tobago had repeatedly failed to engage in discussions notwithstanding Barbadian approaches.[476] Since that time, negotiations have ensued, including at the head of government level,[477] and each State has since discussed signing a treaty that would allow Barbadians and Tobagonians to share fish stocks.[478] It appears that an agreement has not yet been reached as at the time of writing. Nonetheless, in 2014 the States came to an agreement on a protocol concerning procedures for the detention and arrest of fishing vessels flagged to the other State and their crew when in the other's EEZ.[479] Further, it does not appear that arrests of Barbadian fishers have occurred since the issuance of the Award, resolving one of the key points of contention between the parties. However, to the extent that the failure to come to an agreement is attributable to any one State, that State would certainly not be in compliance with the Award. In the absence of an agreement on measures relating to the flying fish stock, full compliance has not yet been achieved with the judgment in its entirety. In any case, the fact that there have been positive steps may reflect an effort at good faith compliance on this aspect of the judgment.

5.4.2 Guyana v. Suriname

In February 2004, Guyana instituted proceedings against Suriname concerning the delimitation of the maritime boundary between the two States in the Atlantic Ocean at the mouth of the Corentyne River, as well as various alleged

475 Ibid., [385(3)].

476 'Barbados Still Seeking Fishing Agreement with Trinidad and Tobago' 7 February 2011, *Caribbean Trakker*, available at: <https://www.caribbeantrakker.com/barbados-still-seeking-fishing-agreement-with-trinidad-and-tobago/>.

477 G. Carter, 'Fishing for Deal' 4 February 2019, *NationNews*, available at: <https://www.nationnews.com/2019/02/04/fishing-for-deal/>.

478 R. de Silva, 'T&T, Barbados, to Negotiate Fishing Treaty' 24 August 2019, *Trinidad & Tobago Guardian*, available at: <https://www.guardian.co.tt/news/tt-barbados-to-negotiate-fishing-treaty-6.2.917177.555001b133>; 'Local Fishermen Encouraged to Meet Counterparts in Tobago' 24 August 2019, *Barbados Today*, available at: <https://barbadostoday.bb/2019/08/24/local-fishermen-encouraged-to-meet-counterparts-in-tobago/>.

479 BGIS, 'Barbados and Trinidad Sign Fishing Protocol' 5 December 2014, *NationNews*, available at: <https://www.nationnews.com/2014/12/05/barbados-and-trinidad-sign-fishing-protocol/>.

breaches of international law in the disputed maritime territory.[480] Attempts to establish boundaries between the two States had been ongoing since the era of colonial rule,[481] and continued following each State gaining their independence.[482] Both States had granted oil concessions and fishing licences in the disputed area for nearly 30 years,[483] which caused conflict between the two States, including approaches by the Surinamese navy to the oil rigs in the disputed area.[484] As a result of this conflict and the subsequent commercial uncertainty, concessionaires licensed by Guyana invoked the *force majeure* clauses in their contracts and refrained from carrying out otherwise lucrative exploration and exploitation activities.[485] Following an impasse in diplomatic negotiations, proceedings were instituted under UNCLOS.[486]

An Annex VII tribunal was convened, which issued its award in September 2007. Guyana sought delimitation by way of a single maritime boundary as well as reparations for Suriname's alleged failure to settle disputes by peaceful means, having purportedly used force to harass the concessionaires in Guyana's maritime zones, which was said to constitute an internationally wrongful act.[487] The Tribunal unanimously held that it had jurisdiction to delimit the territorial sea, continental shelf and EEZ between the two States and proceeded to do so.[488]

The practical result of this delimitation exercise was a ruling effectively in favour of Guyana, with the disputed maritime area containing energy deposits found to be under Guyana's authority. Guyana was said to have "undisputed title to the area" where the concessionaires were operating.[489] Further, Guyana was found to have sovereignty or sovereign rights over some 65 per cent of the disputed area. The Tribunal also held that it had jurisdiction over the question of whether Suriname had committed an internationally wrongful act.[490] It determined that the expulsion of the oil rigs constituted a threat of the use of

480 For context to the dispute, see D. Singh, 'Comment on the Guyana-Suriname Boundary Dispute' (2004) 32 *Georgia Journal of International and Comparative Law* 657. The author was the Attorney-General of Guyana at the time proceedings were instituted.
481 *Guyana v. Suriname* [137]–[143].
482 Ibid., [144]–[146].
483 Ibid., [140]–[141], [149].
484 Ibid., [151]–[152].
485 Ibid., [151]–[152].
486 Ibid., [153]–[156].
487 Ibid., [157].
488 Ibid., [280], [487], [488(1)].
489 Ibid., [451].
490 Ibid., [406], [457], [487(ii)].

force but that no compensation could be payable.[491] Both States were also said to have acted inconsistently with their obligations not to jeopardise or hamper the reaching of a final maritime boundary agreement.[492]

As to compliance, both States immediately welcomed the Award. Guyanese President Jagdeo praised the Award in a national broadcast, while Suriname's President Venetiaan accepted the Award and expressed satisfaction that the dispute was finally resolved.[493] Oil activities by one of the concessionaires harassed by the Surinamese navy recommenced promptly after the Award.[494] President Jagdeo heralded the Award as an opportunity to "lay the foundation for a long future of harmonious relations and cooperation with [Guyana's] brothers and sisters in Suriname".[495] Such an approach may further indicate, beyond compliance, the role of the UNCLOS dispute settlement system in facilitating not only the pacific settlement of disputes but also the building of more amicable relations between States with complex histories.

5.4.3 Bay of Bengal Arbitration (Bangladesh v. India)

The *Bay of Bengal Arbitration*, it will be recalled, was initiated simultaneously with the *Bay of Bengal Delimitation*.[496] The maritime border between Bangladesh and India in the north-western part of the Bay of Bengal had been unresolved since the 1970s, and the two States had engaged in a series of inconclusive negotiations to no avail. In 2009, Bangladesh instituted proceedings against India to resolve the dispute between the two States.

The Tribunal largely followed the example set for it in the *Bay of Bengal Delimitation*, relevantly delimiting the maritime boundaries between the two States, including the continental shelf both within and outside 200 nm (having found, following the *Bay of Bengal Delimitation*, that it possessed the requisite jurisdiction to delimit the outer continental shelf). Further, the Tribunal also,

491 Ibid., [450]–[452], [487(2)].

492 Ibid., [488(2)].

493 A. Kuipers and S. Khan, 'U.N. Favors Guyana in Oil Border Spat with Suriname' 21 September 2007, *Reuters*, available at: <https://www.reuters.com/article/us-suriname-guyana-idUSN2044982420070920>; B. Jagdeo, 'Address to the Nation by His Excellency Bharrat Jagdeo, President of the Republic of Guyana, on the Award of the Guyana-Suriname Arbitral Tribunal' 20 September 2007, *Guyana News and Information*, available at: <http://www.guyana.org/guysur/jagdeo_tribunal_award.html>, cited in H. D. Phan and L. N. Nguyen, 'The *South China Sea* Arbitration: Bindingness, Finality and Compliance with UNCLOS Dispute Settlement Decisions' 36, at fn 44.

494 R. Sanders, 'Guyana to be Oil Rich?' 26 September 2007, *BBC Caribbean*, available at: <https://www.bbc.co.uk/caribbean/news/story/2007/09/070926_sanders240907.shtml>.

495 Jagdeo (n. 493).

496 See above Chapter 5.3.1.

alike in the *Bay of Bengal Delimitation*, created a 'grey area', being an "an area in which the states concerned have shared rights".[497] In the grey area, Bangladesh was accorded the right to explore and exploit the continental shelf, whereas India retained all other sovereign rights over the water column and suprajacent airspace. The Tribunal indicated that it was for India and Bangladesh to determine between themselves how sovereign rights were to be exercised in the grey area, calling upon the States to cooperate.[498] In sum, Bangladesh emerged with the greatest share of the delimited area, being awarded nearly 80 per cent of the area in dispute.

As to compliance, the Award received a favourable reaction from each State. Bangladesh hailed the Award as a "victory for friendship and a win-win situation for the peoples of Bangladesh and India",[499] while India proclaimed that the Award would "enhance mutual understanding and goodwill between India and Bangladesh by bringing closure to a long-pending issue".[500] India further remarked that the Award "paves the way for the economic development of this part of the Bay of Bengal, which will be beneficial to both countries".[501] Indeed, as Nguyen has noted, the arbitral award "ended decades of uncertainty as to the allocation of maritime entitlements, which created political and economic security and stability for all States concerned".[502] Such certainty proved to be particularly important given the discovery of natural gas deposits, which may have provided the commercial confidence necessary for international oil

497 *Bay of Bengal Arbitration* [507]–[508].

498 Ibid., [508]. Though, as noted previously, each State is already under an obligation to negotiate both under UNCLOS and pursuant to customary international law.

499 R. Bhattacharjee, 'Delimitation of Indo-Bangladesh Maritime Boundary' 19 August 2014, *Institute for Defence Studies and Analyses*, available at: <https://www.idsa.in/idsacomments/DelimitationofIndo-Bangladesh_rbhattacharjee_190814>.

500 A. Panda, 'Reclamation, Arbitration, Competition: South China Sea Situation Report' 9 May 2015, *The Diplomat*, available at: <https://thediplomat.com/2015/05/reclamation-arbitration-competition-south-china-sea-situation-report/>; J. Borger and T. Phillips, 'How China's Artificial Islands Led to Tension in the South China Sea' 27 October 2015, *The Guardian*, available at: <https://www.theguardian.com/world/2015/oct/27/tensions-and-territorial-claims-in-the-south-china-sea-the-guardian-briefing>.

501 R. Paul, 'UN Tribunal Rules for Bangladesh in Sea Border Dispute with India' 8 July 2014, *Reuters*, available at: <http://uk.reuters.com/article/2014/07/08/uk-bangladesh-india-seaborder-idUKKBN0FD15N20140708>; Official Spokesperson of the Ministry of External Affairs, 'Official Spokesperson's Response to a Question on the Award of the Tribunal on the Maritime Boundary Arbitration between India and Bangladesh' 8 July 2014, *Government of India*, available at: <https://mea.gov.in/bilateral-documents.htm?dtl/23575/Official+Spokespersons+response+to+a+question+on+the+award+of+the+Tribunal+on+the+Maritime+Boundary+Arbitration+between+India+and+Bangladesh>.

502 Nguyen (n. 493), 99.

and gas companies to commence operations in the formerly disputed area.[503] Since that time, production sharing contracts have been signed between Bangladeshi and Indian oil companies,[504] indicating a compliance approach to cooperation in the 'grey area'.

It should, however, be noted that much like the result in the *Bay of Bengal Delimitation*, India has objected to Bangladesh's amended submission to the CLCS on the basis that the Bangladeshi submission is inconsistent with the Award.[505] India has also objected to Bangladesh's revised basepoints for the purposes of drawing straight baselines arguing that they are "at variance with the base points used in the [Award] ... encroach[ing] into the Indian [EEZ] in the Grey Area recognised by the Tribunal".[506] Accordingly, the conclusion to be reached in relation to compliance is much the same as that in the *Bay of Bengal Delimitation*: while the acceptance of the Award by both States is to be celebrated, problems remain.

5.5 *Compulsory Conciliation: Timor Sea*

Conciliation is anticipated in UNCLOS in two situations: first, as an available mode of dispute settlement to which parties in dispute might agree,[507] or, second, as a required form of dispute resolution at the behest of one party when the subject matter of the dispute is excluded from the scope of arbitration or adjudication.[508] The only conciliation held to date further to the UNCLOS dispute settlement procedures was a compulsory conciliation instituted by Timor-Leste against Australia in 2016 in light of Australia's optional exclusion of maritime boundary delimitation disputes under Article 298(1)(a). Australia initially resisted the conciliation process, challenging the competence

503 Kałduński and Wasilewski (n. 439), 847–848 (noting that "[u]ncertainty over entitlements may have previously deterred firms from investing in offshore blocks ... the Award is expected to open the way for new oil and gas exploration in the Bay of Bengal. Importantly both parties welcomed the Award, emphasizing that it will pave the way for the economic development of this part of the Bay of Bengal, which will in turn be beneficial to both states").

504 Source: <http://www.petrobangla.org.bd/site/page/18628f28-4849-435f-aaf4-dcc3c1e8bea4/nolink/->.

505 Permanent Mission of India to the United Nations, *Letter to the Secretary-General*, 16 April 2021, available at: <https://www.un.org/depts/los/clcs_new/submissions_files/bgd55_11/20210416IndNvUN002.pdf>.

506 Permanent Mission of India to the United Nations, *Letter to the Secretary-General*, 3 August 2017, available at: <https://www.un.org/depts/los/LEGISLATIONANDTREATIES/PDFFILES/2017_08_03_IND_UN.pdf>.

507 UNCLOS, Art. 282, Annex V.

508 UNCLOS, Arts. 298(1)(a), 297(3)(b).

of the Conciliation Commission, in light of a bilateral treaty between Australia and Timor-Leste that was intended to delay the establishment of a maritime boundary between the two States during the joint exploitation of seabed resources.[509]

After Australia's challenge to competence failed,[510] it fully participated in the conciliation process as required under UNCLOS. The Commission proceeded to undertake a series of consultations with the parties in line with its mandate under UNCLOS, which included "draw[ing] the attention of the parties to any measures which might facilitate an amicable settlement of the dispute".[511] The parties differed on their views as to the proper methodology for delimiting the continental shelf boundary between them; Timor-Leste favoured the use of the equidistance line whereas Australia had long maintained the use of natural prolongation in the area given the presence of the Timor Trough.[512] Also of importance were the lateral lines of the maritime boundary in light of the existing continental shelf boundary in place between Australia and Indonesia on either side of Timor-Leste's entitlement in the Timor Sea. The placement of the maritime boundary was of critical importance because of the known existence of significant gas fields in the Timor Sea, most particularly one known as Greater Sunrise, which straddled the eastern side of a joint development area and Australia's continental shelf.[513] This consideration also featured in the conciliation process.[514]

509 Treaty between Australia and the Democratic Republic of Timor-Leste on Certain Maritime Arrangements in the Timor Sea, signed 12 January 2006, entered into force 23 February 2007, [2007] ATS 12 ('CMATS Treaty'), Arts. 4, 12.

510 *Timor Sea Conciliation* (*Timor-Leste v. Australia*), Competence, Decision of 19 September 2016, PCA Case No. 2016–10.

511 UNCLOS, Annex V, Art. 5. In commencing its work, the Commission identified its objectives as:
'(a) to map out and understand the Parties' objectives and interests, as well as their formal positions;
(b) to manage the process for all stakeholders in the Timor Sea ...;
(c) to provide for a suitable interim arrangement ... and
(d) to advance a proposal capable of achieving agreement ... on all elements of their dispute. ...'
Timor Sea Conciliation, [90].

512 Ibid., [231]–[235].

513 The treaties governing the arrangements in the Timor Sea were the CMATS Treaty (n. 121); Agreement between the Government of Australia and the Government of the Democratic Republic of Timor-Leste relating to the Unitisation of the Sunrise Troubadour Fields, signed 6 March 2003, entered into force 23 February 2007, 2483 UNTS 317; Timor Sea Treaty between the Government of East Timor and the Government of Australia, signed 20 May 2002, entered into force 2 April 2003, 2258 UNTS 3.

514 See *Timor Sea Conciliation*, [124], [237], [240]–[241], Annex 19.

Through the intervention of the Conciliation Commission, the parties were able to reach agreement on the delimitation of the maritime boundary,[515] and concluded a maritime boundary treaty on 6 March 2018.[516] Following signature of the treaty, both States then had to undertake domestic processes for the ratification of the treaty,[517] and it entered into force through an exchange of notes in August 2019.[518]

Beyond the delimitation of the boundary, there was also a recommendation of the Conciliation Commission that "the Parties continue their discussions regarding the development of Greater Sunrise with a view to reaching agreement on a concept for the development of the resource".[519] In the 2018 Treaty, the parties agreed to joint rights with upstream revenue divided depending on the development of the field through a Timorese or Darwin (Australian) location.[520] Timor-Leste subsequently purchased a considerable stake in Greater Sunrise but the field has not been developed and there has been some scepticism voiced as to whether it ever will be.[521]

As a conciliation process, neither Australia nor Timor-Leste was legally bound by the recommendations in the Commission's report.[522] Australia has described the resolution of the dispute in the following terms:

> By signing this Treaty, both governments have judged it has delivered a fair and equitable outcome. Our treaty reflects the value and importance of those rules and institutions, and the benefits for states in abiding by

515 *Timor Sea Conciliation*, 'Timor-Leste and Australia Continue Engagement with Greater Sunrise Joint Venture and Agree Timeframe for Signature of Maritime Boundary Treaty', Press Release No. 9, 26 December 2017, PCA Case No. 2016–10.

516 Treaty between Australia and the Democratic Republic of Timor-Leste Establishing their Maritime Boundaries in the Timor Sea, signed 6 March 2018, entered into force 30 August 2019, [2019] ATS 16 ('Maritime Boundary Treaty').

517 Australia adopted legislation in July 2019: *Timor Sea Maritime Boundaries Treaty Consequential Amendments Act 2019* (Cth); *Passenger Movement Charge Amendment (Timor Sea Maritime Boundaries Treaty) Act 2019* (Cth); *Treasury Laws Amendment (Timor Sea Maritime Boundaries Treaty) Act 2019* (Cth).

518 Maritime Boundary Treaty (n. 516).

519 *Timor Sea Conciliation* [306].

520 Ibid., [265]–[266]; Maritime Boundary Treaty (n. 516), Art. 2(2).

521 A. Grigg, 'Less than 20 Years after Independence, Timor-Leste is Running on Fumes' 30 April 2021, *Australian Financial Review*, available at: <https://www.afr.com/companies/energy/less-than-20-years-after-independence-timor-leste-is-running-on-fumes-20210429-p57nc7>.

522 UNCLOS, Annex V, Art. 7(2).

> those rules. In particular, our treaty reflects the importance of the United Nations Convention on the Law of the Sea.[523]

In describing how the Maritime Boundary Treaty was reached, Timor-Leste has stated:

> After a long-running dispute, Timor-Leste triggered this [conciliation] process to bring Australia to the negotiating table so that it could pursue its sovereign rights and secure permanent maritime boundaries in the Timor Sea.[524]

Given Australia's prior steadfast position resisting the delimitation of a maritime boundary with Timor-Leste before the conciliation, Australia's engagement with the process and willingness to reach an agreement on the boundary reflects well on the influence of UNCLOS dispute settlement.[525] The exploitation of Greater Sunrise remains as 'unfinished business' from the process, however.

The conditions for successful conciliation are inevitably varied when account is taken of the relationship between the parties concerned, the influence of domestic constituencies, the influence of other international stakeholders and the national defence and/or economic interests at stake.[526] Whether the *Timor Sea Conciliation* prompts greater use of this form of dispute settlement, or perhaps greater willingness on the part of neighbouring States to negotiate agreements so as to avoid compulsory conciliation, is yet to be realised. The outcomes of the compulsory conciliation process do, though, further support the perspective that the settlement of maritime boundaries

523 Department of Foreign Affairs and Trade, Australian Government, *Australia and Timor-Leste Maritime Boundaries* (March 2018), available at: <https://www.dfat.gov.au/sites/default/files/aus-timor-maritime-boundary-fact-sheet.pdf>.

524 Timor-Leste Maritime Boundary Office, *What is in the Maritime Boundary Treaty: Fact Sheet* (March 2018), available at: <http://www.gfm.tl/wp-content/uploads/2021/01/FACT-SHEET-MARCH-2018.pdf>.

525 Strating has noted how the conciliation, as well as Timor-Leste's threat to withdraw from the CMATS Treaty, compelled the Australian government to change its position: B. Strating, 'Timor-Leste Runs the Risk of a Pyrrhic Victory' 11 January 2017, *The Interpreter*, available at: <https://www.lowyinstitute.org/the-interpreter/timor-leste-runs-risk-pyrrhic-victory>.

526 See, e.g., U. Linderfalk, 'The *Jan Mayen Case* (*Iceland/Norway*): An Example of Successful Conciliation' in C. Tomuschat, R. P. Mazzeschi and D. Thürer (eds), *Conciliation in International Law: The OSCE Court of Conciliation and Arbitration* (Brill, 2017) 193; E. L. Richardson, 'Jan Mayen in Perspective' (1988) 82 *American Journal of International Law* 443.

through third-party processes can prompt compliance because of the interest in resource access.

5.6 *Conclusion*

Compliance with maritime boundary delimitation awards issued by UNCLOS dispute settlement bodies has overall been very positive in relation to EEZ and continental shelf boundaries. In each instance, the parties resolving their disputes through arbitration, adjudication or conciliation under UNCLOS have embraced the awards, and frequently lauded the process by which the awards were reached.[527] The conclusion of the judicial proceedings has often allowed the parties to reinvigorate their bilateral relationships, either in relation to maritime affairs or more generally. Resolution of additional claims beyond the maritime boundary dispute have not always created any separate requirements in complying with the terms of a judgment. This positive compliance record broadly reflects the experience of maritime delimitation before the ICJ; there are two known ICJ cases where the decision on maritime delimitation was rejected by a party to the dispute.[528]

As the discussion has indicated in this Chapter, the resolution of maritime boundary disputes has not been entirely without complication and in some instances, outstanding issues remain. Notably, operationalising an obligation of cooperation has not necessarily been forthcoming in relation to so-called grey areas. The difficulties in implementation may warrant closer consideration as to whether such areas are to be avoided in future maritime boundary disputes. The implications of these outer continental shelf maritime boundaries for the work of the CLCS are still not fully grasped. It is in relation to the outer continental shelf where disagreements between the parties have emerged.[529] In light of the arbitral or judicial decision being final and binding

527 While conciliation does not produce an 'award', the result of the conciliation was nonetheless applauded, as discussed above in Chapter 5.5.

528 Following the ICJ's decision in *Territorial and Maritime Dispute* (*Nicaragua v. Colombia*) (n. 54), Colombia withdrew from the *Pact of Bogotá*, which had formed the basis of jurisdiction before the Court: Helen Murphy, 'Colombia Leaves Pact Recognizing U.N. Court Rulings' 29 November 2012, *Reuters*, available at: <https://www.reuters.com/article/us-colombia-icj-idUSBRE8AR11Q20121128>. Further, Kenya's president rejected the ICJ decision in *Maritime Delimitation in the Indian Ocean* (*Somalia v. Kenya*) (n. 27), which gave Somalia control over disputed waters between the two States: P. Muiruri, 'Kenya Rejects UN Court Judgment Giving Somalia Control of Resource-Rich Waters' 15 October 2021, *The Guardian*, available at: <https://www.theguardian.com/global-development/2021/oct/14/kenya-rejects-un-court-judgment-giving-somalia-control-of-resource-rich-waters>.

529 As noted above in relation to the *Barbados/Trinidad and Tobago* case, as well as following the delimitations in the Bay of Bengal.

on the States, the CLCS should be able to rely on those judgments in the course of its work.

As to other outcomes of the resolution of disputes, the resolution of maritime boundary disputes through the UNCLOS dispute resolution system has also enhanced the commercial confidence of stakeholders seeking to exploit the living and non-living resources of the maritime zones in question. Further, the law of maritime boundary delimitation, which is a field of international law to which primacy has been offered to interpretations of international courts and tribunals rather than to treaty or custom,[530] has been enriched and developed as a result of the contribution of UNCLOS courts and tribunals. Such clarification of the law of maritime boundary delimitation – perhaps better described as *acquis judicaire* – complemented by the generally positive responses of States party to maritime boundary delimitation disputes, may provide greater guidance and exemplar responses to States seeking to resolve outstanding maritime boundary delimitations by negotiation; such outcome being at least partly evident in the commentary surrounding the award in *Barbados v. Trinidad and Tobago*.

A final observation on compliance with maritime boundary delimitation disputes is that the receptivity of the final boundary to the parties does not change depending on whether ITLOS, a special chamber of ITLOS or an arbitral tribunal has issued the decision. Whether the forum has implications for the procedure or the substantive result may still be a source of speculation but at least in terms of compliance, the choice of ITLOS or an Annex VII tribunal has not mattered. Instead, the harmonisation that has occurred between the different tribunals is notable and the predictability that perhaps follows as a result may also positively influence the extent of compliance with the decision on the maritime boundary.

6 Detention of Vessels and Crew

6.1 *Introduction*

Six cases arising under UNCLOS dispute settlement procedures have assessed the actions of coastal States seizing vessels and/or the crew onboard for alleged

530 P. Weil, *The Law of Maritime Delimitation: Reflections* (Cambridge Grotius Publications, 1989), 8:

> [T]he legal conquest of maritime delimitation is not the work of either treaty or custom but of the courts which, far from being a subsidiary source of international law, here play the role of a primary and direct source of law, even if they have chosen modesty to ascribe the credit to customary law.

violations of coastal State laws.[531] The flag States have challenged the coastal State's assertion of jurisdiction over their ships in each instance. These cases have been addressed on the merits rather than under the provisional measures proceedings discussed in Chapter 4, or Article 292 prompt release proceedings discussed in Chapter 3, as Article 292 only applies in relation to the arrest of fishing vessels under Article 73 or specific pollution offences under Articles 220 and 226 of UNCLOS.[532]

Rather than the prompt release of vessels and crew, the proceedings discussed in this Chapter are generally concerned with the question of whether the arresting State had the authority under the Convention to arrest the vessel and/or crew and whether that authority was exercised lawfully. Determination of this question may turn on whether the arrest was validly within the enforcement jurisdiction of the arresting State pursuant to the Convention, whether the actions of the arresting State in conducting the arrest were reasonable and proportionate in the circumstances, and whether the procedural elements of the Convention concerning arrest, such as the duty to inform the flag State,[533] were followed. If the Tribunal finds that the State has illegally arrested and detained vessels and crew, general international law provides that the offending State is under an obligation to make full reparation for the injury caused, whether material or moral.[534] Such reparation may take the form of restitution (*restitutio in integrum*), compensation and/or satisfaction.[535]

Other than maritime boundary delimitation cases, the three other contentious cases decided on the merits by ITLOS all concerned the arrest of vessels: *Saiga*, *Virginia G* and *Norstar*. These three cases are the first focus of our consideration in the discussion below for assessing compliance with ITLOS judgments on the merits. Among the cases decided on the merits in Annex VII arbitration, three were primarily concerned with the arrest of vessels and/or crew: *Duzgit Integrity*, *Enrica Lexie*, and *Arctic Sunrise*. Each of these cases involved two or three stages of proceedings, with the *Duzgit Integrity* and

531 *Saiga (No. 2)*, Merits; *Virginia G*; *Norstar*, Merits; *Duzgit Integrity*, Merits; *Enrica Lexie*, Merits; *Arctic Sunrise*, Merits. The *Louisa* case also sought to challenge the arrest of a vessel and its crew but ITLOS determined it lacked jurisdiction to resolve the merits of this dispute. *San Padre Pio (No. 2)*, which concerned Switzerland's challenge of Nigeria's arrest and detention of a vessel engaged in ship-to-ship transfers, was settled.

532 See Chapter 3.1.

533 UNCLOS, Art. 73(4). Note that this duty under Article 73(4) of UNCLOS only arises in relation to fishing vessels.

534 International Law Commission, *Report of the International Law Commission on the Work of Its Fifty-Third Session*, UN GAOR, 56th sess., Supp. No. 10, UN Doc. A/56/10 (2001) ('*Articles on the Responsibility of States for Internationally Wrongful Acts*'), Art. 31.

535 Ibid., Arts. 34–37.

Arctic Sunrise cases each having a reparations phase resulting in an award of damages.[536] The compliance of the respondent State is also examined for each of these cases in this Chapter. Some other outcomes are also highlighted.

Two cases currently pending before Annex VII arbitral tribunals are not discussed because they have not concluded or otherwise not progressed to a substantive stage at the time of writing. First, *Three Ukrainian Naval Vessels*, which involves legal claims against Russia associated with the arrest and detention of Ukrainian vessels and their crew. As a judgment on the merits is yet to be rendered, we do not consider that case in this Chapter but have addressed it in relation to provisional measures in Chapter 4.[537] Second, in relation to *Heroic Idun*, the Marshall Islands initially flagged its intent to constitute an Annex VII tribunal in relation to its claim against Equatorial Guinea for the arrest of the Heroic Idun, which the Marshall Islands claims occurred within the EEZ of São Tomé and Principe, and thereby in excess of Equatorial Guinea's enforcement jurisdiction pursuant to the Convention. The parties subsequently agreed to the formation of a Special Chamber of ITLOS to resolve their dispute and written proceedings had commenced at time of writing.[538]

6.2 *Saiga (No. 2)*

As discussed above in relation to the *Saiga* prompt release case,[539] the first ITLOS decision on the merits, *Saiga* (*No. 2*), concerned Guinea's arrest of the M/V Saiga, which was flagged to Saint Vincent and the Grenadines and was arrested for allegedly importing fuel into Guinean territory without prior authorisation. Under Guinean law, the importation, storage, transportation and distribution of fuel, as well as acts of bunkering, were prohibited within the State's 'customs area'.[540] The Guinean Customs Code in force at the time provided that the 'customs area' of the State extended 250 km from the State's coast, which constitutes, at least in part, an area of Guinea's EEZ.[541] The

536 *Duzgit Integrity*, Compensation; *Arctic Sunrise*, Compensation.

537 See Chapter 4.10.

538 *The M/T "Heroic Idun" (No. 2) Case* (Marshall Islands/Equatorial Guinea), Order of 27 April 2023. The short-lived prompt release proceedings are mentioned in the listing of cases in Chapter 3. No substantive steps in those judicial proceedings occurred before the application was withdrawn. See Chapter 3.1.

539 For a more fulsome recitation of the facts, see above Chapter 4.6.

540 Law L/94/007/CTRN, 15 March 1994 (Guinea), relevantly translated and reproduced in *Saiga* (*No. 2*), Merits, 49–50 [112].

541 *Code des douanes* (*Customs Code*) (Guinea), Art. 34, relevantly translated and reproduced in ibid., 50 [114].

Tribunal found it had jurisdiction and dismissed all objections to the admissibility of the dispute.[542]

On the merits, the Tribunal first considered whether Guinea's enforcement of its domestic law on the transport of oil was permitted under the Convention.[543] Having regard to Articles 56 and 58 of the Convention, each of which provide the rights and jurisdiction of States in the EEZ, the Tribunal determined that Guinea's customs law could not be extended to the EEZ.[544] Given that the exercise of power was invalid as a matter of international law, ITLOS determined that the arrest, detention and prosecution of the M/V Saiga and its crew, as well as the confiscation of its cargo, were unlawful.[545] The Tribunal further determined that the arrest was a violation of the right of hot pursuit under the Convention,[546] and that Guinea's decision to indiscriminately fire upon an unarmed and otherwise compliant vessel entailed an excessive use of force contrary to international law.[547] On 1 July 1999, Guinea was ordered to pay US$2 million compensation.[548] The Saiga and its crew had been released as a result of the earlier proceedings under Article 292 of UNCLOS.[549]

From communications by Saint Vincent and the Grenadines to the Tribunal, it appears that there was no immediate compliance with the judgment of the Tribunal. It was not until April 2001 that Saint Vincent and the Grenadines informed the Tribunal that the parties had reached an amicable agreement to resolve outstanding issues in relation to the implementation of the Tribunal's judgment.[550] The compensation was paid in instalments, with the full amount paid by 31 December 2002.[551] Full compliance with the order for compensation was thus achieved.

---

542 These objections included concerns about the nationality of claims and genuine link. See ibid., 30–48 [40]–[109].

543 Ibid., 54 [126].

544 Ibid., 56 [136]. The contiguous zone does overlap with the EEZ, but in the case of Guinea's customs law, the customs radius extended further than the permissible breadth of the contiguous zone under Article 33 of the Convention.

545 Ibid., 69 [183].

546 Ibid., 59–60 [147]–[149].

547 Ibid., 62–63 [157]–[159].

548 Ibid., 65–66 [172]–[175].

549 See Chapter 3 above.

550 ITLOS, *Annual Report of the International Tribunal for the Law of the Sea for* 2001, ITLOS Doc. SPLOS/74 (2002).

551 H. D. Phan, 'International Courts and State Compliance: An Investigation of the Law of the Sea Cases' (2019) 50(1) *Ocean Development and International Law* 70, fn 36.

One question of compliance that also arose in relation to *Saiga* (*No. 2*) was the status of Guinea's customs law. The Tribunal made no order requiring Guinea to bring its domestic law into conformity with the Convention as authoritatively interpreted by the Tribunal, despite its determination that Guinea lacked legal authority to exercise its customs jurisdiction within the EEZ beyond its contiguous zone.[552] It is, however, arguable that good faith compliance with the Tribunal's decision necessitated that Guinea cease to enforce its customs jurisdiction within the EEZ.

The resulting question for the purpose of compliance is whether Guinea subsequently changed its national law in light of the Tribunal's decision. The authors understand that the former Customs Code was repealed and has since been replaced.[553] Article 59 of the new Customs Code provides that the 'customs radius' (*rayon des douanes*) of the State extends only to the outer limit of its territorial sea, being 12 nm from the baselines of the State.[554] Without taking any view on the complete consistency of the revised Customs Code with the Convention, it appears that the confinement of the customs jurisdiction of the State to the territorial sea is compliant with both the Convention and the Tribunal's judgment.[555] Notwithstanding the difficulty in proving a causal link between the revision of Guinea's Customs Code and the Tribunal's judgment, the later revision of the law does reflect full compliance. Such compliance demonstrates a further outcome of UNCLOS dispute resolution, being the clarification of the content of the law of the sea through the interpretation of the Convention. Revision of domestic law pursuant to the views of the Tribunal is likely to send broader signals to other parties to the Convention to ensure their domestic law is in conformity with the Convention, thereby improving overall compliance with international law.

6.3 *Virginia G*

The *Virginia G* case concerned the arrest of the Virginia G, a Panamanian bunkering vessel, by Guinea-Bissau. Guinea-Bissau alleged that the Virginia G had violated its fishing laws and regulations in refuelling foreign fishing vessels (an

---

552 *Saiga* (*No. 2*), Merits, 54 [127].

553 *Code des douanes* (*Customs Code*), Law L/2015/007/1, 25 May 2015 (Guinea).

554 In the original French:

1. Le rayon des douanes comprend une zone maritime et une zone terrestre.
2. La zone maritime du rayon des douanes est comprise entre le littoral et la limite extérieure de la mer territoriale située en mer à 12 mille marins des côtes.

555 See generally UNCLOS, Arts. 2, 18 and 33; States are permitted to exercise control in the territorial sea and contiguous zone to prevent the breach of, inter alia, their customs laws and may prevent non-innocent passage to this effect.

act commonly known as 'bunkering') in Guinea-Bissau's EEZ. On 21 August 2009, the Virginia G and its gas oil were confiscated, and domestic legal action ensued. All of the eleven crew on board the Virginia G at the time of its arrest had their passports returned in January 2010; some chose to leave Guinea-Bissau while others remained on board the vessel until it too was released in September 2010, over a year following the initial arrest.[556]

In assessing Guinea-Bissau's enforcement actions in arresting the Virginia G, the Tribunal found on 14 April 2014 that Guinea-Bissau's laws on bunkering were within its coastal State jurisdiction pursuant to Article 73(1).[557] However, its confiscation of the Virginia G's gas oil constituted a violation of that Article because it was, considering the gravity of the offence and in the circumstances as a whole, an unreasonable and disproportionate enforcement mechanism.[558] Further, while the arrest and detention of the vessel were not unreasonable,[559] Guinea-Bissau's failure to notify Panama of the detention and arrest of the Virginia G constituted a breach of Article 73(4) of UNCLOS.[560]

As reparations, ITLOS awarded compensation to Panama for the confiscation of gas oil and for repairs to the vessel.[561] This order was the only operative provision in the *dispositif* against which compliance can be assessed. Following the delivery of the judgment, communication ensued between the parties regarding payment of compensation to Panama. Guinea-Bissau reported to the Tribunal that it was 'making all necessary diligences' to comply with the decision.[562] It is unclear if compensation was ultimately paid.[563] Accepting Guinea-Bissau's statement about compliance would indicate that there was good faith compliance with the award. In any event, it has been reported that the Virginia G broke down and drove aground in Senegal and became a total loss due to looting in 2015.[564]

6.4 *Norstar*

The *Norstar* case was instituted before ITLOS by Panama against Italy in November 2015. From 1994 until 1998, the MV Norstar, which was flagged to

556 *Virginia G*, 36–37 [82], [84].
557 Ibid., 78 [256], 123 [452(7)].
558 Ibid., 81–82 [269]–[271], 124 [452(8)].
559 Ibid., 90 [310].
560 Ibid., 125 [452(11)].
561 Ibid., 121 [446].
562 ITLOS, *Annual Report of the International Tribunal for the Law of the Sea for 2014*, ITLOS Doc. SPLOS/278 (2015), 18.
563 Phan (n. 551) notes: "That there has been no further reported request for payment from Panama might be indicative that the compensation has been delivered": 74.
564 Source: <http://www.shipspotting.com/gallery/photo.php?lid=1013771>.

Panama, operated in the EEZ of various States, supplying gas oil to mega yachts. An Italian public prosecutor issued a decree of seizure against the MV Norstar in the context of criminal proceedings against eight individuals for the sale of fuel purchased in Italy and supplied on the high seas without the payment of the appropriate customs and duties.[565] At the request of Italy, the vessel was seized by Spanish authorities when it was anchored in a Spanish port in 1998. Domestic legal proceedings, including the criminal trials of those accused, proceeded and concluded in 2003. The Italian courts ordered the release of the vessel to the shipowners.[566] The shipowners were apparently not alerted to this outcome and never took possession of the Norstar.[567] Following their failure to take possession, in March 2015 the Spanish authorities auctioned the vessel for scrap,[568] leading to the institution of these proceedings.

As to the merits, Panama filed an application alleging that Italy's exercise of its criminal jurisdiction and application of its customs laws to bunkering activities carried out on the high seas violated its freedom of navigation, which is protected under Article 87(1) and (2) of the Convention.[569] For its part, Italy contended that the act of bunkering was a component of a broader series of smuggling crimes perpetrated within Italian jurisdiction, entitling it to arrest the vessel.[570]

A judgment on the merits was issued on 10 April 2019, following a preliminary objections phase.[571] The Tribunal found that the impugned act of bunkering had occurred on the high seas.[572] Considering that the act of bunkering is a freedom of the high seas within the meaning of Article 87(1),[573] the Tribunal decided that Italy's exercise of both prescriptive and enforcement jurisdiction constituted breaches of Article 87(1) by interfering with Panama's right to freedom of navigation in the high seas.[574] As such, the Tribunal awarded compensation for the loss of the Norstar in the amount of US$285,000 plus interest.[575]

565 *Norstar*, Merits, 32 [70].
566 Ibid., 34–35 [80]–[84].
567 Ibid., 35 [83].
568 Ibid., 35–36 [85]–[86].
569 Ibid., 30–31 [68].
570 Ibid., 53–54 [162].
571 *Norstar*, Preliminary Objections.
572 *Norstar*, Merits, 65 [186].
573 Ibid., 73–74 [219].
574 Ibid., 74–76 [222]–[230], 124 [469(1)].
575 Ibid., 114 [417], 123 [462], 125 [469(4)]. This amount was well below the sum of approximately US$52 million sought by Panama. See ibid., [68].

Panama subsequently communicated with the agent of Italy requesting information about compliance.[576] It has been informally reported that Italy did pay compensation albeit with some delay given that the police directly involved in the case were disappointed with the Tribunal's decision.[577] Assuming this information to be correct, and in the absence of information to the contrary, it appears there was full compliance with the judgment.

6.5 *Duzgit Integrity*

The *Duzgit Integrity* was a Maltese-flagged chemical tanker that was arrested and confiscated by officials in São Tomé and Principe. Malta claimed, *inter alia*, that São Tomé was in violation of obligations under Article 49(3) of UNCLOS concerning the exercise of its sovereignty in archipelagic waters. The Annex VII tribunal found that São Tomé violated Article 49(3) in light of unreasonable and disproportionate penalties imposed by the State for an attempted, albeit unauthorised, ship-to-ship transfer between two vessels of the same charterer.[578]

Consequently, the case proceeded to a reparations phase, but São Tomé did not participate in this stage of the proceedings.[579] An award on reparations was issued in December 2019. The master and vessel were released during the arbitral proceedings on the merits pursuant to a settlement agreement between the owner and São Tomé.[580] Despite this agreement, the Tribunal determined that São Tomé was liable under multiple heads of damages in relation to the vessel and ordered compensation of approximately US$13 million.

Judge Kateka, in dissent, was critical of the quantum of compensation ordered,[581] which has been described as "crippling compensation" awarded against a developing State.[582] As far as is possible to determine, the amount is yet to be paid. This result is not surprising given that the amount ordered

576 ITLOS, *Annual Report of the International Tribunal for the Law of the Sea for 2019*, ITLOS Doc. SPLOS/278 (2020), 17.

577 Correspondence on file with the authors.

578 *Duzgit Integrity*, Merits [256].

579 *Duzgit Integrity*, Reparations [3]–[4]. For discussion of potential motivations behind São Tomé's decision not to participate, see P. Tzeng, 'A Strategy of Non-Participation before International Courts and Tribunals' (2020) 19 *The Law and Practice of International Courts and Tribunals* 5, 25–26.

580 *Duzgit Integrity*, Merits, [117]–[118].

581 *Duzgit Integrity*, Reparations (Dissenting Opinion of Judge Kateka), [25]–[26]. See further R. Churchill, 'Dispute Settlement in the Law of the Sea: Survey for 2019' (2020) 35 *International Journal of Marine and Coastal Law* 621, 652.

582 M. Paparinskis, 'Crippling Compensation in the International Law Commission and Investor – State Arbitration' (2021) 37(1–2) *ICSID Review* 289.

reflected some 3 percent of São Tomé's GDP,[583] and that it is one of the world's poorest States. Such circumstances raise the question of whether a State ought to be regarded as violating an obligation to make reparations further to the order of an international court or tribunal in circumstances where doing so would be extremely difficult due to economic conditions that could be, at least in part, beyond the State's control. In these circumstances, there may be merit in the declaratory effect of a judgment in finally pronouncing fault and clarifying the application of the relevant international law requirements to prevent future violations. The extent and likelihood of compliance in this instance thus prompts broader considerations about calculations of compensation under international law, as well as the nature of reparations more generally, in inter-State disputes.

6.6 *Enrica Lexie*

In *Enrica Lexie*, Italy challenged India's detention, arrest and prosecution of two Italian marines who had been serving as a vessel protection detachment on an Italian oil tanker, the Enrica Lexie. The two marines fired on an Indian fishing vessel, believing it to be a potential piratical attack, killing two of the fishers. Italy's arguments included submissions that India could not lawfully exercise jurisdiction over the two Italian marines, both because of a lack of authority under UNCLOS and because of immunity enjoyed by the marines as Italian naval officers.[584]

Court proceedings had commenced in India,[585] as well as investigations and criminal proceedings in Italy,[586] but each was stayed pursuant to the provisional measures order of ITLOS issued under Article 290(5).[587] Following a request for the prescription of provisional measures, the Annex VII Tribunal ordered that the two marines be returned to Italy in light of Italian assurances that they would be returned to India for trial if required following a decision on the merits.[588]

In adjudicating on the merits, the Annex VII Tribunal decided that the marines were immune from prosecution in India,[589] and that Italy had breached Articles 87(1)(a) and 90 of the Convention because of its interference

583 Source: <https://data.worldbank.org/indicator/NY.GDP.MKTP.CD?locations=ST>.

584 *Enrica Lexie*, Merits [68].

585 Ibid., [155]–[172], [179]–[193] (outlining investigation, arrest and judicial proceedings against the marines in India).

586 Ibid., [194]–[216].

587 *Enrica Lezie*, ITLOS Provisional Measures [141(1)]. See Chapter 4.9.

588 *Enrica Lexie*, Annex VII Provisional Measures [126]–[132].

589 *Enrica Lexie*, Merits [229]–[248].

with the Indian fishing vessel.[590] In light of the latter breach, the Tribunal held that "India is entitled to payment of compensation in connection with loss of life, physical harm, material damage to property … and moral harm suffered by the captain and other crew members".[591] The amount of compensation was not calculated but left to the parties to determine in first instance.[592] The Tribunal retained jurisdiction over the matter in the event that the parties were unable to reach agreement on an amount of compensation over the following twelve months.[593]

A year passed before agreement was reached and the parties sought an extension of time for discussions prior to initiating further proceedings before the arbitral tribunal.[594] In June 2021, India's courts closed the domestic cases after Italy paid compensation of 100 million rupees.[595] (The equivalent of US$1.3 million as at the time of settlement.) India subsequently agreed with Italy's request that the arbitral proceedings be closed following Italy's assurances "in relation to the prosecution of the Marines in Italy".[596] The Annex VII proceedings were closed on 12 October 2021.[597] However, Italian authorities dropped their investigations over the Marines on 31 January 2022 for lack of evidence.[598] While Italy's decision not to proceed with the prosecution of the marines would appear to be in violation of the assurances provided as part of its compliance with the Annex VII tribunal's decision, if it is assumed that Italy acted in good faith and consistently with requirements of its national laws in relation to the prosecution then India could not fault Italy for non-compliance.

6.7 *Arctic Sunrise*

In 2013, the Arctic Sunrise – a Dutch-flagged vessel owned and operated by the environmental organisation Greenpeace – and its 30 crew were involved in a protest at a Russian oil platform, the *Prirazlomnaya*. Russia arrested the vessel

590 Ibid., [1041]–[1043].

591 Ibid., [1094(B)(6)].

592 Ibid., [1089].

593 Ibid., [1090].

594 *Enrica Lexie* (*Italy v. India*), Closing of the Proceedings, Order of 12 October 2021, PCA Case No. 2015–28.

595 'Italian Marines: India Closes Criminal Cases in 2012 Shooting' 15 June 2021, *BBC News*, available at: <https://www.bbc.com/news/world-asia-india-57479761>.

596 *Enrica Lexie* (*Italy v. India*), Closing of the Proceedings, Order of 12 October 2021, PCA Case No. 2015–28.

597 Ibid.

598 'Italy Drops Probe against Marines Who Killed Indian Fishermen in 2012' 1 February 2022, *The Week*, available at: <https://www.theweek.in/news/world/2022/02/01/italy-drops-probe-against-marines-who-killed-indian-fishermen-in-20-12.html>.

and crew, prompting the Netherlands to institute proceedings under UNCLOS. As discussed in Chapter 4, the Netherlands initially sought provisional measures at ITLOS pending the constitution of the Annex VII tribunal. Following the provisional measures proceedings, the crew and vessel were eventually released.[599]

Russia refused to participate in the Annex VII arbitral proceedings, as it had done at the provisional measures stage before ITLOS.[600] Nonetheless, the Annex VII tribunal determined it had jurisdiction,[601] and proceeded to resolve the dispute on the merits. The Tribunal found that Russia's actions in "boarding, investigating, inspecting, arresting, detaining, and seizing the Arctic Sunrise without the prior consent of the Netherlands, and by arresting, detaining, and initiating judicial proceedings against the Arctic 30" violated obligations owed to the Netherlands "as the flag State under Articles 56(2), 58(1), 58(2), 87(1)(a), and 92(1) of the Convention".[602]

The Tribunal ordered that compensation be paid as a result of Russia's breaches of international law, consisting of heads of damage for physical damage to the vessel, costs incurred to prepare it for its return voyage and the loss of the use of the vessel during the period of its detention, compensation to the Arctic 30 for their illegal arrest and detention, as well as for the refund of their bail and departure from Russia, and ancillary costs incurred by the Netherlands to produce bank guarantees in the course of the proceedings.[603] In light of this decision, a further round of proceedings on compensation was undertaken to determine the quantum to be paid in relation to the heads of damage identified in the merits phase.[604] The Tribunal determined that Russia should pay over €5 million in compensation to the Netherlands.[605]

On 17 May 2019, Russia and the Netherlands reached agreement on a settlement payment, estimated at €2.7 million (or, about half of the award sum).[606] While the agreement was between the Netherlands and Russia, the compensation was to be paid to Greenpeace, which announced that compensation would be given as required to the protestors and the remainder would be

599 See Chapter 4.7.

600 Shortly before the Tribunal's decision on the merits, Russia submitted a memorandum outlining its position but the Tribunal refused to take it into account given the late stage of proceedings: *Arctic Sunrise*, Merits [68].

601 *Arctic Sunrise*, Jurisdiction.

602 *Arctic Sunrise*, Merits [401(C)].

603 Ibid., [401(F)].

604 *Arctic Sunrise*, Compensation.

605 Ibid., [128].

606 'Netherlands, Russia Agree Deal on Arctic Sunrise Compensation' 17 May 2019, *Dutch News*, available at: <https://www.dutchnews.nl/news/2019/05/netherlands-russia-agree-deal-on-arctic-sunrise-compensation>.

utilised for Greenpeace campaigns.[607] The settlement payment was made on a without prejudice basis as to the legal positions of both States thereby potentially preserving Russia's objections to the Award.[608] The nature of this settlement raises questions as to whether it was truly in compliance with the Award. Alternatively, the settlement may represent an outcome separate to, albeit perhaps inextricably related to, the Award. The assessment of this potentially semantic issue may depend on a definition of compliance and whether there is insistence on the causative connection with the judgment.[609] In any case, given that the amount of compensation to be paid by Russia pursuant to the agreement was substantially lower than that ordered by the Tribunal, Russia could not be considered as compliant with the Award. The dispute was nonetheless resolved between the parties.

6.8 *Conclusion*

In sum, the cases concerning disputes as to a State's assertion of authority over vessels and, in some instances, the on board crew have challenged the legality of arrest, the conduct of State officials during arrest, the detention of vessel and crew, and the treatment during detention. A primary concern for the flag State instituting proceedings under UNCLOS has been to secure the release of vessels and crew. In the six cases addressed in this Chapter, a successful outcome was achieved with a judicial order for such release – even if occurring at the provisional measures stage and vindicated on the merits.

Where an award of compensation has also followed the assessment of the legality of the respondent State's assertion of authority over a vessel, the stakes become much higher. The record of compliance with orders for compensation is seemingly mixed, given some uncertainty arising from the information readily available. Most positively, it could be asserted that amounts were paid in five out of six cases. A stricter reading of judgment-compliance relying only on information publicly available suggests full compliance in two cases: *Saiga (No. 2)* and *Enrica Lexie*. While some uncertainty may persist as to a definitive

---

607 'Settlement of the Arctic Sunrise Case between the Netherlands and Russia' 17 May 2019, *Greenpeace International*, available at: <https://www.greenpeace.org/international/press-release/22071/settlement-of-the-arctic-sunrise-case-between-the-netherlands-and-russia/>. Greenpeace also instituted proceedings against Russia before the European Court of Human Rights but that case is pending as of time of writing: *Bryan v Russia*, European Court of Human Rights, Application No. 22515/14.

608 See A. O. Elferink, 'Settlement of the *Dispute concerning the Arctic Sunrise*: A Belated Recognition of the Relevance of the Award on the Merits in the *Arctic Sunrise* Case' 8 July 2019, *NCLOS* Blog, at: <https://site.uit.no/nclos/2019/07/08/settlement-of-the-dispute-concerning-the-arctic-sunrise-a-belated-recognition-of-the-relevance-of-the-award-on-the-merits-in-the-arctic-sunrise-case/>.

609 See Chapter 2.3.

view on compliance in these cases, it may still be observed that the extent of compliance (and the availability of information concerning compliance) does appear to have occurred more readily in cases that have proceeded before ITLOS, rather than before an Annex VII tribunal. It is only a slight trend, however, given the small number of cases involved.

Where amounts of compensation are ordered, the experience with Part XV proceedings under UNCLOS is that securing the payment is not always straight forward but may require further negotiations and compromise. Whether and how compensation is paid may be dependent on the sovereign wealth of the country, the importance of the maritime industry to the country and its reputation therein, and the inter-relationship between the parties in dispute. In these situations, it could well be argued that what matters is the resolution of the dispute between the parties concerned rather than the precise amounts of money paid in full compliance with all orders of the tribunal.

7 Annex VII Arbitrations Involving Mixed Disputes

7.1 *Introduction*

Five cases concerning the interpretation or application of the Convention have involved underlying territorial sovereignty disputes, as well as controversies relating to maritime entitlements and the exercise of maritime rights and duties. These so-called 'mixed disputes' instituted under UNCLOS are comprised of one case before ITLOS, *Mauritius/Maldives*, and four Annex VII arbitrations: *Chagos MPA*, *South China Sea*, *Coastal State Rights in the Black Sea, Sea of Azov and Kerch Strait*, and *Detention of Ukrainian Naval Vessels and Servicemen*. The latter two cases, which concern Ukrainian challenges to Russian activities in maritime areas adjoining Crimea, had not been decided on the merits at time of writing. At the jurisdictional phase of *Coastal State Rights*, the arbitral tribunal determined that it lacked jurisdiction to resolve disputes where the "real issue of contention between the parties" was sovereignty over Crimea.[610] The issues in dispute not related to the question of sovereignty are proceeding to the merits phase. The underlying sovereignty dispute has not been the focal point of *Detention of Ukrainian Naval Vessels and Servicemen*, which thus far has centred on the arrest and detention of the vessels and crew.

This Chapter focusses on compliance with the judgments issued in the *Chagos MPA* and *South China Sea* arbitrations. Given the underlying territorial sovereignty claims in these mixed disputes, the jurisdiction of UNCLOS courts

610 *Coastal State Rights* [161], [197]–[198].

and tribunals was contested. Further, arbitrations involving these questions of territorial sovereignty tend to be intrinsically tied to issues of national identity and geopolitics. In this Chapter, we examine whether these significant factors have influenced the compliance record of UNCLOS disputes to any material extent. We begin by outlining some general considerations relevant to these disputes before turning to a discussion of each case in turn.

7.2 *Factors Influencing Compliance in Cases Involving Mixed Disputes*

In this section, we propose two general factors that may negatively impact on compliance in cases with an incidental question concerning territorial sovereignty before UNCLOS courts and tribunals: the jurisdictional limits of UNCLOS courts and tribunals, and the socio-political factors surrounding such disputes.

7.2.1 The Jurisdictional Limitations of UNCLOS Courts and Tribunals

Article 288 of the Convention vests UNCLOS courts and tribunals with jurisdiction *ratione materiae* over 'any dispute concerning the interpretation or application of the Convention'[611] and other international agreements related to the purpose of the Convention, such as bilateral fisheries agreements and maritime delimitation treaties.[612] Determining the disputes that fall within this jurisdiction is not always straightforward, as disputes arising under UNCLOS and disputes arising under other international agreements or at general international law often share the same factual substratum and many of the same issues of law.[613] As Boyle has noted, there is not a "neat division between a law of the sea case and other types of disputes. In some cases, the delimitation of a maritime boundary may necessarily require a decision concerning disputed sovereignty over land".[614]

In such cases instituted under UNCLOS, the question of whether jurisdiction *ratione materiae* exists where sovereignty is disputed over the land territory from which the maritime zones emanate has been controversial.[615] While the

611 UNCLOS, Art. 288(1).

612 UNCLOS, Art. 288(2).

613 For discussion, see C. Harris, 'Claims with an Ulterior Purpose: Characterising Disputes Concerning the "Interpretation or Application" of a Treaty' (2020) 18(3) *Law and Practice of International Courts and Tribunals* 279.

614 A. Boyle, 'Dispute Settlement and the Law of the Sea Convention: Problems of Fragmentation and Jurisdiction' (1997) 46 *International and Comparative Law Quarterly* 37, 49.

615 See general discussion in N. Klein and K. Parlett, *Judging the Law of the Sea: Judicial Interpretations of the UN Convention on the Law of the Sea* (Oxford University Press, 2022) 103–116. See, eg, B. B. Jia, 'The Principle of the Domination of the Land over the Sea: A Historical Perspective on the Adaptability of the Law of the Sea to New Challenges' (2014) 57 *German Yearbook of International Law* 1, 20–31; A. Proelss, 'The Limits of

general position appears to be that UNCLOS courts and tribunals must decline "jurisdiction regarding disputed title to *terra firma*",[616] whether the UNCLOS court or tribunal in question asserts jurisdiction is likely to turn on the characterisation of the dispute. The tribunal may decide that the issues presented may be resolved without any implication for or need to resolve the underlying territorial sovereignty dispute.[617] If the dispute arising under the Convention is merely incidental to the land sovereignty dispute, then that dispute is unlikely to be within the jurisdiction of the tribunal;[618] if the land sovereignty dispute is minor in nature and regarded as ancillary to the UNCLOS dispute, then tribunals may exercise jurisdiction.[619]

Jurisdiction *Ratione Materiae* of UNCLOS Tribunals' (2018) 46 *Hitotsubashi Journal of Law and Politics* 47, 60 (noting that "the scope and limits of jurisdiction of UNCLOS tribunals under Art. 288 (1) UNCLOS are still surrounded by a considerable degree of controversy, in particular as far as the issue of incidental sovereignty is concerned"); P. Tzeng, 'The Implicated Issue Problem: Indispensable Issues and Incidental Jurisdiction' (2018) 50 *New York University Journal of International Law and Politics* 447, 450, 492; B. Kunoy, 'The Scope of Compulsory Jurisdiction and Exceptions Thereto under the *United Nations Convention on the Law of the Sea*' (2020) 58 *Canadian Yearbook of International Law* 78, 129, 141; P. C. Irwin, 'Settlement of Maritime Boundary Disputes: An Analysis of the Law of the Sea Negotiations' (1980) 8 *Ocean Development and International Law* 105, 114; S. Yee, 'The *South China Sea* Arbitration (The Philippines v. China): Potential Jurisdictional Obstacles or Objections' (2014) 13 *Chinese Journal of International Law* 663, 688–89; *Bay of Bengal Arbitration*, 891 (Separate Concurring and Dissenting Opinion of Judge Rao).

616 Kunoy (n. 615), 141.

617 For instance, note that in the *South China Sea* dispute, the Philippines "stated at all stages of [the] arbitration that it is not asking [the] Tribunal to rule on the territorial sovereignty aspect of its disputes with China", a position adopted by the Tribunal: *South China Sea*, Jurisdiction and Admissibility [8].

618 As concluded in *Coastal State Rights*.

619 The Tribunal in the *Chagos MPA* arbitration refused to "categorically exclude that in some instances a minor issue of territorial sovereignty could indeed be ancillary to a dispute concerning the interpretation or application of the convention", noting that determination of this question depends on "where the relative weight of the dispute lies"; in effect leaving it as a matter of characterisation. See generally J. Harrison, 'Defining Disputes and Characterizing Claims: Subject-Matter Jurisdiction in Law of the Sea Convention Litigation' (2017) 48(3–4) *Ocean Development and International Law* 269, 278–79 (observing that "[a]ny distinction between major and minor issues of territorial sovereignty is not one that can be the subject of a strict test, but must be determined by a Tribunal exercising a degree of discretion in its assessment of the evidence before it … The question of what is a minor territorial dispute will doubtless be subject to litigation in the future"); Proelss (n. 615), 56 (proposing a three-step process by which tribunals determine the extent of their jurisdiction, in which the final step involves characterising the "relative weight of the dispute").

For the purposes of this study, it suffices to say that this debate as to the jurisdiction of UNCLOS courts and tribunals has the potential to affect post-award compliance and has seemingly impacted whether respondent States participate in the proceedings. Llamazon has argued that even the most powerful States are likely to comply with adverse judgments of international courts and tribunals "so long as the Court's jurisdiction and competence to rule is unquestionable".[620] As such, should States party to disputes involving questions of sovereignty over land territory regard UNCLOS courts and tribunals as actually or ostensibly acting in excess of the jurisdiction provided by the Convention, they may not only fail to comply with that award but also refrain from participating in UNCLOS dispute settlement system more broadly.

7.2.2 Socio-Political Factors

The second factor influencing compliance in the disputes discussed in this Chapter is their relative political, cultural, and national importance vis-à-vis other disputes settled pursuant to the UNCLOS dispute settlement system. It has been suggested that the submission of such disputes to compulsory dispute resolution, let alone compliance, "are something of a puzzle for the study of international relations, which traditionally assumes that states generally desire to preserve their legal sovereignty, particularly in an area as central to the national interest as title to territory".[621] As we discussed in Chapter 5 regarding maritime boundary delimitation disputes, cases concerning the territory of a State are subject to strong domestic factors influencing compliance.[622] While we resolved that the compliance record with respect to maritime delimitation disputes was largely good, albeit with some persisting issues,[623] we anticipate that factors influencing compliance in cases with elements of sovereignty over land territory are significantly greater. As Buga has noted:

620 A. P. Llamzon, 'Jurisdiction and Compliance in Recent Decisions of the International Court of Justice', (2008) 18(5) *European Journal of International Law* 815, 851.

621 B. A. Simmons, 'Capacity, Commitment and Compliance: International Institutions and Territorial Disputes' (2002) 46(6) *Journal of Conflict Resolution* 829, 831. For a background on the importance of territorial integrity to realist theories of international relations, see S. M. Walt, 'Realism and Security' in R. A. Denemark (ed), *The International Studies Encyclopedia* (Wiley, 2010) (noting that "realist theories define 'security' as the security of the state and place particular emphasis on the preservation of the state's territorial integrity ..."), citing S. M. Walt, 'The Renaissance of Security Studies' (1991) 35(2) *International Studies Quarterly* 211.

622 See Chapter 5.2.

623 See Chapter 5.6.

> Disputes over *land* in particular often touch upon historically or culturally rooted sensitivities of great national significance (geopolitics), and even a small loss of claimed territory can be seen as a threat to State sovereignty and security, providing 'fertile ground for nationalistic rhetoric and flag-waving' ... Mixed disputes are more likely to give rise to conflict than 'pure' maritime delimitations, and are frequently a symptom of traditionally rooted antagonism between the disputing States ... These conflicts often affect not only the States directly concerned, but also the international community as a whole.[624]

It is likely that the intrinsic connection between land, culture, national identity and domestic politics, along with the history of the States party to the dispute, including their bilateral relationship, experiences of colonisation and position in the international system, will strongly influence compliance decisions in cases wherein territorial sovereignty is challenged. The potential influence of these factors was recognised by the *Chagos MPA* tribunal, which noted the "inherent sensitivity of States to questions of territorial sovereignty ... Such sensitivities arise to an even greater degree in relation to land territory" vis-à-vis maritime territory.[625]

Further, and recalling the doctrine of domination (or, 'the land dominates the sea'), given that it is sovereignty over land territory that determines the extent of the maritime zones to which a State is entitled, significant economic motivators arise from control over the living and non-living resources of maritime zones, which may also influence compliance decisions to a significant degree.[626] In sum, it is anticipated that internal political and economic factors

624 I. Buga, 'Territorial Sovereignty Issues in Maritime Disputes: A Jurisdictional Dilemma for Law of the Sea Tribunals' (2012) 27 *International Journal of Marine and Coastal Law* 59, 62 (emphasis in original), citing R-J. Dupuy and D. Vignes (eds), *A Handbook on the New Law of the Sea*, vol. 1, (Martinus Nijhoff, 1991), 292; J. Guoxing, 'Sino-Japanese Jurisdictional Delimitation in East China Sea: Approaches to Dispute Settlement' in S-Y. Hong and J. M. van Dyke (eds), *Maritime Boundary Disputes, Settlement Processes, and the Law of the Sea* (Martinus Nijhoff, 2009), 77; S. A. Kocs, 'Territorial Disputes and Interstate War, 1945–1987' (1995) 57 *The Journal of Politics* 159. See also N. Klein, 'Land and Sea: Resolving Contested Land and Disappearing Land Disputes under the UN Convention on the Law of the Sea' in C. Giorgetti and N. Klein (eds), *Resolving Conflicts in the Law: Essays in Honour of Lea Brilmayer* (Brill, 2019) 249, 271 (noting that "[t]he national interest (or pride) associated with title to territory may be too strong for a State to give up possession, or its claim in the face of an adverse ruling"); H. L. Jones, 'Why Comply? An Analysis of Trends in Compliance with Judgments of the International Court of Justice since *Nicaragua*' (2012) 12 *Chicago-Kent Journal of International and Comparative Law* 58, 84–85.

625 *Chagos MPA*, [216], [219].

626 Simmons (n. 621), 846.

are very likely to influence decisions of States as to whether to comply with judgments of UNCLOS courts and tribunals concerning mixed disputes, more so than the decisions examined in the preceding Parts.

7.3 *Chagos Marine Protected Area* and *Mauritius/Maldives*

In the *Chagos MPA* arbitration, Mauritius challenged the United Kingdom's declaration of a marine protected area ('MPA') around the Chagos Archipelago before an Annex VII tribunal. The land territory of the Chagos Archipelago, consisting of some 60 islands located in the Indian Ocean, has been subject to a long-running sovereignty dispute between Mauritius and the United Kingdom. The United Kingdom exercises *de facto* control over the Archipelago, and has administered it as the British Indian Ocean Territory since 1965. It has leased Diego Garcia, the largest island in the Chagos Archipelago, to the United States for use as a military base. Mauritius has claimed that the Archipelago was illegally separated from it when it gained independence from the United Kingdom, arguing that it is entitled to exercise sovereignty *de jure* over the Archipelago.

In the Annex VII arbitration, instituted in December 2010, Mauritius argued that the United Kingdom was not the 'coastal State' within the meaning of the Convention as it did not exercise *de jure* sovereignty over the Archipelago. It was submitted that the United Kingdom therefore had no legal authority to proclaim or enforce the MPA, nor to exercise sovereignty or sovereign rights over the relevant maritime zones, for the purposes of UNCLOS. Alternatively, it was said that the United Kingdom's actions in proclaiming the MPA had violated the substantive and procedural due process requirements of UNCLOS.[627]

The Annex VII tribunal handed down its award in March 2015. The Tribunal considered that the 1965 Lancaster House Undertakings between the two States, in which the United Kingdom provided the newly independent Mauritius with a reversionary interest in the Chagos Archipelago, as well as compensation, and fishing, mineral and oil rights in the surrounding maritime zones, enlivened obligations of due regard and good faith.[628] As such, the Tribunal held that the declaration of the MPA by the United Kingdom was a violation of UNCLOS and its general international law requirements relating to due regard and good faith owed to Mauritius. As to the sovereignty dispute, the Tribunal found that it lacked jurisdiction pursuant to Article 288 to determine if the United Kingdom was the 'coastal State' for the purposes of UNCLOS,[629] and

627 *Chagos MPA*, [158].
628 Ibid., [294]–[295].
629 Ibid., [547].

therefore declined to consider the questions raised by Mauritius as to territorial sovereignty and the entitlement to sovereign rights and jurisdiction over the relevant maritime zones. This decision meant that the issue of contested sovereignty over the Chagos Archipelago was not addressed by the majority of the Tribunal.[630]

In sum, the Tribunal did not consider whether the MPA itself was lawful or not but was only concerned with the process by which it was declared.[631] That process indicated insufficient consultations with Mauritius and a failure to show due regard to the rights of Mauritius around the Chagos Archipelago. As a result of the Tribunal's decision, the United Kingdom engaged in further bilateral consultations with Mauritius about establishing the MPA,[632] and has indicated that it 'remains committed to implementing the [arbitral award]'.[633] Certainly, further and better consultations with Mauritius were required for the United Kingdom to meet its due regard requirements and hence efforts to do so subsequent to the award reflected an effort at compliance.

Determining whether actual compliance has been achieved is a more difficult question. Given that it has been some seven years since the Tribunal issued its award in *Chagos MPA* and that the same MPA declared by the Commissioner of the British Indian Ocean Territory in 2010 continues to exist unamended, one may question the extent to which these consultations bore fruit. To this end, determination of whether the United Kingdom complied with the Award depends on the way in which compliance is framed. If one interprets the Tribunal's ruling as requiring only good faith consultations with Mauritius, then the United Kingdom may have complied. Alternatively, if one considers that full compliance requires the United Kingdom to give effect to the product of those consultations, such that the MPA is adjusted to better reflect Mauritian interests, then the lack of any amendment may indicate a non-compliant attitude. It may also be the case that Mauritius did not consider it necessary or desirable to engage in consultations with the United Kingdom on the basis that it does not recognise the United Kingdom's claim to sovereignty over the Chagos Archipelago. In such a case, the United Kingdom could

630 The minority did consider whether the Chagos Archipelago had been lawfully excised at the time of Mauritius' independence, concluding that it had not been. See ibid., (Dissenting Opinion of Wolfrum and Kateka) [70]–[80].

631 *Chagos MPA* [544].

632 'Marine Protected Area', *British Indian Ocean Territory*, available at: <https://biot.gov.io/environment/marine-protected-area/>.

633 'Environment', *British Indian Ocean Territory*, available at: <https://biot.gov.io/environment/>; 'British Indian Ocean Territory', *United Kingdom Government*, available at: <https://www.gov.uk/world/organisations/british-indian-ocean-territory>.

hardly be said to be in ongoing breach of the Tribunal's ruling. Either way, coming to a clear answer as to the extent of compliance is difficult due to the lack of publicly available information as to the nature of the negotiations – and, indeed, whether they have taken place at all – as well as the specific demands made, if any, by Mauritius. This experience also indicates the perennial difficulties in determining the appropriate yardstick for the measurement and evaluation of compliance.[634]

Chagos MPA was followed by an ICJ advisory opinion in *Legal Consequences of the Separation of the Chagos Archipelago from Mauritius in 1965* ('*Chagos Advisory Opinion*')[635] and a contentious ITLOS decision in *Mauritius/Maldives*. While these proceedings are functionally separate from the *Chagos MPA* arbitration, being concerned with different factual and legal issues, each consider to varied extents the question of sovereignty over the Chagos Archipelago.

In the *Chagos Advisory Opinion*, handed down in February 2019, the ICJ relevantly held that "the United Kingdom has an obligation to end its administration of the Chagos Archipelago as rapidly as possible".[636] The Court found that the Archipelago was an "integral part" of Mauritian territory in 1965, and that its detachment by the United Kingdom violated Mauritius' right to self-determination.[637] As such, the Court considered that the United Kingdom's occupation of the Archipelago constitutes an ongoing breach of international law.[638] Subsequently, Mauritius and the Maldives, the latter sharing an undelimited maritime boundary with the coastal State exercising sovereignty over the Archipelago, instituted proceedings by *compromis* before a special chamber of ITLOS in September 2019. In its preliminary objections judgment of January 2021, the Chamber confirmed the ICJ's finding and asserted jurisdiction over maritime delimitation proceedings between Mauritius and the Maldives, rejecting the Maldives' jurisdictional arguments that *inter alia* the United Kingdom was a necessary party to the proceedings in accordance with the *Monetary Gold* principle.[639] The *Mauritius/Maldives* decision on preliminary objections was significant as it bypassed the jurisdictional issues contemplated by the *Chagos MPA* tribunal by giving effect to the *Chagos*

634 See further Chapter 2.
635 *Legal Consequences of the Separation of the Chagos Archipelago from Mauritius in 1965*, Advisory Opinion, *ICJ Reports* 2019.
636 Ibid., [178], [182].
637 Ibid., [174].
638 Ibid., [177].
639 *Mauritius/Maldives* [247].

Advisory Opinion and declarations of the United Nations General Assembly implementing that Opinion.[640]

While not formally 'overruling' the decision of the *Chagos MPA* tribunal, *Mauritius/Maldives* is somewhat in conflict with that decision because of the direct engagement with a question of disputed territorial sovereignty. One implication of these subsequent cases is the creation of tension in the nature and form of compliance. To the extent that the ICJ found that the United Kingdom's continued assertion of sovereignty over the Chagos Archipelago constitutes a breach of international law, then *a fortiori* consulting with Mauritius as ordered by the *Chagos MPA* tribunal, such that the United Kingdom purports to have the sovereign right to deal with the Archipelago, would constitute a further breach of international law. Indeed, it must now be questioned whether the MPA is of any legal consequence or effect given that the practical import of the *Chagos Advisory Opinion* is that, at least in theory, the ordinances of the British Indian Ocean Territory should be considered void *ab initio*, vitiating the core of the subject matter over which compliance was ordered by the *Chagos MPA* tribunal. To this end, any consultations undertaken by the United Kingdom in compliance with the order of the *Chagos MPA* tribunal would at worst draw the United Kingdom in further breach of international law and at best be ineffectual, raising questions as to the necessity of compliance.

7.4 *South China Sea*

In January 2013, the Philippines initiated proceedings against China pursuant to Articles 286 and 287 of the Convention in relation to the latter's assertion of maritime rights in the South China Sea, which extended to the prevention of the Philippines' rights to exercise sovereignty or sovereign rights in those maritime spaces. This challenge raised questions as to the maritime entitlements of certain land features in the South China Sea, as well as the competing exercise of rights in the maritime zones generated by those features. The Philippines further contested China's claim to a large portion of the South China Sea on the basis of what is often referred to as the 'nine-dash line'. While only the Philippines and China were party to the arbitration, the underlying issue is much larger in scope, concerning territorial and maritime rights of all South China Sea littoral States.[641] Further, the dispute is deeply rooted in regional history and international geopolitics, garnering a great deal of popular attention

640 See generally, J. McNally, 'The Metamorphosis of Soft Law in *Mauritius/Maldives*' (2021) 28 *Australian International Law Journal* 195.

641 The claimants are Brunei, China, Indonesia, Malaysia, the Philippines, Taiwan and Viet Nam.

both from the domestic polities impacted as well as the international community more generally.

The *dispositif* in the *South China Sea* arbitration reflected the vast scope of issues considered in these Annex VII arbitral proceedings and the many claims resolved in favour of the Philippines at its conclusion. The instances of claims being rejected either on the evidence provided or for lack of jurisdiction were extremely limited.[642] For the purposes of assessing China's compliance with the final award, the Tribunal's findings may be roughly described as relating to: maritime limits and entitlements; fishing; protection of the marine environment; construction of islands; surveillance on the continental shelf; and unsafe navigation during law enforcement. There was a further finding concerning China's aggravation of the dispute during the course of the arbitration as violations of Articles 279, 296, 300 and general international law.[643] This latter determination related to an assessment of behaviour during the arbitration and hence does not necessitate consideration in post-arbitration compliance actions.

At the outset of any assessment of compliance with the *South China Sea* rulings, it must be acknowledged that China rejected the binding award in its entirety when issued in 2016.[644] Over 40 States have voiced support for the *South China Sea* award,[645] and the Philippines has recently affirmed its acceptance and the importance of the award.[646] In 2021, commentators observed that "China is still holding onto its 'Four Noes' policy in the South China Sea: that is, no acceptance, no participation, no recognition, and no implementation of the South China Sea arbitration".[647] Yet suggestions have also been made that there have been some (small) shifts in China's policy and practices

642 For example, the Tribunal could not ascertain if an environmental impact assessment was undertaken in the context of land reclamation activities and construction of artificial islands: at [991]. A 'quintessential' military confrontation was considered outside jurisdiction because of the exception under Article 298(1)(b): at [1161].

643 Ibid., [1181].

644 A lengthy refutation of the award was subsequently published by the Chinese Society of International Law: Chinese Society of International Law, 'The South China Sea Arbitration Awards: A Critical Study' (2018) 17(2) *Chinese Journal of International Law* 207.

645 See 'Arbitration Support Tracker' 2 August 2021, *Asia Maritime Transparency Initiative*, available at: <https://amti.csis.org/arbitration-support-tracker/>.

646 N. H. Thao and N. T. L. Huong, 'The South China Sea Arbitration Award: 5 Years and Beyond' 12 July 2021, *The Diplomat*, available at: <https://thediplomat.com/2021/07/the-south-china-sea-arbitration-award-5-years-and-beyond/> (citing statements from the President and Foreign Minister to this effect).

647 Ibid.

that align with the findings of the Tribunal.[648] The discussion below seeks to update some of the initial assessments as to China's compliance with the Tribunal's findings and notes the influence achieved, even if a distinct reversal or shift in position or practice is not immediately discernible.

The Tribunal's views on maritime limits and entitlements can be generally divided between those relating to historic rights and the nine-dash line on the one hand and, on the other, the maritime entitlements of specific land features in the South China Sea as islands, rocks or low-tide elevations. On the former, the Tribunal determined that China's claims to historic rights or other sovereign rights arising from the nine-dash line were contrary to the Convention and that China was not permitted to extend the limits of its maritime zones beyond those provided in UNCLOS. On the latter, the Tribunal concluded that none of the features in question were entitled to a continental shelf or EEZ claim in line with Article 121(3), or otherwise the features were low-tide elevations that do not generate any entitlements to maritime zones.[649]

At the time the arbitral award was rendered, China issued a White Paper in which it not only claimed the maritime zones recognised in UNCLOS but "[i]n addition, China has historic rights in the South China Sea".[650] This statement left some ambiguity as to whether the historic rights claimed were those that exist in the territorial sea, which the Tribunal recognised as persisting following the adoption of UNCLOS,[651] or whether China still claims a more expansive maritime area based on its historic rights. The latter position would be inconsistent, and non-compliant, with the final award. China does not seemingly rely on the nine-dash line to the same extent as before the arbitration, but now refers to the Four Sha approach, which involves drawing archipelagic baselines around the claimed island groups.[652] This argument does not align with the Tribunal's determination that China may not claim maritime entitlements beyond those

648 See J. Ku and C. Mirasola, 'Tracking China's Compliance with the South China Sea Arbitral Award' 3 October 2016, *Lawfare*, available at: <https://www.lawfareblog.com/tracking-chinas-compliance-south-china-sea-arbitral-award>; 'Failing or Incomplete? Grading the South China Sea Arbitration' 11 July 2019, *Asia Maritime Transparency Initiative*, available at: <https://amti.csis.org/failing-or-incomplete-grading-the-south-china-sea-arbitration/> ('Failing or Incomplete?').

649 UNCLOS, Art. 13.

650 State Council Information Office of the People's Republic of China, *China Adheres to the Position of Settling through Negotiation the Relevant Disputes between China and the Philippines in the South China Sea* (2016), available at: <http://english.www.gov.cn/state_council/ministries/2016/07/13/content_281475392503075>, [70].

651 *South China Sea* [270].

652 J. I. Goldenziel, 'Law as a Battlefield: The US, China, and the Global Escalation of Lawfare' (2021) 106 *Cornell Law Review* 1085, 1127.

allowed in UNCLOS.[653] However, in line with the Tribunal's decision, China has not explicitly claimed an EEZ or continental shelf off the islands determined to be 'rocks' in the arbitration. Some ambiguity around compliance persists because of the ongoing disputed territorial sovereignty issues; for example, China's continued presence on Gaven Reef and Hughes Reef would only be problematic if China was not sovereign over the neighbouring islands.[654]

China continues to occupy Mischief Reef and make claims over Second Thomas Shoal, with Mischief Reef used for military and civilian purposes, despite the Tribunal's conclusion that both features are low-tide elevations falling within the EEZ and continental shelf area of the Philippines. China's construction of the artificial island on Mischief Reef was determined to be a violation of Articles 60 and 80 of UNCLOS.[655] Nonetheless, China has continued to expand its facilities on Mischief Reef, including by upgrading radar facilities, and adding a two-mile runway, concrete buildings, and underground storage for ammunition.[656] In November 2021, the Chinese coastguard blocked and fired water cannons on two Philippine supply boats within the Philippines' EEZ near Second Thomas Shoal.[657] China has also demanded that the Philippines remove the grounded BRP Sierra Madre from Second Thomas Shoal.[658] China has said that the vessel is "illegally grounded",[659] notwithstanding the fact it is within the Philippines' EEZ.

---

653 Article 47 defines the proper use of archipelagic baselines, which does not include their use around mid-sea islands that are distinct from an 'archipelagic State': UNCLOS, Arts. 46(a), 47(1). See also *South China Sea*, [573].

654 See Ku and Mirasola (n. 648).

655 *South China Sea* [1043].

656 M. Specia and M. Takkunen, 'South China Sea Photos Suggest a Military Building Spree by Beijing' 8 February 2018, *The New York Times*, available at: <https://www.nytimes.com/2018/02/08/world/asia/south-china-seas-photos.html?>; 'A Constructive Year for Chinese Base Building' 14 December 2017, *Asia Maritime Transparency Initiative*, available at: <https://amti.csis.org/constructive-year-chinese-building/>.

657 See 'Philippines tells China to "Back Off" after South China Sea Clash' 18 November 2021, *Al Jazeera*, available at: <https://www.aljazeera.com/news/2021/11/18/philippines-tells-china-to-back-off-after-south-china-sea-clash>. See also R. Pedrozo, 'China Again Uses Force to Bully Its Neighbours' 10 December 2022, *Lawfare*, available at: <https://www.lawfareblog.com/china-again-uses-force-bully-its-neighbors>.

658 'Under China's Shadow, Philippines Clings to Rusting Maritime Outpost' 29 November 2021, *Radio Free Asia*, available at: <https://www.rfa.org/english/news/china/philippines-southchinasea-11292021151419.html>.

659 R. Robles, 'Philippines Says China Is "The Trespasser" as it Refuses to Move Ship from Disputed South China Sea Shoal' 25 November 2021, *South China Morning Post*, available at: <https://www.scmp.com/week-asia/politics/article/3157403/philippines-says-china-trespasser-it-refuses-move-ship-disputed>.

China's record in relation to the Tribunal's determinations on fishing are mixed. Compliance was initially discerned in relation to traditional fishing rights around Scarborough Shoal. A notable change in Chinese behaviour in line with the award was China permitting the return of traditional fishers from the Philippines, which apparently resulted from a deal struck between the presidents of China and the Philippines in 2016.[660] However, other reports have noted that China has continued to block or harass Philippine fishers in this area.[661]

China has maintained a fishing moratorium during summer months in the South China Sea, ostensibly as a conservation and management measure. This measure was found to be a violation of Article 56 of UNCLOS in the *South China Sea* arbitration. In 2021, the moratorium prohibited all fishing except with hand tackle in South China Sea waters, including the Gulf of Tonkin.[662] Chinese State media reported that the 2021 moratorium "was considered the toughest ever, with a number of new technologies such as satellite positioning, video surveillance and big data management used for maritime law enforcement".[663] The Philippines advised its fishers to ignore the fishing ban,[664] and explicitly tied its rejection of the moratorium to the arbitral award.[665]

The *South China Sea* Tribunal further determined that China's failure to prevent its fishers from undertaking fishing in what the Tribunal considered the Philippines' EEZ was a violation of Article 58(3) of UNCLOS.[666] Moreover,

660 J. M. Aurelio, 'Duterte-Xi Fishing Deal Verbal – Palace' 2 July 2019, *Inquirer*, available at: <https://globalnation.inquirer.net/177292/duterte-xi-fishing-deal-verbal-palace>.

661 F. Mangosing, 'China Still Harassing Filipino Fishermen in Scarborough Shoal – US Navy Official' 13 February 2019, *Inquirer*, available at: <https://newsinfo.inquirer.net/1085307/china-still-harassing-filipino-fishermen-in-scarborough-shoal-us-navy-official>; A. Barker, 'China and the Philippines' Tense Stand-Off over Scarborough Shoal Leaves Fishermen in Fear' 26 May 2021, *ABC News*, available at: <https://www.abc.net.au/news/2021-05-26/china-philippines-stand-off-over-scarborough-shoal/100145586>.

662 L. Zhen, 'South China Sea: Countdown to a New Fishing Season in Troubled Waters' 13 August 2021, *South China Morning Post*, available at: <https://www.scmp.com/news/china/diplomacy/article/3144844/south-china-sea-countdown-new-fishing-season-troubled-waters>.

663 L. Shumei, 'China Ends Fishing Moratorium in South China Sea, Foreign Media Speculation Rejected' 16 August 2021, *Global Times*, available at: <https://www.globaltimes.cn/page/202108/1231625.shtml?id=11>.

664 See 'Philippines Tells Fishermen to Ignore Beijing's Ban on Fishing in South China Sea' 5 May 2021, *Reuters*, available at: <https://www.reuters.com/world/asia-pacific/philippines-tells-fishermen-ignore-beijings-ban-fishing-south-china-sea-2021-05-05/>.

665 P. L. Viray, 'Manila Protests Beijing's Unilateral Fishing Ban in South China Sea' 18 May 2021, *Philippines Star*, available at: <https://www.philstar.com/headlines/2021/05/18/2099224/manila-protests-beijings-unilateral-fishing-ban-south-china-sea>.

666 *South China Sea* [757].

China's law enforcement actions in the vicinity of Scarborough Shoal also violated Article 94 of UNCLOS and related provisions in the COLREGS[667] for the unsafe navigation involved.[668] China has maintained its aggressive approach to law enforcement, including prevention of Philippine fishing in its EEZ.[669] One example is a June 2019 incident where a Chinese fishing vessel rammed and partially sank a Philippine fishing vessel, leaving them to await rescue from a Vietnamese fishing vessel.[670] Connected with unsustainable or unlawful fishing practices, the Tribunal concluded that China had violated obligations pursuant to Articles 192 and 194(5) of UNCLOS to protect and preserve the marine environment.[671] While harmful fishing practices to harvest the endangered giant clams dropped off in the aftermath of the award, this practice subsequently resumed.[672]

Violations of the obligation to protect and preserve the marine environment were also found in relation to China's wide-scale land reclamation activities, which involved construction of artificial islands at different locations in the South China Sea. China has not engaged in any comparable constructions since the issuance of the award, including most notably at Scarborough Shoal, which is considered an act (or omission) of compliance.[673] Hayton suggests that, from an optimistic perspective, China has not occupied new territory, even though it has built military bases on reefs that it already controlled.[674] It may be the case that the award has influenced China's conduct in some small ways, but proving a causal link is not possible, especially in the face of China's

667 *Convention on the International Regulations for Preventing Collisions at Sea*, adopted 20 October 1972, entered into force 15 July 1977, 1050 UNTS 16.

668 *South China Sea* [1109].

669 See 'Failing or Incomplete?' (n. 648); Mangosing (n. 661); Barker (n. 661).

670 R. C. de Castro, 'Incident at Reed Bank: A Crisis in the Philippines' China Policy' 20 June 2019, *Asia Maritime Transparency Initiative*, available at: <https://amti.csis.org/incident-at-reed-bank-a-crisis-in-the-philippines-china-policy/>; J. Gutierrez, 'Philippines Accuses Chinese Vessel of Sinking Fishing Boat in Disputed Waters' 12 June 2019, *The New York Times*, available at: <https://www.nytimes.com/2019/06/12/world/asia/philippines-china-fishing-boat.html>.

671 *South China Sea* [992].

672 'China's Most Destructive Boats Return to the South China Sea' 20 May 2019, *Asia Maritime Transparency Initiative*, available at: <https://amti.csis.org/chinas-most-destructive-boats-return-to-the-south-china-sea/>.

673 See, e.g., S. Gupta, 'Beijing's Creative Compliance and Non-compliance in the South China Sea' 11 October 2021, *East Asia Forum*, available at: <https://www.eastasiaforum.org/2021/10/11/beijings-creative-compliance-and-non-compliance-in-the-south-china-sea/>; 'Failing or Incomplete?' (n. 648).

674 B. Hayton, 'Denounce but Comply: China's Response to the South China Sea Arbitration Ruling' (2017) 18(2) *Georgetown Journal of International Affairs* 104, 107.

statements rejecting the arbitration. On the whole, the response of China is more so non-compliant than otherwise.

7.4 *Conclusion*

The *South China Sea* arbitration reflects the gravest situation of non-compliance following an award from UNCLOS dispute settlement proceedings. The case will likely continue to hold relevance, despite this fact, because of the detailed assessment of the law of the sea undertaken by the Tribunal across diverse issue areas. While the members of the Annex VII tribunal were all distinguished jurists in the law of the sea, China's firm rejection of the award (and the subsequent challenge to its validity through the publication of the Chinese Society of International Law[675]) casts a shadow on the authority of the judgment in future cases and more generally in State decision-making.

The *Chagos MPA* arbitration also presented a number of complexities. As with the *South China Sea* arbitration, the question of contested territorial sovereignty was difficult to extricate from the issues over which the Annex VII tribunal did have jurisdiction. The final decision necessitating action on the United Kingdom's behalf was ultimately quite a small one: improved consultation in declaring an MPA. The larger issue of sovereignty in relation to the Chagos Archipelago could not be resolved before the Annex VII tribunal and further proceedings were needed to achieve this outcome. It may be recalled that the narrowing of jurisdictional scope of the *Coastal State Rights* case will also likely lead to more limited determination of the merits that necessitate compliance.

As to what may be discerned from the compliance record in these disputes, it may be worth considering whether compliance is less likely when the jurisdictional basis of the proceedings is contested between the States concerned, especially because of a connected or underlying territorial sovereignty dispute. One benchmark for comparison is with maritime boundary disputes, which necessarily implicate sovereignty and sovereign rights over maritime space. Jurisdictional challenges have been far less common in maritime boundary cases. As indicated above in Chapter 5.3, compliance has been generally good with respect to maritime boundary delimitation, in no small part due to the benefits of marketable title. A comparable result does not appear to have been achieved in mixed disputes such as those considered in this Chapter. It would be premature, however, to attempt to discern any trends from the cases considered in this Chapter, given the limited sample size and their intrinsic interaction with contested issues of jurisdiction, geopolitics, and national

675 Chinese Society of International Law (n. 644).

identity. Instead, it suffices to say that there may be a diverse range of factors that contribute to judgment compliance for mixed disputes instituted under UNCLOS. The overall compliance trends are set out in the final Chapter that follows.

8 Assessing Compliance

8.1 *Introduction*

International dispute settlement is a complex process that inevitably involves a range of dynamics, actors and perspectives. Compliance with judicial decision-making is just one small aspect of this process; it does not define the success or effectiveness of a particular avenue of dispute settlement. While it may be a fundamental component of the operation of domestic legal systems, the distinctive aspects of the international legal system render compliance as one factor among many that contributes to how and why disputes are resolved. Compliance may be seen as a form of communication among actors in international dispute settlement; it is a message as to the views of the States party to the dispute on the value accorded to the judicial statements rendered, their commitment to the rule of law and international dispute settlement, and the importance they attribute to restoring inter-State relationships. The communication extends to other stakeholders: the shipping or fishing companies deciding where to register vessels or where to conduct their activities, the individuals who set sail with expectations as to their treatment at sea, and to the judges and international institutions who are tasked with contributing to this form of dispute settlement.

Compliance also influences our understanding of the specific legal systems of which compliance forms a part. In the context of UNCLOS dispute settlement, the record of compliance provides additional information about the dispute settlement proceedings and what was achieved from the process. In occasionally referencing some of the other outcomes from the cases, we have further sought to underline that the mere fact of compliance is indeed one factor among many in understanding the operation of UNCLOS and its role in governing inter-State relations in respect of ocean space and use. Other works have examined the significance of the content of the judgments for the development of UNCLOS and for the law of the sea;[676] understanding how

676 See, e.g., A. Del Vecchio and R. Virzo (eds), *Interpretations of the United Nations Convention on the Law of the Sea by International Courts and Tribunals* (Springer, 2019); Ø. Jensen (ed),

States have responded after a judgment is rendered should also inform this examination.

To conclude our study of compliance with decisions of ITLOS and Annex VII tribunals in UNCLOS dispute settlement, we first seek to bring together the record of compliance across all the decisions that emerged in UNCLOS case law and highlight if there are trends or distinct commonalities. In doing so, we note that the sample of cases is relatively small and there will no doubt be opinions on the extent it is possible to extrapolate general views based on this sample size. Second, we suggest how reporting requirements under Article 95 of the ITLOS Rules for provisional measures could be extended so as to enhance transparency and accountability at least in relation to the decisions of ITLOS. Third, we contemplate how to assess compliance in light of the broad aims associated with the UNCLOS dispute settlement system. These aims include protecting the compromises reached during negotiations, balancing the rights and duties of different actors, and providing a means to elaborate on some of the broad obligations included in the Convention.[677] More fundamentally, we consider that the UNCLOS dispute settlement procedures contribute to the over-arching obligation to settle disputes by peaceful means.[678] Further, through recourse to legal methods, UNCLOS dispute settlement is important for upholding the rule of law in international relations and contributing to overall good ocean governance or the public order of the oceans.[679] Ultimately, we ask whether, or to what extent, the compliance record meets these varied aims of UNCLOS dispute settlement.

8.2 *Overall Trends in Compliance*

In Chapter 2, we indicated that compliance did not involve a binary assessment but rather a spectrum of responses from full compliance through to defiance. In our discussion of the cases, we indicated our views on whether there had been 'full compliance', 'non-compliance' or whether the actions taken may be understood as 'good faith', 'nominal' or 'part' compliance. Good faith compliance was intended to indicate that a State had made efforts to comply but there might have been reasons, external to the State, that meant the State fell short of full compliance. We used the label nominal compliance to address situations where the goals of the applicant State may have been achieved but the orders of the international court or tribunal were not satisfactorily executed or

The Development of the Law of the Sea Convention: The Role of International Courts and Tribunals (Elgar, 2020).

677 See Chapter 1.1.

678 Reflected in Article 2(3) of the UN Charter.

679 N. Klein and K. Parlett, *Judging the Law of the Sea: Judicial Interpretations of the UN Convention on the Law of the Sea* (Oxford University Press, 2022), 11–12.

executed for reasons other than the bona fide implementation of that order. In such cases, it may be wise not to confuse correlation with causation. Part compliance emerged when a State complied with some aspects of the judgment, but not all. In some instances, we could not determine if compliance was achieved, either because of lack of publicly available data or because the requirements of the judgment were inherently vague.

In Table 3, we have sought to summarise our findings. Yet even with the various categories developed across a spectrum, it is not always evident how to label the result. The table below should not be read in isolation but should also be referenced to the fuller discussion in each Chapter.

TABLE 3 Table of compliance with UNCLOS decisions

Case	Type of case / Outcome	Compliance status
M/V Saiga (*Saint Vincent and the Grenadines v. Guinea*)	Prompt release	Good faith compliance
M/V Saiga (*No. 2*) (*Saint Vincent and the Grenadines v. Guinea*)	Provisional measures; decision on merits	Full compliance
Southern Bluefin Tuna (*New Zealand v. Japan; Australia v. Japan*)	Provisional measures	Full compliance
Camouco (*Panama v. France*)	Prompt release	Good faith compliance (or full compliance if considered sufficiently prompt)
Monte Confurco Case (*Seychelles v. France*)	Prompt release	Good faith compliance (or full compliance if considered sufficiently prompt)
MOX Plant (*Ireland v. United Kingdom*)	Provisional measures	Indeterminate
Volga (*Russian Federation v. Australia*)	Prompt release	Non-compliance by applicant in paying bond; respondent's compliance indeterminate

TABLE 3 Table of compliance with UNCLOS decisions (*cont.*)

Case	Type of case / Outcome	Compliance status
Land Reclamation by Singapore in and around the Straits of Johor (Malaysia v. Singapore)	Provisional measures	Full compliance
Juno Trader (Saint Vincent and the Grenadines v. Guinea-Bissau)	Prompt release	Good faith compliance (may be part or full compliance if more information was available)
Hoshinmaru (Japan v. Russian Federation)	Prompt release	Full compliance
Delimitation of the Maritime Boundary between Bangladesh and Myanmar in the Bay of Bengal (Bangladesh/Myanmar)	Decision on merits	Full compliance (though some contestation remains indicating potential part compliance)
M/V Virginia G (Panama/ Guinea-Bissau)	Decision on merits	Good faith compliance (seemingly on information available)
ARA *Libertad (Argentina v. Ghana)*	Provisional measures	Full compliance
Arctic Sunrise (Netherlands v. Russian Federation)	Provisional measures	Non-compliance
Delimitation of the Maritime Boundary between Ghana and Côte d'Ivoire in the Atlantic Ocean (Ghana/Côte d'Ivoire)	Provisional measures	Full compliance
Delimitation of the Maritime Boundary between Ghana and Côte d'Ivoire in the Atlantic Ocean (Ghana/Côte d'Ivoire)	Decision on merits	Full compliance
Enrica Lexie (Italy v. India),	Provisional measures	Full compliance
M/V Norstar (Panama v. Italy)	Decision on merits	Full compliance (seemingly on information available)

TABLE 3 Table of compliance with UNCLOS decisions (*cont.*)

Case	Type of case / Outcome	Compliance status
Detention of Three Ukrainian Naval Vessels (*Ukraine v. Russian Federation*)	Provisional measures	To be determined by Annex VII Tribunal in merits phase.
M/T San Padre Pio (*Switzerland v. Nigeria*)	Provisional measures	Indeterminate (or part compliance)
Guyana v. Suriname	Decision on merits; maritime boundary delimitation	Full compliance
Barbados v. Trinidad and Tobago	Decision on merits; maritime boundary delimitation	Part compliance
Bay of Bengal Maritime Boundary Arbitration (*Bangladesh v. India*)	Decision on merits; maritime boundary delimitation	Full compliance (though some contestation remains indicating potential part compliance)
Chagos Marine Protected Area (*Mauritius v. United Kingdom*)	Decision on merits	Indeterminate
South China Sea Arbitration (*Philippines v. China*)	Decision on merits	Non-compliance
Arctic Sunrise (*Netherlands v. Russian Federation*)	Decision on merits, compensation.	Nominal compliance
Duzgit Integrity (*Malta v. São Tomé and Príncipe*)	Decision on merits and reparation	Non-compliance
Enrica Lexie (*Italy v. India*)	Decision on merits	Full compliance

From these 28 decisions, if a generous count of full compliance is undertaken then it could be said there was full compliance in 14 of these cases, as well as 5 instances of good faith compliance. There are three examples of what might be cast as nominal compliance, each instance involving Russia; in the one prompt release case where the vessel was not released (*Volga*), it was because of Russia's failure to pay any bond to the coastal State. The range of cases involving nominal compliance may be extended to include the *MOX Plant* and *Chagos MPA* cases, both involving the United Kingdom as respondent, which are cast above as 'indeterminate' because the benchmark for compliance was too obtuse to reach a firm decision on whether the required behaviour had occurred to the standard expected or set by the tribunals. The information available about *San Padre Pio* left some ambiguity as to whether there was compliance with the provisional measures order; did the behaviour align? Was the behaviour at the domestic level in the court proceedings involving the vessel and crew different because of the provisional measures order?

If a strict reading of compliance is undertaken – putting aside assumptions of good faith and ambiguous or deficient information – the record is weaker. Full compliance is manifest in relation to eight cases (*Saiga* (*No. 2*); the *Southern Bluefin Tuna* cases; *Land Reclamation*; *Hoshinmaru*; *ARA Libertad*; *Ghana/Côte d'Ivoire*; *Enrica Lexie*; *Guyana v. Suriname*); the majority of these cases of full compliance involved ITLOS decisions rather than Annex VII awards. As noted in Chapter 2, understanding what counts as compliance is not straightforward.

When good faith is assumed because the information available may be less fulsome, the compliance record with UNCLOS dispute settlement processes indicates that compliance is far more likely than not. While caveats are necessary, some degree of compliance has been achieved in all but two of the 28 cases. Yet even with the *South China Sea* arbitration, there are arguments that nominal compliance in some small instances is discernible. Chapter 7 indicated that some of China's decisions with regards to fishing around the Spratly Islands had initially been in line with the award, as were the omissions on the part of China to undertake further land reclamation activities at similar scale or to declare an EEZ or continental shelf from the disputed islands.[680] The other case of non-compliance, *Duzgit Integrity*, involved a specific, albeit large, sum to be paid by the respondent State. The parties had previously pursued settlement negotiations prior to the issuance of the reparations award,[681] and, as noted in Chapter 6, an agreement had been reached as between the ship owner and São Tomé.[682] While the passage of time may indicate otherwise, this dispute may yet lead to a negotiated result even if São Tomé and Príncipe is unable to pay the full amount awarded. Even taking these instances of non-compliance into account, it cannot be doubted that the resort to arbitration or adjudication under UNCLOS clearly makes a difference in contributing to the peaceful settlement of disputes between States.

680 See Chapter 7.4.

681 Permanent Court of Arbitration, *Annual Report* (2019), available at: <https://docs.pca-cpa.org/2020/03/7726c41e-online-pca-annual-report-2019-final.pdf>, 21.

682 *Duzgit Integrity*, Merits, [117]–[118].

Any assessment of UNCLOS dispute settlement must account for the possibility that these disputes may go before a variety of courts or tribunals. This flexibility in choice of forum was essential for agreement on the inclusion of compulsory jurisdiction in the Convention. It is thus notable that in cases with similar subject matter arising for decision before both ITLOS and Annex VII tribunals, which primarily concern maritime boundary delimitations and release of arrested vessels and/or crew, the compliance record was largely comparable.[683] On this basis, it would appear that compliance is not a factor for decision-makers considering whether to refer a dispute to ITLOS or to ad hoc arbitration. Further, there is no suggestion that States are more likely to comply with orders of standing dispute settlement institutions like ITLOS as opposed to ad hoc tribunals, such as those constituted under Annex VII. Perhaps this assessment might change if ITLOS was to engage more openly in reporting on the implementation of its orders and judgments, as discussed below.[684]

There does, though, appear to be a correlation between participation in proceedings and compliance. China did not participate in the *South China Sea* arbitration, São Tomé and Príncipe did not participate in the reparations phase of *Duzgit Integrity*, and Russia's participation in UNCLOS proceedings may be described as inconsistent, with its compliance record equally sporadic. Yet outcomes from these cases may still be observed, as noted in the previous Chapters, and the judgments have still impacted State decision-making in different ways. Equally, the (arguably) most wide-reaching decisions on jurisdiction have arisen in cases where compliance was not perfect, or indeterminate; notably the cases involving Russia and the *South China Sea* arbitration.

Another overall trend, albeit from our small sample of cases, is that vessels and their crews are most usually released when challenged in UNCLOS dispute settlement. Bonds are also most commonly paid, especially because it facilitates the release of a vessel. Yet compensation for seized vessels is more difficult to obtain. There may be an interesting difference at stake where the fishing or shipping company has the necessary finances and facilities in place to pay bonds to secure the release of vessels,[685] whereas sovereign payments of compensation are less likely or forthcoming. Respect for the delimitation of maritime boundaries is also a discernible trend and may similarly be

683 As noted in Chapter 6, the compliance record in relation to ITLOS was potentially slightly better than with Annex VII arbitrations. See Chapter 6.8.

684 See Chapter 8.3 below.

685 The private nature of the dispute involving, indirectly, ship owners and other commercial stakeholders in the shipping and fishing industries is noted in Chapter 3.1.

attributed to the economic interests at stake. Again, the financial concerns of private stakeholders may impact in supporting the decision of an UNCLOS tribunal on this point and payments by a sovereign State are not required for compliance. These findings align with views that there is compliance with international commercial arbitration and investment treaty disputes or trade disputes because of the economic imperatives that are involved.[686] When political interests are at stake, as apparent in the mixed disputes discussed in the previous Chapter, compliance has been less readily observable.

8.3 *Enhancing Compliance by Improved Transparency and Accountability*

Some of the uncertainties indicated in our conclusions above demonstrate the desirability of more transparent reporting on actions taken pursuant to the decisions of courts or tribunals constituted under UNCLOS. As discussed in Chapter 1, the UNCLOS dispute settlement system does not have any separate enforcement process as established in, for example, regional human rights regimes.[687] Article 95 of the Rules of ITLOS does, however, anticipate that the parties will report on implementation and compliance with provisional measures orders of ITLOS, irrespective of whether the Tribunal has acted under Article 290(1) or Article 290(5).[688] The competence to monitor implementation switches to an Annex VII tribunal once it is constituted in relation to provisional measures adopted under Article 290(5).[689] At least in relation to provisional measures, ITLOS anticipates a "proactive role to ensure … implementation".[690] The reports on compliance with provisional measures submitted by parties to the dispute provide an insight into the parties' views on compliance, as well as how and whether any order has been complied with.

A comparable rule on reporting in relation to a judgment may arguably be beyond the power of ITLOS on the basis that a judgment is a "final" decision,[691]

686 See discussion in G. B. Born, 'A New Generation of International Adjudication' (2012) 61 *Duke Law Journal* 775.

687 See Chapter 1.2.

688 This rule is based on Article 78 of the ICJ Rules. P. Chandrasekhara Rao and Ph. Gautier, *The Rules of the International Tribunal for the Law of the Sea: A Commentary* (Martinus Nijhoff, 2006), 260.

689 Ibid., 261. See also *Land Reclamation*, 138 [11], which notes that this power rests with an Annex VII tribunal "unless the arbitral tribunal decides otherwise". The authority of an Annex VII tribunal to require reports for provisional measures orders may depend on whether a rule comparable to Article 95 of the ITLOS Rules is included in the rules for the ad hoc tribunal.

690 Chandrasekhara Rao and Gautier (n. 688), 261.

691 UNCLOS, Annex VI, Art. 33(1).

ending the dispute that was presented to ITLOS for resolution and thereby terminating the grant of jurisdiction under Article 288(1). In the absence of requests from the parties for the Tribunal to remain seised with jurisdiction pending the final resolution of any aspect of the dispute,[692] it could be argued that ITLOS does not have any powers to conduct any monitoring of compliance. However, the counter-argument is that such a role exists by virtue of Article 33(1) of the Statute, which provides that the decision of the Tribunal "shall be complied with by all the parties to the dispute". It then falls to the Tribunal to "frame rules for carrying out its functions".[693] The judicial function necessarily includes oversight of judgments, especially since ITLOS has explicit authority to construe the meaning or scope of its decisions at the request of a party.[694] ITLOS thus arguably has the authority to include a rule that parties are to report on compliance with its decisions, comparable to Article 95 in relation to provisional measures. Even in the absence of such a rule, a party could submit a dispute concerning the interpretation or application of Article 33(1) of the ITLOS Statute under Article 288 of Part XV of UNCLOS as a distinct case.

ITLOS has several avenues available to indicate what actions have been taken in light of its decisions. In its early years, the ITLOS Yearbook occasionally published "selected communications from parties on matters of implementation of judgments and orders" in an Annex.[695] These communications were "published without comment" (although selected extracts are sometimes published rather than the full communication) and with the view that the Registry would not accept responsibility in relation to those communications.[696] The communications included references to the reports filed by parties pursuant to provisional measures orders, but these reports were not included within the Yearbook.[697] In any event, the practice of extracting communications from

692 As happens, for example, where orders for compensation anticipate that the parties will negotiate an amount in light of the judicial findings and only return to the court or tribunal if those discussions are unsuccessful. This approach was followed in *Enrica Lexie*. See Chapter 6.6.

693 UNCLOS, Annex VI, Art. 16.

694 UNCLOS, Annex VI, Art. 33(3).

695 Such an Annex started appearing in 2000 and was subsequently included in 2001 and 2002.

696 See, e.g., ITLOS, 'Selected Communications from Parties on Matters of Implementation of Judgments and Orders' (2000) 4 *Yearbook of the International Tribunal for the Law of the Sea* 147.

697 See, e.g., ITLOS, 'Selected Communications from Parties on Matters of Implementation of Judgments and Orders' (2002) 6 *Yearbook of the International Tribunal for the Law of the Sea* 137, 137–138 (in relation to the *MOX Plant* provisional measures order). Instead, these reports are included in the published pleadings.

the parties to publish in the Yearbook appears to have been short-lived. Other reports of compliance have been limited to a press release from ITLOS,[698] or in one of its newsletters.[699] In more recent cases, ITLOS has published reports on compliance with provisional measures as part of the online case file.[700]

There are undoubted opportunities for ITLOS to enhance compliance through consistent practices that would improve transparency, and concomitantly accountability. Publishing the Article 95 reports with regards to provisional measures orders as part of the case file is an important development. Correspondence from the parties relating to the case could equally be published by ITLOS, as was initially the case with the Yearbooks. The very availability of the information may be advantageous in relation to compliance without ITLOS necessarily having to take any further steps in relation to enforcement, as is formally authorized for other international courts and tribunals. Yet, given ITLOS' past practice, the authority to publish information regarding its cases exists and will improve transparency with regards to the practice of parties to disputes before ITLOS.

The situation in relation to Annex VII tribunals is different as compared to ITLOS. Apart from the *Southern Bluefin Tuna* cases, all Annex VII arbitrations have been instituted under the auspices of the PCA. The PCA records do not extend to implementation or compliance efforts with judgments in either the documentation pertaining to each of the cases instituted under UNCLOS, as published on the PCA's website, or seemingly in any specific fashion in the annual reports of the PCA.[701] As an ad hoc institution, the arbitral tribunals established under Annex VII of UNCLOS are less likely to have authority to publish information about, let alone assess, compliance with their decisions. Doing so would be dependent on the agreement of the parties when formulating the procedural rules for the arbitration. Otherwise, it would fall to the

698 See, e.g., ITLOS, 'The *"Hoshinmaru" Case* (*Japan v. Russian Federation*): Release of the Vessel and Crew after Posting of the Bond Ordered by the Tribunal' (Press Release, 17 August 2007).

699 ITLOS, '*Ghana/Cote d'Ivoire* delimitation case' (Newsletter 2018/1, February 2018), available at: <https://www.itlos.org/en/main/press-media/itlos-newsletters/itlos-newsletter-2018/1/>.

700 Reports of compliance are available on the ITLOS website for *San Padre Pio, Three Ukrainian Naval Vessels* and the *Arctic Sunrise* (although not for *Enrica Lexie* nor *Ghana/Côte d'Ivoire*, which involved measures being prescribed after the *Arctic Sunrise* decision where the practice appears to have begun).

701 The 2021 Annual Report does reference the closure of the proceedings in the *Enrica Lexie* further to the agreement of the parties on implementation: Permanent Court of Arbitration, *Annual Report* (2021), 23.

secretariat within the PCA to determine whether information relating to compliance could be published pursuant to its annual reporting.

To this end, while ITLOS may arguably be able to carve out a greater role in securing post-judgment compliance by changing its rules, or by receiving an application from a party, such a role is unlikely to attach to Annex VII tribunals. A lacuna therefore exists in the monitoring of post-judgment compliance of the decisions of Annex VII tribunals. One potential solution could be the formation of a body to oversee compliance with decisions rendered by all UNCLOS courts and tribunals. However, such a development would require substantial amendment to UNCLOS,[702] which the authors consider unlikely to occur. Whether this lacuna may act as a motivator for States to submit their disputes to ITLOS rather than Annex VII tribunals remains to be seen.

Providing UNCLOS courts and tribunals with a function in publishing information about State conduct is not entirely novel in light of the record of UNCLOS courts and tribunals in assessing compliance with provisional measures orders at the merits stage of the dispute.[703] Given that provisional measures have a binding character, a finding that a State has failed to comply with the provisional measures ordered constitutes an internationally wrongful act,[704] invoking the responsibility of the respondent State to make "full reparation for the injury caused by the internationally wrongful act [in the] form of restitution, compensation or satisfaction, either singly or in combination".[705] In the circumstances, judicial supervision may serve as a powerful motivator to comply as it requires a State to articulate their steps toward compliance or their reasons for failing to comply. This articulation of a legal position is likely a statement of which the broader community of States may take note. There are missed opportunities not only to showcase how decisions of the UNCLOS dispute settlement bodies have mattered, but also to enhance compliance practice through the transparency and accountability that are entailed in publicising what has happened after a judgment or order. However, while judicial supervision "is noteworthy as an attempt to ensure

702 UNCLOS, Annex VI, Art. 41; UNCLOS, Art. 313.

703 See Chapter 4.

704 See C. Miles, *Provisional Measures before International Courts and Tribunals* (Cambridge University Press, 2017), 320 (noting that, "[a]s far as a State is concerned, the content of an order for provisional measures constitutes an international obligation breach of which is an internationally wrongful act – nothing more, nothing less.")

705 International Law Commission, *Report of the International Law Commission on the Work of Its Fifty-Third Session*, UN GAOR, 56th sess., Supp. No. 10, UN Doc. A/56/10 (2001) ('*Articles on Responsibility of States for Internationally Wrongful Acts*'), Art. 34.

effective implementation of provisional measures",[706] it is unlikely to be the panacea for securing full compliance. Instead, judicial supervision can only secure compliance to a certain extent,[707] and should be regarded as an important tool in a broader arsenal of techniques aimed at securing compliance.

8.4 *Compliance and Achieving the Purposes of the UNCLOS Dispute Settlement Regime*

The extent we criticise or laud the track record of adherence (or not) to judgments issued in UNCLOS dispute settlement proceedings depends in some measure on what we perceive to be the purpose of those cases. For example, if a flag State simply wants its vessel and crew released so they can return to operations then that goal may be achieved through the prompt release proceedings or even through a provisional measures order before a full assessment of jurisdiction and merits of the case. Out of a total of 16 cases challenging the arrest of vessels (not including *Enrica Lexie*, which was more so concerned with the arrest of crew members),[708] all but one of the vessels (the Volga) were released. Where third-party assistance was sought to resolve a maritime boundary dispute, a maritime boundary resulted,[709] including at the conclusion of the *Timor Sea Conciliation*.

Alternatively, the success of the compliance record may depend on what we perceive to be the purpose(s) of UNCLOS dispute settlement. In this regard, Shany has pursued the claim that "the significance of judgment-compliance ought to be understood in the light of its contribution to attainment of international courts' goals, such as changing the practices of third parties, resolving disputes, and advancing regime goals".[710] In relation to UNCLOS dispute settlement, we have suggested that judgment-compliance is only one part of the picture. In this regard, we have sought to highlight other outcomes of UNCLOS dispute settlement, including the clarification or development of the law of the sea. In relation to cases that did not proceed to merits and were settled, sometimes after a provisional measures order, Phan speculates, "[t]he

706 Y. Tanaka, 'Juridical Insights into the Protection of Community Interests through Provisional Measures: Reflections on the ITLOS Jurisprudence' in G. Ziccardi Capaldo (ed.), *The Global Community Yearbook of International Law and Jurisprudence* (Oxford University Press, 2014), vol. 1, 249, 271.

707 Y. Tanaka, 'Provisional Measures Prescribed by ITLOS and Marine Environmental Protection' (2014) 208 *Proceedings of the Annual Meeting of the American Society of International Law* 365.

708 The *Heroic Idun* decision is also excluded as the proceedings are currently pending.

709 Not always entirely without subsequent questions emerging, as discussed in Chapter 6.

710 Y. Shany, *Assessing the Effectiveness of International Courts* (Oxford University Press, 2014), 118–119.

availability of UNCLOS dispute settlement, including the imposition of provisional measures, motivated the parties to reach an out-of-court agreement to settle their disputes."[711] Thus disputes may be settled even when a judgment is not reached, or when a judgment is reached and the parties proceed to resolve their issues beyond the precise terms of the judgment.[712] To this end, the dispute settlement regime provided for in UNCLOS may, entirely separate from the question of compliance, lead to improved relations between States party to the dispute; this outcome may be more powerful than strict compliance with a decision of an UNCLOS court or tribunal.

Following the *Saiga (No. 2)* judgment, in its efforts to secure Guinea's compliance with the judgment, Saint Vincent and the Grenadines wrote to ITLOS, noting:

> Along with other maritime countries, having neither the resources nor the desire to deploy substantial armed force on the oceans, Saint Vincent and the Grenadines relies on respect for the rules of international law. We take the view that if Contracting States can, without adverse consequences, fail to comply with judgments of the Tribunal, grave damage will be done to the authority of the Tribunal itself and to the law that it interprets and enforces. Contracting Parties are bound, by Article 33 of Annex VI to the Convention, to respect the finality and binding force of decisions of the International Tribunal. That engagement, solemnly undertaken by the Contracting Parties, must not become a dead letter.[713]

The views expressed in this statement undoubtedly hold validity but, as noted above, are not the only benchmarks of "authority", for the dispute settlement bodies under UNCLOS.

The compliance record alone thus does not necessarily reflect on whether the goals of the UNCLOS dispute settlement system are entirely achieved; the substance of the judgments is the relevant benchmark for determining if

711 H. D. Phan, 'International Courts and State Compliance: An Investigation of the Law of the Sea Cases' (2019) 50(1) *Ocean Development & International Law* 70, 76. See also A. P. Llamzon, 'Jurisdiction and Compliance in Recent Decisions of the International Court of Justice' (2008) 18(5) *European Journal of International Law* 815, 848 ("on some occasions, the very act of submitting a dispute before [an international court or tribunal] bears considerable positive effect upon the ultimate settlement of an international dispute").

712 As was the case, for example, in *Enrica Lexie* and in relation to *Arctic Sunrise*.

713 ITLOS, 'Selected Communications from Parties on Matters of Implementation of Judgments and Orders' (2000) 4 *Yearbook of the International Tribunal for the Law of the Sea* 147.

the balance of the 'package deal' is maintained or if the laws are being interpreted and expounded in a manner that is acceptable to the parties to the regime. A State may have chosen to comply even if it did not agree entirely with the reasoning or specific findings of the UNCLOS court or tribunal. The importance of some of the other outcomes that have been identified in this study perhaps better demonstrate how the UNCLOS dispute settlement regime has been operating further to the broader goals of that regime.

There were several instances noted where States responded to judgments through domestic court proceedings (as happened, for example, with the prompt release cases involving France) or within national legislatures. Contributions to the rule of law and good ocean governance arguably emerge when States change their positions domestically to align better with the requirements of UNCLOS. Guinea's redraft of its customs legislation[714] and Ghana's confirmation of the immunity of warships[715] further support this perspective. The changes in national laws were not necessarily a predicate for compliance but reflect an outcome of UNCLOS dispute settlement proceedings worthy of note and aligning with the overarching goals of the regime.

Weaknesses in compliance with judgments and orders arising from UNCLOS dispute settlement are weaknesses shared with other international courts and tribunals. National interests in the subject matter of the dispute may mean that a State will not brook interference from international institutions, including international courts and tribunals, in State decisions taken in pursuit of that national interest. The extent that more powerful States may be 'brought to heel' by international judicial proceedings and/or by a judgment against those States has not always been a feature of UNCLOS dispute settlement, but where it has, compliance has not been readily forthcoming. It is nonetheless necessary to note that of the two clear cases of non-compliance to date – *South China Sea* and *Duzgit Integrity* – the latter case was a developing State as respondent with its actions challenged by a more affluent State.

Decisions about compliance are not only political, however. Assessments of the compliance record with judgments of the ICJ in the last thirty years have suggested that "external political influence, the internal need for a definitive solution, the substance of the judgment issued, and internal political influence" are all factors that influence a State's reaction to a judgment.[716] Yet, as indicated above, economic factors may also hold high relevance in UNCLOS

714 See Chapter 6.2.

715 See Chapter 4.6.

716 See H. L. Jones, 'Why Comply? An Analysis of Trends in Compliance with Judgments of the International Court of Justice since *Nicaragua*' (2012) 12(1) *Chicago-Kent Journal of International and Comparative Law* 57, 60–83.

dispute settlement and hence in the outcomes of and in compliance with judgments. The weight of any of these factors will vary in the different cases and in decisions regarding compliance so as to bring the dispute to an end.

8.5 *Conclusion*

This study has highlighted three key dimensions to UNCLOS dispute settlement. First, there is a relative paucity of decisions that have emerged from UNCLOS dispute settlement proceedings. So much is true when compared to other international courts, tribunals or panels and when regard is had to the modest total of 28 decisions over almost thirty years of operation. Decisions as to lack of jurisdiction or the inadmissibility of the dispute are not included in this account. Nor are the pending cases, settled cases or advisory opinions. Where these other cases are included, the judicial and arbitral activity further to Part XV of UNCLOS still only rises to 47 cases.[717] The implication is that a third of the cases have not ended in a decision necessitating compliance.

Second, where disputes did proceed and court decisions were reached (including under Article 292 of UNCLOS, as well as in relation to provisional measures ordered and judgments on the merits), the likelihood of judgment compliance was high. Perhaps the high compliance rate, coupled with the relatively low number of cases, suggest that compliance with UNCLOS itself is generally strong. In this vein, instances of law of the sea violations are the exceptions to the rule. State practice indicating to the contrary may be considered outweighed by a diversity of actions consistent with UNCLOS provisions. Alternatively, when account is taken of the vast scope of ocean activities and the regime complex involved in ocean affairs, it may perhaps be the case that UNCLOS dispute settlement is a minor aspect in ocean governance and the results of its dispute settlement processes are more commonly 'low stakes' for the parties involved.

Third, while compliance with the decisions of UNCLOS courts and tribunals is undoubtedly important, it is not the only, or even necessarily the most desirable outcome, of the UNCLOS dispute settlement system. Decisions rendered by UNCLOS courts and tribunals have led to the greater clarification and development of the law, the improvement of relations between States party to a dispute, and modifications to national laws to align with international requirements. These other outcomes of UNCLOS dispute settlement may arise notwithstanding a failure by a State to comply with the decision in question, or in cases where that compliance is less than full compliance. As such, when considering the overall health of the UNCLOS dispute settlement system, it is important not simply to correlate compliance with success, but to take a more

717 See Chapter 1 for the full list of cases.

nuanced view as to how the broader network of relationships between States and international law may be influenced and improved as a result of dispute settlement processes.

Overall, as an international regime that seeks to promote the peaceful settlement of disputes and contribute to the rule of law and good ocean governance, it is noteworthy that judgment-compliance occurs more often than not. UNCLOS dispute settlement proceedings may not solve every contentious issue in ocean affairs, but so much should not be expected. Instead, it is a multi-purpose dispute settlement system that can perform well when acting within the constraints expected of it by the participants.

Author Biographies

Dr. Natalie Klein is a Professor at UNSW Sydney's Faculty of Law & Justice, Australia, and an Australian Research Council Future Fellow. She is currently President of the Australian Branch of the International Law Association and a Trustee for the UK-based charity, Human Rights at Sea. Professor Klein was previously Dean of Macquarie Law School (2011–2017), as well as Acting Head of the Department for Policing, Intelligence and Counter-Terrorism at Macquarie University (2013–2014). Prior to joining Macquarie, Professor Klein worked at Debevoise & Plimpton LLP, for the Government of Eritrea (1998–2002) and in the Office of Legal Affairs at the United Nations. Professor Klein teaches and researches in different areas of international law, with a focus on law of the sea and international dispute settlement. Her masters and doctorate in law were earned at Yale Law School and she is a Fellow of the Australian Academy of Law.

Jack McNally is a Research Fellow at UNSW Sydney's Faculty of Law & Justice, Australia, and a Solicitor at an international law firm in Sydney. He previously served as Tipstaff (Judicial Clerk) to a Judge of the Supreme Court of New South Wales and worked for a Member of the Parliament of Australia. The recipient of the International Law Association's Brennan Prize in Public International Law, Jack practises and researches in international arbitration and public international law, with a focus on the law of the sea, international dispute settlement, international procedural law and complex international disputes. His work has been published in the *Columbia Journal of Transnational Law*, the *Australian International Law Journal*, in edited collections and in other public media. Jack holds a Bachelor of Laws (Hons I) and a Bachelor of Arts (International Relations) with Distinction from UNSW Sydney.

Bibliography

Cases

International Court of Justice

Interpretation of Peace Treaties with Bulgaria, Hungary and Romania, Advisory Opinion (First Phase), ICJ *Reports* 1950.

North Sea Continental Shelf (Federal Republic of Germany/Netherlands), Judgment, ICJ *Reports* 1969.

Fisheries Jurisdiction (Federal Republic of Germany v. Iceland), Provisional Measures, ICJ *Reports* 1972.

Delimitation of the Maritime Boundary in the Gulf of Maine Area (Canada/United States of America), Judgment, ICJ *Reports* 1984.

Arbitral Award of 31 July 1989 (Guinea-Bissau v. Senegal), Provisional Measures, ICJ *Reports* 1990.

Maritime Delimitation and Territorial Questions between Qatar and Bahrain (Qatar v. Bahrain), Judgment, ICJ *Reports* 1994.

Armed Activities on the Territory of the Congo (Democratic Republic of the Congo v. Uganda), Provisional Measures, Order of 1 July 2000, ICJ *Reports* 2000.

Land and Maritime Boundary (Cameroon v. Nigeria), Judgment, ICJ *Reports* 2002.

Land and Maritime Boundary between Cameroon and Nigeria (Cameroon v. Nigeria; Equatorial Guinea intervening), Judgment, ICJ *Reports* 2002.

Maritime Delimitation in the Black Sea (Romania v. Ukraine), Judgment, ICJ *Reports* 2009.

Territorial and Maritime Dispute (Nicaragua v. Colombia), Judgment, ICJ *Reports* 2012.

Alleged Violations of Sovereign Rights and Maritime Spaces in the Caribbean Sea (Nicaragua v. Colombia), Preliminary Objections, ICJ *Reports* 2016.

Delimitation of the Continental Shelf between Nicaragua and Colombia beyond 200 Nautical Miles from the Nicaraguan Coast (Nicaragua v. Colombia), Preliminary Objections, ICJ *Reports* 2016.

Legal Consequences of the Separation of the Chagos Archipelago from Mauritius in 1965, Advisory Opinion, ICJ *Reports* 2019.

Maritime Delimitation in the Indian Ocean (Somalia v. Kenya), Judgment, ICJ *Reports* 2021.

Alleged Violations of Sovereign Rights and Maritime Spaces in the Caribbean Sea (Nicaragua v. Colombia), Judgment, 21 April 2022, General List No. 155.

Guatemala's Territorial, Insular and Maritime Claim (Guatemala v. Belize), General List No. 177.

Land and Maritime Delimitation and Sovereignty over Islands (Gabon v. Equatorial Guinea), General List No. 179.

International Tribunal for the Law of the Sea

M/V Saiga (*Saint Vincent and the Grenadines v. Guinea*), Prompt Release, Judgment of 4 December 1997, *ITLOS Reports* 1997.

M/V Saiga (*No. 2*) (*Saint Vincent and the Grenadines v. Guinea*), Provisional Measures, Order of 11 March 1998, *ITLOS Reports* 1998.

M/V Saiga (*No. 2*) (*Saint Vincent and the Grenadines v. Guinea*), Merits, Judgment of 1 July 1999, *ITLOS Reports* 1999.

Southern Bluefin Tuna Cases (*New Zealand v. Japan; Australia v. Japan*), Provisional Measures, Order of 27 August 1999, *ITLOS Reports* 1999.

Camouco (*Panama v. France*), Prompt Release, Judgment of 7 February 2000, *ITLOS Reports* 2000.

Monte Confurco (*Seychelles v. France*), Prompt Release, Judgment of 18 December 2000, *ITLOS Reports* 2000.

Grand Prince (*Belize v. France*), Prompt Release, Judgment of 20 April 2001, *ITLOS Reports* 2001.

Chaisiri Reefer 2 (*Panama v. Yemen*), Prompt Release, Order 2001/4 of 13 July 2001.

MOX Plant (*Ireland v. United Kingdom*), Provisional Measures, Order of 3 December 2001, *ITLOS Reports* 2001.

Volga (*Russian Federation v. Australia*), Prompt Release, Judgment of 23 December 2002, *ITLOS Reports* 2002.

Land Reclamation by Singapore in and around the Straits of Johor (*Malaysia v. Singapore*), Provisional Measures, Order of 8 October 2003, *ITLOS Reports* 2003.

Juno Trader (*Saint Vincent and the Grenadines v. Guinea-Bissau*), Prompt Release, Judgment of 18 December 2004, *ITLOS Reports* 2004.

Hoshinmaru (*Japan v. Russian Federation*), Prompt Release, Judgment of 6 August 2007, *ITLOS Reports* 2007.

Tomimaru (*Japan v. Russian Federation*), Prompt Release, Judgment of 6 August 2007, *ITLOS Reports* 2007.

Conservation and Sustainable Exploitation of Swordfish Stocks in the South-Eastern Pacific Ocean (*Chile/European Union*), Termination of Proceedings, Order 2009/1 of 16 December 2009, *ITLOS Reports* 2009.

M/V Louisa (*Saint Vincent and the Grenadines v. Spain*), Provisional Measures, Order of 23 December 2010, *ITLOS Reports* 2010.

Responsibilities and Obligations of States Sponsoring Persons and Entities with Respect to Activities in the Area (*Request for Advisory Opinion submitted to the Seabed Disputes Chamber*), Advisory Opinion of 1 February 2011, *ITLOS Reports* 2011.

Delimitation of the Maritime Boundary between Bangladesh and Myanmar in the Bay of Bengal (*Bangladesh/Myanmar*), Merits, Judgment of 14 March 2012, *ITLOS Reports* 2012.

ARA Libertad (*Argentina v. Ghana*), Provisional Measures, Order of 15 December 2012, ITLOS *Reports* 2012.

M/V Louisa (*Saint Vincent and the Grenadines v. Spain*), Merits, Judgment of 28 May 2013, ITLOS *Reports* 2013.

Arctic Sunrise (*Netherlands v. Russian Federation*), Provisional Measures, Order of 22 November 2013, ITLOS *Reports* 2013.

M/V Virginia G (*Panama/Guinea-Bissau*), Merits, Judgment of 14 April 2014, ITLOS *Reports* 2014.

Request for an Advisory Opinion submitted by the Sub-Regional Fisheries Commission (SRFC) (*Request for Advisory Opinion submitted to the Tribunal*), Advisory Opinion of 2 April 2015, ITLOS *Reports* 2015.

Delimitation of the Maritime Boundary between Ghana and Côte d'Ivoire in the Atlantic Ocean (*Ghana/Côte d'Ivoire*), Provisional Measures, Order of 25 April 2015, ITLOS *Reports* 2015.

Enrica Lexie (*Italy v. India*), Provisional Measures, Order of 24 August 2015, ITLOS *Reports* 2015.

M/V Norstar (*Panama v. Italy*), Preliminary Objections, Judgment of 4 November 2016, ITLOS *Reports* 2016.

Delimitation of the Maritime Boundary between Ghana and Côte d'Ivoire in the Atlantic Ocean (*Ghana/Côte d'Ivoire*), Merits, Judgment of 23 September 2017, ITLOS *Reports* 2017.

M/V Norstar (*Panama v. Italy*), Merits, Judgment of 10 April 2019, ITLOS *Reports* 2019.

Detention of Three Ukrainian Naval Vessels (*Ukraine v. Russian Federation*), Provisional Measures, Order of 25 May 2019, ITLOS *Reports* 2019.

Three Ukrainian Naval Vessels, Report of the Russian Federation, 25 June 2019, ITLOS Case No. 26.

Three Ukrainian Naval Vessels, Supplementary Report of Ukraine to the Registry, 26 June 2019, ITLOS Case No. 26.

M/T San Padre Pio (*Switzerland v. Nigeria*), Provisional Measures, Order of 6 July 2019, ITLOS *Reports* 2019.

San Padre Pio, Additional Report of the Swiss Confederation, 8 November 2019, ITLOS Case No. 27.

San Padre Pio (*No. 2*), Special Agreement and Notification, 17 December 2019, ITLOS Case No. 29.

San Padre Pio (*No. 2*), Memorial of Switzerland, 23 June 2020, ITLOS Case No. 27.

San Padre Pio, Additional Report of the Swiss Confederation, 5 November 2020, ITLOS Case No. 27.

M/T San Padre Pio (*No. 2*) (*Switzerland/Nigeria*), Merits, Order 2021/6 of 29 December 2021.

Delimitation of the Maritime Boundary between Mauritius and Maldives in the Indian Ocean (Mauritius/Maldives), Preliminary Objections, Judgment of 28 January 2021, ITLOS Case No. 28.

Heroic Idun (Marshall Islands v. Equatorial Guinea), Prompt Release, Order 2022/3 of 15 November 2022.

Request for an Advisory Opinion submitted by the Commission of Small Island States on Climate Change and International Law (Request for an Advisory Opinion submitted to the Tribunal), ITLOS Case No. 31.

Other International Courts and Tribunals

Delimitation of Maritime Areas between Canada and France (Canada/France), Decision of 10 June 1992, 21 *RIAA* 265.

In the matter of an Arbitration Pursuant to an Agreement to Arbitrate dated 3 October 1996 (Eritrea/Yemen), Award of the Arbitral Tribunal in the Second Stage of the Proceedings (Maritime Delimitation), 17 December 1999, 22 *RIAA* 335.

Southern Bluefin Tuna (New Zealand v. Japan; Australia v. Japan), Jurisdiction and Admissibility, Decision of 4 August 2000, 23 *RIAA* 1.

MOX Plant, Annex VII Provisional Measures, Reply of Ireland, 7 March 2003, PCA Case No. 2002-01.

Land Reclamation by Singapore in and around the Straits of Johor (Malaysia v. Singapore), Merits, Award on Agreed Terms of 1 September 2005, 27 *RIAA* 133.

Judgment of the European Court of Justice (ECJ) in Case C-459/03 *Commission of the European Communities v. Ireland* (2006).

Barbados v. Trinidad and Tobago, Merits, Award of 11 April 2006, 27 *RIAA* 147.

Guyana v. Suriname, Merits, Award of 17 September 2007, 30 *RIAA* 1.

MOX Plant (Ireland v. United Kingdom), Termination of Proceedings, Order No. 6 of 6 June 2008, PCA Case No. 2002-01.

ARA Libertad (Argentina v. Ghana), Agreement between Argentina and Ghana, 27 September 2013, PCA Case No. 2013-11.

ARA Libertad (Argentina v. Ghana), Termination of Proceedings, Order of 11 November 2013, PCA Case No. 2013-11.

Arctic Sunrise (Netherlands v. Russian Federation), Merits, Award of 14 August 2015, PCA Case No. 2014-02.

Atlanto-Scandian Herring (Denmark in respect of the Faroe Islands v. the European Union), Termination Order of 23 September 2014, PCA Case No. 2013-30.

Arctic Sunrise (Netherlands v. Russian Federation), Jurisdiction, Award of 26 November 2014, PCA Case No. 2014-02.

Chagos Marine Protected Area Arbitration (Mauritius v. United Kingdom), Merits, Award of 18 March 2015, PCA Case No. 2011-03.

South China Sea Arbitration (Philippines v. China), Jurisdiction and Admissibility, Award of 29 October 2015, PCA Case No. 2013-19.

Enrica Lexie (*Italy v. India*), Provisional Measures, Order of 29 April 2016, PCA Case No. 2015-28.

South China Sea Arbitration (*Philippines v. China*), Merits, Award of 12 July 2016, PCA Case No. 2013–19.

Duzgit Integrity (*Malta v. São Tomé and Príncipe*), Merits, Award of 5 September 2016, PCA Case No. 2014-07.

Timor Sea Conciliation (*Timor-Leste v. Australia*), Competence, Decision of 19 September 2016, PCA Case No. 2016-10.

In the matter of an Arbitration under the Arbitration Agreement between the Government of the Republic of Croatia and the Government of the Republic of Slovenia signed on 4 November 2009, Final Award, 29 June 2017, PCA Case No. 2012-04.

Arctic Sunrise (*Netherlands v. Russian Federation*), Compensation, Award of 10 July 2017, PCA Case No. 2014-02.

Conciliation between the Democratic Republic of Timor-Leste and the Commonwealth of Australia, Report and Recommendations of the Compulsory Conciliation Commission, 9 May 2018, PCA Case No. 2016-10.

Duzgit Integrity (*Malta v. São Tomé and Príncipe*), Reparation, Award of 18 December 2019, PCA Case No. 2014-07.

Coastal State Rights in the Black Sea, Sea of Azov, and Kerch Strait (*Ukraine v. Russian Federation*), Preliminary Objections, Award of 21 February 2020, PCA Case No. 2017-16.

Enrica Lexie (*Italy v. India*), Merits, Award of 21 May 2020, PCA Case No. 2015-28.

Enrica Lexie (*Italy v. India*), Closing of the Proceedings, Order of 12 October 2021, PCA Case No. 2015-28.

Detention of Ukrainian Naval Vessels and Servicemen (*Ukraine v. Russian Federation*), Preliminary Objections, Award of 27 June 2022, PCA Case No. 2019-28.

Bryan v. Russia, European Court of Human Rights, Application No. 22515/14.

Domestic Cases

Australia

Director of Public Prosecutions (Cth) v. Lijo [2002] WASC 154 (14 June 2002).

Lijo v. Director of Public Prosecutions [2003] WASCA 4 (16 December 2002).

Olbers v. Commonwealth of Australia (No. 4) [2004] FCA 229 (12 March 2004).

Olbers Co Ltd v. Commonwealth of Australia [2004] FCAFC 262 (16 September 2004).

Olbers Co Ltd v. Commonwealth of Australia [2005] HCATrans 228 (22 April 2005).

France

Decision No 052/AM/99 of the *Tribunal d'Instance de Saint Paul* of 14 December 1999.

Merce Pesca Company v. The French State, Judgment of the Court of Appeal of Saint Denis of 21 March 2000, Judgment No 267/2000.

Ghana

The Republic v. High Court (Comm Div) Accra, ex parte; Attorney General (Supreme Court of Ghana, Case No J5/10/2013, 20 June 2013).

United States

Republic of Argentina v. NML Capital, Ltd. (2014) 573 U.S. 134.

International Instruments

Statute of the International Court of Justice.

Convention for the Protection of Human Rights and Fundamental Freedoms (European Convention on Human Rights), adopted 4 November 1950, entered into force 3 September 1953, 212 UNTS 221.

Convention on the Territorial Sea and the Contiguous Zone, opened for signature, 29 April 1958, entered into force 10 September 1964, 516 UNTS 205.

Vienna Convention on the Law of Treaties, opened for signature 23 May 1969, entered into force 27 January 1980, 1155 UNTS 331.

American Convention on Human Rights (Pact of San José), adopted 22 November 1969 entered into force 18 July 1978, 1144 UNTS 123.

UNGA Res. 2625(XXV) (24 October 1970), *Declaration on Principles of International Law concerning Friendly Relations and Cooperation among States in Accordance with the Charter of the United Nations*, UN Doc. A/RES/2625(XXV).

Convention on the International Regulations for Preventing Collisions at Sea, adopted 20 October 1972, entered into force 15 July 1977, 1050 UNTS 16.

United Nations Convention on the Law of the Sea, adopted 10 December 1982, entered into force 16 November 1994, 1833 UNTS 397.

Marrakesh Agreement establishing the World Trade Organization, adopted 15 April 1994, entered into force 1 January 1995, 1869 UNTS 401.

Rules of the International Tribunal for the Law of the Sea, adopted 28 October 1997.

Commonwealth of Australia, *Declaration under the United Nations Convention on the Law of the Sea concerning the Application to Australia of the Dispute Settlement Provisions of that Convention*, adopted and entered into force 21 March 2002.

Timor Sea Treaty between the Government of East Timor and the Government of Australia, signed 20 May 2002, entered into force 2 April 2003, 2258 UNTS 3.

Treaty between Australia and the Democratic Republic of Timor-Leste on Certain Maritime Arrangements in the Timor Sea, signed 12 January 2006, entered into force 23 February 2007, [2007] ATS 12.

Agreement between the Government of Australia and the Government of the Democratic Republic of Timor-Leste relating to the Unitisation of the Sunrise Troubadour Fields, signed 6 March 2003, entered into force 23 February 2007, 2483 UNTS 317.

Treaty between Australia and the Democratic Republic of Timor-Leste Establishing their Maritime Boundaries in the Timor Sea, signed 6 March 2018, entered into force 30 August 2019, [2019] ATS 16.

Legislation

Australia

International Arbitration Act 1974 (Cth).
Fisheries Management Act 1991 (Cth).
Foreign Judgments Act 1991 (Cth).
Passenger Movement Charge Amendment (Timor Sea Maritime Boundaries Treaty) Act 2019 (Cth).
Timor Sea Maritime Boundaries Treaty Consequential Amendments Act 2019 (Cth).
Treasury Laws Amendment (Timor Sea Maritime Boundaries Treaty) Act 2019 (Cth).

Guinea

Law L/94/007/CTRN, 15 March 1994 (Guinea).
Code des douanes (*Customs Code*) (undated) (Guinea).
Code des douanes (*Customs Code*), Law L/2015/007/1, 25 May 2015 (Guinea).

Primary Sources

Bangladesh, *Submission by the People's Republic of Bangladesh to the Commission on the Limits of the Continental Shelf* (2020), available at: <https://www.un.org/depts/los/clcs_new/submissions_files/bgd55_11/Executive%20summary_BGD_AMD.pdf>.
Bureau of Oceans and International Environmental and Scientific Affairs, United States Department of State, *Limits in the Seas No. 131 – Trinidad and Tobago: Archipelagic and Other Maritime Claims and Boundaries* (31 January 2014).
Department of Foreign Affairs and Trade, Australian Government, *Australia and Timor-Leste Maritime Boundaries* (March 2018), available at: <https://www.dfat.gov.au/sites/default/files/aus-timor-maritime-boundary-fact-sheet.pdf>.
Government of Barbados, *Continental Shelf Submission: Executive Summary* (2008), available at: <https://www.un.org/depts/los/clcs_new/submissions_files/brb08/brb08_executive_summary.pdf>.
ITLOS, *Annual Report of the International Tribunal for the Law of the Sea for 2000*, ITLOS Doc. SPLOS/63 (2001).
ITLOS, *Annual Report of the International Tribunal for the Law of the Sea for 2001*, ITLOS Doc. SPLOS/74 (2002).
ITLOS, *Annual Report of the International Tribunal for the Law of the Sea for 2005*, ITLOS Doc. SPLOS/136 (2006).
ITLOS, *Annual Report of the International Tribunal for the Law of the Sea for 2007*, ITLOS Doc. SPLOS/174 (2008).

ITLOS, *Annual Report of the International Tribunal for the Law of the Sea for 2014*, ITLOS Doc. SPLOS/278 (2015).

ITLOS, *Annual Report of the International Tribunal for the Law of the Sea for 2019*, ITLOS Doc. SPLOS/278 (2020).

ITLOS, 'Documents' (2012) 18 *Pleadings, Minutes of Public Sittings and Documents* 359.

ITLOS, 'Minutes of Public Sittings held from 8 March to 20 March 1999' (1999) 3 *Pleadings, Minutes of Public Sittings and Documents* 493.

ITLOS, 'Selected Communications from Parties on Matters of Implementation of Judgments and Orders' (2000) 4 *Yearbook of the International Tribunal for the Law of the Sea* 147.

ITLOS, 'Selected Communications from Parties on Matters of Implementation of Judgments and Orders', (2001) 5 *Yearbook of the International Tribunal for the Law of the Sea* 152.

ITLOS, 'Selected Communications from Parties on Matters of Implementation of Judgments and Orders' (2002) 6 *Yearbook of the International Tribunal for the Law of the Sea* 137.

Joint Report by Australia and New Zealand on Compliance with the Provisional Measures Ordered by the International Tribunal for the Law of the Sea in the Southern Bluefin Tuna Cases in ITLOS, 'Communications from Parties on Matters of Implementation of the Tribunal's Orders' (1999) 4 *Pleadings, Minutes of Public Sittings and Documents* 602.

Joint Standing Committee on Treaties, Parliament of the Commonwealth of Australia, *Report 47: Treaties Tabled on 18 and 25 June 2002* (2002), available at: <https://www.aph.gov.au/parliamentary_business/committees/house_of_representatives_committees?url=jsct/18_25_june_2002/report/chapter4.pdf>.

Letter from Bozo A Dabinovic (Agent of St Vincent and the Grenadines) to Hartmut von Brevern (Agent for Guinea) dated 7 April 1998 in ITLOS, 'Report under Article 95, Paragraph 1, of the Rules of the Tribunal Submitted by Saint Vincent and the Grenadines' (1998) 2 *Pleadings, Minutes of Public Sittings and Documents* 255.

Myanmar, *Continental Shelf Submission* (July 2015), available at: <https://www.un.org/depts/los/clcs_new/submissions_files/mmr08/Myanmar_Amended_Ex_Summary.pdf>.

Official Spokesperson of the Ministry of External Affairs, 'Official Spokesperson's Response to a Question on the Award of the Tribunal on the Maritime Boundary Arbitration between India and Bangladesh' 8 July 2014, *Government of India*, available at: <https://mea.gov.in/bilateral-documents.htm?dtl/23575/Official+Spokespersons+response+to+a+question+on+the+award+of+the+Tribunal+on+the+Maritime+Boundary+Arbitration+between+India+and+Bangladesh>.

Permanent Mission of Bangladesh to the United Nations, *Letter to the Secretary-General*, 22 October 2015, available at: <https://www.un.org/depts/los/clcs_new/submissions_files/mmr08/2015_10_22_BGD_NV_UN.pdf>.

Permanent Mission of Bangladesh to the United Nations, *Letter to the Secretary-General*, 6 May 2021, available at: <https://www.un.org/depts/los/clcs_new/submissions_files/bgd55_11/20210506BgdNvUn009.pdf>.

Permanent Mission of Bangladesh to the United Nations, *Letter to the Secretary-General*, 13 September 2021, available at: <https://www.un.org/depts/los/clcs_new/submissions_files/bgd55_11/20210913BgdNvUn010.pdf>.

Permanent Mission of India to the United Nations, *Letter to the Secretary-General*, 16 April 2021, available at: <https://www.un.org/depts/los/clcs_new/submissions_files/bgd55_11/20210416IndNvUN002.pdf>.

Permanent Mission of India to the United Nations, *Letter to the Secretary-General*, 3 August 2017, available at: <https://www.un.org/depts/los/LEGISLATIONANDTREATIES/PDFFILES/2017_08_03_IND_UN.pdf>.

Permanent Mission of Myanmar to the United Nations, *Letter to the Secretary-General*, 26 January 2021, available at: <https://www.un.org/Depts/los/clcs_new/submissions_files/bgd55_11/20210126MmrNvUn002.pdf>.

Republic of Trinidad and Tobago, *Submission to the Commission on the Limits of the Continental Shelf pursuant to Article 76, Paragraph 8 of the United Nations Convention on the Law of the Sea* (12 May 2009), available at: <https://www.un.org/depts/los/clcs_new/submissions_files/tto49_09/tto2009executive_summary.pdf>.

Rural and Regional Affairs and Transport Legislation Committee, Parliament of Australia, *Answers to Questions on Notice: Additional Estimates February 2015 (Agriculture)*, at: <https://www.aph.gov.au/~/media/Committees/rrat_ctte/estimates/add_1415/ag/Answers/AFMAQoN9-13.pdf>.

Timor-Leste Maritime Boundary Office, *What is in the Maritime Boundary Treaty: Fact Sheet* (March 2018), available at: <http://www.gfm.tl/wp-content/uploads/2021/01/FACT-SHEET-MARCH-2018.pdf>.

Secondary Sources

Alter, K. J., 'Agents or Trustees? International Courts in their Political Context' (2008) 14(1) *European Journal of International Relations* 33.

Alter, K. J., 'Do International Courts Enhance Compliance with International Law?' (2003) 25 *Review of Asian and Pacific Studies* 51.

Alter, K. J., 'The International Court of Justice in Comparison: Understanding the Court's Limited Influence' (2021) 21 *Melbourne Journal of International Law* 676.

Anderson, D. H., 'Delimitation of the Maritime Boundary in the Bay of Bengal (Bangladesh/Myanmar)' (2012) 106(4) *American Journal of International Law* 817.

Anderson, D., 'The Role of ITLOS as a Means of Dispute Settlement under UNCLOS' in D. Anderson (ed), *Modern Law of the Sea: Selected Essays* (2008, Martinus Nijhoff) 547.

Baird, R. 'Coastal State Fisheries Management: A Review of Australian Enforcement Action in the Heard and McDonald Islands Australian Fishing Zone' (2004) 9(1) *Deakin Law Review* 91.

Bantz, V. P., 'View from Hamburg: The Juno Trader Case or How to Make Sense of the Coastal State's Rights in the Light of Its Duty of Prompt Release' (2005) 24 *University of Queensland Law Journal* 415.

Bernard, L., 'The Effect of Historic Fishing Rights in Maritime Boundaries Delimitation' (Law of the Sea Institute Conference, Seoul, May 2012), available at: <https://www.law.berkeley.edu/files/Bernard-final.pdf>.

Bernard, L. and C. Schofield, 'Disputes concerning the Delimitation of the Continental Shelf beyond 200 Nautical Miles' in T. Heidar (ed), *New Knowledge and Changing Circumstances in the Law of the Sea* (Brill Nijhoff, 2020) 157.

Bhattacharjee, R., 'Delimitation of Indo-Bangladesh Maritime Boundary' 19 August 2014, *Institute for Defence Studies and Analyses*, available at: <https://www.idsa.in/idsacomments/DelimitationofIndo-Bangladesh_rbhattacharjee_190814>.

Borgese, E. M., 'A Constitution for the Oceans: Comments and Suggestions regarding Part XI of the Informal Composite Negotiating Text' (1978) 15 *San Diego Law Review* 371.

Born, G. B., 'A New Generation of International Adjudication' (2012) 61 *Duke Law Journal* 775.

Boyle, A., 'Dispute Settlement and the Law of the Sea Convention: Problems of Fragmentation and Jurisdiction' (1997) 46 *International and Comparative Law Quarterly* 37.

Boyle, A., 'The Environmental Jurisprudence of the International Tribunal for the Law of the Sea' (2007) 22(3) *International Journal of Marine and Coastal Law* 369.

Brilmayer, L. and N. Klein, 'Land and Sea: Two Sovereignty Regimes in Search of a Common Denominator' (2001) 33 *New York University Journal of International Law and Politics* 704.

Brown, C., *A Common Law of International Adjudication* (Oxford University Press, 2007).

Brown, C., 'Provisional Measures before the ITLOS: The Mox Plant Case' (2002) 17(2) *International Journal of Marine and Coastal Law* 267.

Buga, I., 'Territorial Sovereignty Issues in Maritime Disputes: A Jurisdictional Dilemma for Law of the Sea Tribunals' (2012) 27 *International Journal of Marine and Coastal Law* 59.

Busch, S. V., *Establishing Continental Shelf Limits beyond 200 Nautical Miles by the Coastal State: A Right of Involvement for Other States?* (Brill, 2016).

Cabrera Mirassou, M., 'ARA Libertad' in A. Peters (ed), *Max Planck Encyclopedia of Public International Law* (Oxford University Press, 2014).

Chayes, A. and A. Chayes, 'On Compliance' (1993) 47(2) *International Organization* 175.

Chinese Society of International Law, 'The South China Sea Arbitration Awards: A Critical Study' (2018) 17(2) *Chinese Journal of International Law* 207.

Churchill, R., 'Dispute Settlement in the Law of the Sea: Survey for 2019' (2020) 35(4) *International Journal of Marine and Coastal Law* 621.

Churchill, R., 'Dispute Settlement under the UN Convention on the Law of the Sea: Survey for 2004' (2006) 21(1) *International Journal of Marine and Coastal Law* 1.

Churchill, R., 'Dispute Settlement under the UN Convention on the Law of the Sea: Survey for 2005' (2006) 21(4) *International Journal of Marine and Coastal Law* 377.

Churchill, R., 'MOX Plant Arbitration and Cases' in A. Peters (ed), *Max Planck Encyclopedia of Public International Law* (Oxford University Press, June 2018).

Churchill, R., 'The Bangladesh/Myanmar Case: Continuity and Novelty in the Law of Maritime Boundary Delimitation' (2012) 1(1) *Cambridge International Law Journal* 137.

Churchill, R., 'The International Tribunal for the Law of the Sea: Survey for 2003' (2004) 19(4) *International Journal of Marine and Coastal Law* 369.

de Herdt, S. W., 'The Relationship between the Delimitation of the Continental Shelf beyond 200 nm and the Delineation of Its Outer Limits' (2020) 51(3) *Ocean Development and International Law* 263.

de la Rasilla, I. and J. Viñuales (eds), *Experiments in International Adjudication* (Cambridge University Press, 2018).

Del Vecchio, A. and R. Virzo (eds), *Interpretations of the United Nations Convention on the Law of the Sea by International Courts and Tribunals* (Springer, 2019).

Devereux, A., and S. McCosker, 'International Law and Australian Law', in D. R. Rothwell and E. Crawford (eds), *International Law in Australia* (3rd edn., Thomson Reuters, 2017).

Donoghue, J. E., 'The Effectiveness of the International Court of Justice' (2014) 108 *Proceedings of the American Society of International Law Annual Conference* 114.

Dupuy, R-J. and D. Vignes (eds), *A Handbook on the New Law of the Sea*, vol. 1, (Martinus Nijhoff, 1991).

Elferink, A. O., 'Settlement of the *Dispute concerning the Arctic Sunrise*: A Belated Recognition of the Relevance of the Award on the Merits in the *Arctic Sunrise* Case' 8 July 2019, *NCLOS* Blog, at: <https://site.uit.no/nclos/2019/07/08/settlement-of-the-dispute-concerning-the-arctic-sunrise-a-belated-recognition-of-the-relevance-of-the-award-on-the-merits-in-the-arctic-sunrise-case/>.

Fietta, S. and R. Cleverly, *A Practitioner's Guide to Maritime Boundary Delimitation* (Oxford University Press, 2016).

Foster, M. J. C., 'The *Mox Plant* Case: Provisional Measures in the International Tribunal for the Law of the Sea' (2003) 16 *Leiden Journal of International Law* 611.

Franck, T. M., *The Power of Legitimacy Among Nations* (Oxford University Press, 1990).

Gao, J., 'The Delimitation Method for the Continental Shelf beyond 200 Nautical Miles: A Reflection on the Judicial and Arbitral Decisions' (2020) 51(2) *Ocean Development and International Law* 116.

Gautier, P., 'Some Reflections on the "New Law of the Sea"' (2022) 99 *International Law Studies* 1051.

Ginsburg, T., 'International Judicial Lawmaking' (University of Illinois College of Law, Law and Economics Working Paper No. 26).

Giorgetti, C., 'What Happens after a Judgment is Given? Judgment Compliance and the Performance of International Courts and Tribunals' in Theresa Squatrito, et al. (eds), *The Performance of International Courts and Tribunals* (Cambridge University Press, 2018) 324.

Goldenziel, J. I., 'Law as a Battlefield: The US, China, and the Global Escalation of Lawfare' (2021) 106 *Cornell Law Review* 1085.

Grossman, N., H. G. Cohen, A. Follesdal and G. Ulfstein (eds), *Legitimacy and International Courts* (Cambridge University Press, 2018).

Guoxing, J., 'Sino-Japanese Jurisdictional Delimitation in East China Sea: Approaches to Dispute Settlement' in S-Y. Hong and J. M. van Dyke (eds), *Maritime Boundary Disputes, Settlement Processes, and the Law of the Sea* (Martinus Nijhoff, 2009).

Guzman, A. T., 'A Compliance-Based Theory of International Law' (2002) 90 *California Law Review* 1825.

Guzman, A. T., 'International Tribunals: A Rational Choice Analysis' (2008) 157 *University of Pennsylvania Law Review* 171.

Harris, C., 'Claims with an Ulterior Purpose: Characterising Disputes Concerning the "Interpretation or Application" of a Treaty' (2020) 18(3) *Law and Practice of International Courts and Tribunals* 279.

Harrison, J., 'Defining Disputes and Characterizing Claims: Subject-Matter Jurisdiction in Law of the Sea Convention Litigation' (2017) 48(3–4) *Ocean Development and International Law* 269.

Hart, H. L. A., *The Concept of Law* (Oxford University Press, 1961).

Hawkins, D. and W. Jacoby, 'Partial Compliance: A Comparison of the European and Inter-American Courts of Human Rights' (2010) 6(1) *Journal of International Law and International Relations* 35.

Hayton, B., 'Denounce but Comply: China's Response to the South China Sea Arbitration Ruling' (2017) 18(2) *Georgetown Journal of International Affairs* 104.

Helfer, L. R. and A. Slaughter, 'Toward a Theory of Effective Supranational Adjudication' (1997) 107 *Yale Law Journal* 273.

Helfer, L. R. and A-M. Slaughter, 'Why States Create International Tribunals: A Response to Professors Posner and Yoo' (2005) 93 *California Law Review* 899.

Helfer, L. R., 'The Effectiveness of International Adjudicators' in C. P. Romano, K. J. Alter and Y. Shany (eds), *The Oxford Handbook of International Adjudication* (Oxford University Press, 2014) 464.

Henkin, L., *How Nations Behave* (Columbia University Press, 1979).

Howse, R. and R. Teitel, 'Beyond Compliance: Rethinking Why International Law Really Matters' (2010) 1(2) *Global Policy* 127.

Huneeus, A., 'Compliance with Judgments and Decisions' in C. P. Romano, K. J. Alter and Y. Shany (eds), *The Oxford Handbook of International Adjudication* (Oxford University Press, 2014) 437.

International Law Commission, *Report of the International Law Commission on the Work of Its Fifty-Third Session*, UN GAOR, 56th sess., Supp. No. 10, UN Doc. A/56/10 (2001).

Irwin, P. C., 'Settlement of Maritime Boundary Disputes: An Analysis of the Law of the Sea Negotiations' (1980) 8 *Ocean Development and International Law* 105.

Jennings, R., 'Presentation', in C. Peck and R. S. K. Lee (eds), *Increasing the Effectiveness of the International Court of Justice: Proceedings of the ICJ/UNITAR Colloquium to Celebrate the 50th Anniversary of the Court* (Kluwer, 1997).

Jensen, Ø. (ed), *The Development of the Law of the Sea Convention: The Role of International Courts and Tribunals* (Elgar, 2020).

Jia, B. B., 'The Principle of the Domination of the Land over the Sea: A Historical Perspective on the Adaptability of the Law of the Sea to New Challenges' (2014) 57 *German Yearbook of International Law* 1.

Jing, G., 'An Analysis of the Jurisdiction over Provisional Measures of the ITLOS' [2007](1) *China Oceans Law Review* 413.

Jones, H. L., 'Why Comply? An Analysis of Trends in Compliance with Judgments of the International Court of Justice since *Nicaragua*' (2012) 12(1) *Chicago-Kent Journal of International and Comparative Law* 57.

Kałduński, M. and T. Wasilewski 'The International Tribunal for the law of the sea on maritime delimitation: the Bangladesh v. Myanmar case' (2014) 45(2) *Ocean Development & International Law* 123.

Kałduński, M., 'A Commentary on Maritime Boundary Arbitration between Bangladesh and India Concerning the Bay of Bengal' (2015) 28(4) *Leiden Journal of International Law* 799.

Karim, Md. S., 'Conflicts over Protection of Marine Living Resources: The Volga Case Revisited' (2011) 3 *Goettingen Journal of International Law* 101.

Keyuan, Z., 'International Tribunal for the Law of the Sea: Procedures, Practices, and Asian States' (2010) 41(2) *Ocean Development and International Law* 131.

Kingsbury, B., 'The Concept of Compliance as a Function of Competing Conceptions of International Law' (1998) 19 *Michigan Journal of International Law* 345.

Klein, N. and K. Parlett, *Judging the Law of the Sea: Judicial Interpretations of the UN Convention on the Law of the Sea* (Oxford University Press, 2022).

Klein, N., *Dispute Settlement in the UN Convention on the Law of the Sea* (Cambridge University Press, 2005).

Klein, N., 'Land and Sea: Resolving Contested Land and Disappearing Land Disputes under the UN Convention on the Law of the Sea' in C. Giorgetti and N. Klein (eds), *Resolving Conflicts in the Law: Essays in Honour of Lea Brilmayer* (Brill, 2019) 249.

Klein, N., 'Resolving Disputes under UNCLOS when the Coastal and User States are Disputed' in N. Hong and G. Houlden (eds), *Maritime Order and the Law in East Asia* (Routledge, 2018).

Kocs, S. A., 'Territorial Disputes and Interstate War, 1945–1987' (1995) 57 *The Journal of Politics* 159.

Koh, H. H., 'Why Do Nations Obey International Law?' (1997) 106(8) *Yale Law Journal* 2599.

Kunoy, B., 'The Scope of Compulsory Jurisdiction and Exceptions Thereto under the *United Nations Convention on the Law of the Sea*' (2020) 58 *Canadian Yearbook of International Law* 78.

Kwiatkowska, B., '*Barbados/Trinidad and Tobago*. Award on Jurisdiction and Merits' (2007) 101 *American Journal of International Law* 156.

Lando, M., 'Provisional Measures and the Link Requirement' (2020) 19 *The Law and Practice of International Courts and Tribunals* 177.

Lando, M., *Maritime Delimitation as a Judicial Process* (Cambridge University Press, 2019).

Lathrop, C. (ed.), *International Maritime Boundaries* (2020, Brill Nijhoff).

Levy, M. A., 'European Acid Rain: The Power of Tote-Board Diplomacy' in P. M. Haas, et al. (eds), *Institutions for the Earth: Sources of Effective Environmental Protection* (MIT Press, 1993) 75.

Linderfalk, U., 'The *Jan Mayen Case* (*Iceland/Norway*): An Example of Successful Conciliation' in C. Tomuschat, R. P. Mazzeschi and D. Thürer (eds), *Conciliation in International Law: The OSCE Court of Conciliation and Arbitration* (Brill, 2017) 193.

Liwanga, R-C. and C. Turner, 'Demystifying the Legitimacy of International Tribunals: Case Study of the International Court of Justice and its Decisions on Armed Activities in the Congo' (2021) 35(3) *Emory International Law Review* 413.

Llamzon, A. P., 'Jurisdiction and Compliance in Recent Decisions of the International Court of Justice' (2007) 18(5) *European Journal of International Law* 815.

Mackenzie, R., C. P. Romano, Y. Shany and P. Sands (eds), *The Manual on International Courts and Tribunals* (2nd edn., Oxford University Press, 2010).

Magnússon, B. M., 'The Grey Areas in the Bay of Bengal' (2016) 56 *Indian Journal of International Law* 41.

Mansfield, B., 'Letter to the Editor' (2001) 95 *American Journal of International Law* 624.

Mansfield, B., 'The Southern Bluefin Tuna Arbitration, Comments on Professor Barbara Kwiatkowska's Article' (2000) 16 *International Journal of Marine and Costal Law* 361.

Marchuk, I., 'Powerful States and International Law: Changing Narratives and Power Struggles in International Courts' (2019) 26(1) *UC Davis Journal of International Law and Policy* 65.

Martin, L. L., 'Against Compliance' in J. L. Dunoff and M. A. Pollack (eds), *Interdisciplinary Perspectives on International Law and International Relations* (Cambridge University Press, 2012) 591.

McCreath, M. and Z. Scanlon, 'The Dispute Concerning the Delimitation of the Maritime Boundary Between Ghana and Côte d'Ivoire: Implications for the Law of the Sea' (2019) 50(1) *Ocean Development & International Law* 1.

McLaughlin Mitchell, S. and A. P. Owsiak, 'Judicialization of the Sea: Bargaining in the Shadow of UNCLOS' (2021) 115 *American Journal of International Law* 579.

McNally, J., 'The Metamorphosis of Soft Law in *Mauritius/Maldives*' (2021) 28 *Australian International Law Journal* 195.

Merrills, J. G., *International Dispute Settlement* (6th edn., Cambridge University Press, 2017).

Miles, C., *Provisional Measures before International Courts and Tribunals* (Cambridge University Press, 2018).

Mirasola, C., *Ghana/Côte d'Ivoire: A Case Summary for the Maritime Dispute Resolution Project*, available at: <https://static1.squarespace.com/static/55d21ffee4b0d22e803fdca1/t/5f4d05bc29cfe63ea87eb389/1598883268056/GhanavCotedIvoire.pdf>.

Miron, A., 'The *Acquis Judiciaire*, a Tool for Harmonization in a Decentralized System of Litigation?' in C. Giorgetti and M. Pollack (eds), *Beyond Fragmentation: Cross-Fertilization, Cooperation and Competition among International Courts and Tribunals* (Cambridge University Press, 2022).

Mishra, R., 'The Grey Area in the Northern Bay of Bengal: A Note on a Functional Cooperative Solution' (2016) 47(1) *Ocean Development and International Law* 29.

Morgenthau, H. J., *Politics Among Nations* (A. A. Knopf, 1948).

Neyer, J., and D. Wolf, 'The Analysis of Compliance with International Rules: Definitions, Variables and Methodology' in M. Zürn and C. Joerges (eds), *Law and Governance in Postnational Europe* (Cambridge University Press, 2005) 40.

Nguyen, L. N., 'The UNCLOS Dispute Settlement System: What Role Can It Play in Resolving Maritime Disputes in Asia' (2018) 8(1) *Asian Journal of International Law* 91.

Oral, N., 'Ukraine v the Russian Federation: Navigating Conflict over Sovereignty under UNCLOS' (2021) 97 *International Law Studies* 478.

Oude Elferink, A. G., 'ITLOS's Approach to the Delimitation of the Continental Shelf beyond 200 Nautical Miles in the *Bangladesh/Myanmar* Case: Theoretical and Practical Difficulties' in R. Wolfrum, M. Seršić, and T. Šošić (eds), *Contemporary Developments in International Law: Essays in Honour of Budislav Vukas* (Brill Nijhoff, 2016) 230.

Oude Elferink, A. G., T. Henriksen and S. V. Busch, 'The Judiciary and the Law of Maritime Delimitation' in A. G. Oude Elferink, T. Henriksen and S. V. Busch (eds), *Maritime Boundary Delimitation: The Case Law* (Oxford University Press, 2018).

Oude Elferink, A. G., T. Henriksen and S. V. Busch (eds), *Maritime Delimitation: The Case Law – Is It Consistent and Predictable?* (Cambridge University Press, 2018).

Oxman, B. H., 'The *Barbados/Trinidad & Tobago* Arbitration – The Law of Maritime Delimitation: Back to the Future', available at: <https://media.law.miami.edu/faculty-administration/pdf/bernard-oxman/oxman-barbados-trinidad-arbitration.pdf>.

Paparinskis, M., 'Crippling Compensation in the International Law Commission and Investor – State Arbitration' (2021) 37(1–2) *ICSID Review* 289.

Patel, B. N., 'Recommendations on the Enhancement of the Role and Effectiveness of the International Court of Justice and State Practice: The Gap between Recommendation and Practice (1971–2006)' (2007) 11 *Singapore Yearbook of International Law* 99.

Peat, D., *Comparative Reasoning in International Courts and Tribunals* (Cambridge University Press, 2019).

Phan, H. D. and L. N. Nguyen, 'The *South China Sea* Arbitration: Bindingness, Finality and Compliance with UNCLOS Dispute Settlement Decisions' (2018) 8(1) *Asian Journal of International Law* 36.

Phan, H. D., 'International Courts and State Compliance: An Investigation of the Law of the Sea Cases' (2019) 50(1) *Ocean Development & International Law* 70.

Posner, E. A. and J. C. Yoo, 'Judicial Independence in International Tribunals' (2005) 93(1) *California Law Review* 1.

Prescott, J. R. V., 'On the Resolution of Marine Boundary Conflicts' in J. P. Craven, J. Schneider and C. Stimson (eds), 'The International Implications of Extended Maritime Jurisdiction in the Pacific' (1987) 21 *Proceedings of the Law of the Sea Institute Conference* 33.

Proelss, A., 'The Limits of Jurisdiction *Ratione Materiae* of UNCLOS Tribunals' (2018) 46 *Hitotsubashi Journal of Law and Politics* 47.

Proelss, A., *The United Nations Convention on the Law of the Sea: A Commentary* (C. H. Beck Hart Nomos, 2017).

Ramírez, W. A., 'Resistance to Territorial and Maritime Delimitation Judgments of the International Court of Justice and Clashes with "Territory Clauses" in the Constitutions Of Latin American States' (2022) 35 *Leiden Journal of International Law* 185.

Raustiala, K., 'Compliance and Effectiveness in International Regulatory Cooperation' (2000) 3 *Case Western Reserve Journal of International Law* 387.

Rayfuse, R., 'The Future of Compulsory Dispute Settlement under the Law of the Sea Convention' (2005) 36(1) *Victoria University of Wellington Law Review* 683.

Richardson, E. L., 'Jan Mayen in Perspective' (1988) 82 *American Journal of International Law* 443.

Rosenne, S., *The Law and Practice of the International Court 1920–1996*, vol. 1, (5th edn., Brill, 2016).

Schofield, C., P. Bekker and R. van de Poll, 'The World Court Fixes the Somalia-Kenya Maritime Boundary: Technical Considerations and Legal Consequences' (2021) 25(25) *American Society of International Law Insights*.

Serdy, A., *The Other Australia/Japan Living Resources Dispute: Inferences on the Merits of the Southern Bluefin Tuna Arbitration in Light of the Whaling Case* (Brill, 2017).

Shany, Y., 'Assessing the Effectiveness of International Courts: A Goal-Based Approach' (2012) 106 *American Journal of International Law* 225.

Shany, Y., *Assessing the Effectiveness of International Courts* (Oxford University Press, 2014).

Shapiro, M., *Courts: A Comparative Political Analysis* (University of Chicago Press, 1981).

Shaw, M. N., *International Law* (Cambridge University Press, 2008).

Siegfreid, A., 'Preface' in J. Ancel, *Géographie Des Frontières* (Gallimard, 1938).

Simmons, B., 'International Law and State Behavior: Commitment and Compliance in International Monetary Affairs' (2000) 94 *American Political Science Review* 819.

Simmons, B. A., 'Capacity, Commitment and Compliance: International Institutions and Territorial Disputes' (2002) 46(6) *Journal of Conflict Resolution* 829.

Simmons, B. A., 'Compliance with International Agreements' (1998) 1 *Annual Review of Political Science* 75.

Singh, D., 'Comment on the Guyana-Suriname Boundary Dispute' (2004) 32 *Georgia Journal of International and Comparative Law* 657.

Squatrito, T. O., R. Young, A. Follesdal and G. Ulfstein (eds), *The Performance of International Courts and Tribunals* (Cambridge University Press, 2018).

Tanaka, Y., 'Juridical Insights into the Protection of Community Interests through Provisional Measures: Reflections on the ITLOS Jurisprudence' in G. Ziccardi Capaldo (ed.), *The Global Community Yearbook of International Law and Jurisprudence* (Oxford University Press, 2014), vol. 1, 249.

Tanaka, Y., 'Provisional Measures Prescribed by ITLOS and Marine Environmental Protection' (2014) 108 *Proceedings of the Annual Meeting of the American Society of International Law* 365.

Tanaka, Y., *The International Law of the Sea* (Cambridge University Press, 2012).

Tanaka, Y., *The Peaceful Settlement of International Disputes* (Cambridge University Press, 2018).

Treves, T., 'The International Tribunal for the Law of the Sea' (2004) 14 *Italian Yearbook of International Law* 289.

Trevisanut, S., 'Twenty Years of Prompt Release of Vessels: Admissibility, Jurisdiction, and Recent Trends' (2017) 48(3–4) *Ocean Development & International Law* 300.

Tuerk H., 'The Contribution of the International Tribunal for the Law of the Sea to International Law' (2007) 26(2) *Penn State International Law Review* 289.

Tzeng, P., 'A Strategy of Non-Participation before International Courts and Tribunals' (2020) 19 *The Law and Practice of International Courts and Tribunals* 5.

Tzeng, P., 'The Implicated Issue Problem: Indispensable Issues and Incidental Jurisdiction' (2018) 50 *New York University Journal of International Law and Politics* 447.

van Logchem, Y., 'The Rights and Obligations of States in Disputed Maritime Areas: What Lessons Can Be Learned from the Maritime Boundary Dispute between Ghana and Cote d'Ivoire' (2019) 52 *Vanderbilt Journal of Transnational Law* 121.

von Stein, J., 'The Engines of Compliance' in J. L. Dunoff and M. A. Pollack (eds), *Interdisciplinary Perspectives on International Law and International Relations: The State of the Art* (Cambridge University Press, 2012) 477.

Walt, S. M., 'Realism and Security' in R. A. Denemark (ed), *The International Studies Encyclopedia* (Wiley, 2010).

Walt, S. M., 'The Renaissance of Security Studies' (1991) 35(2) *International Studies Quarterly* 211.

Weil, P., *The Law of Maritime Delimitation: Reflections* (Cambridge Grotius Publications, 1989).

White, M. W. D., *Australian Offshore Laws* (Federation Press, 2009).

Yee, S., 'The *South China Sea* Arbitration (The Philippines v. China): Potential Jurisdictional Obstacles or Objections' (2014) 13 *Chinese Journal of International Law* 663.

Young, O. R., *Compliance and Public Authority* (John Hopkins University Press, 1979).

Zhang, F., 'Assessing China's Response to the South China Sea Arbitration' (2017) 71(4) *Australian Journal of International Affairs* 440.

News, Blogs and Other Internet Materials

'A Constructive Year for Chinese Base Building' 14 December 2017, *Asia Maritime Transparency Initiative*, available at: <https://amti.csis.org/constructive-year-chinese-building/>.

'Akufo-Addo Reciprocates Ivorian Gesture; Honours Ouattara' 17 October 2017, *Ghana News Page*, available at: <https://ghananewspage.com/akufo-addo-reciprocates-ivorian-gesture-honours-ouattara/>.

'ARA Libertad Joins Velas Latinoamérica 2022' 15 February 2022, available at: <https://seawaves.com/?p=19191>.

'Arbitration Support Tracker' 2 August 2021, *Asia Maritime Transparency Initiative*, available at: <https://amti.csis.org/arbitration-support-tracker/>.

'Bangladesh Hails UN Ruling in Myanmar Border Dispute' 15 March 2012, *Reuters*, available at: <https://www.reuters.com/article/bangladesh-myanmar-maritime-idUKL5E8EE40F20120314?edition redirect=uk>.

'Barbados Still Seeking Fishing Agreement with Trinidad and Tobago' 7 February 2011, *Caribbean Trakker*, available at: <https://www.caribbeantrakker.com/barbados-still-seeking-fishing-agreement-with-trinidad-and-tobago/>.

'China's Most Destructive Boats Return to the South China Sea' 20 May 2019, *Asia Maritime Transparency Initiative*, available at: <https://amti.csis.org/chinas-most-destructive-boats-return-to-the-south-china-sea/>.

'Failing or Incomplete? Grading the South China Sea Arbitration' 11 July 2019, *Asia Maritime Transparency Initiative*, available at: <https://amti.csis.org/failing-or-incomplete-grading-the-south-china-sea-arbitration/>.

'Ghana and Côte d'Ivoire Sign Strategic Partnership Agreement' 18 October 2017, *Ghana Business News*, available at: <https://www.ghanabusinessnews.com/2017/10/18/ghana-and-cote-divoire-sign-strategic-partnership-agreement/>.

'Ghana, Côte d'Ivoire Agree on Delimiting Maritime Boundary' 13 August 2018, *GhanaWeb*, available at: <https://www.ghanaweb.com/GhanaHomePage/business/Ghana-Cote-d-Ivoire-agree-on-delimiting-maritime-boundary-676235>.

'Illegal Fishers Face Bill' 26 November 2003, *Sydney Morning Herald*, available at: <https://www.smh.com.au/national/illegal-fishers-face-chase-bill-20031126-gdhuwh.html>.

'Italian Marines: India Closes Criminal Cases in 2012 Shooting' 15 June 2021, *BBC News*, available at: <https://www.bbc.com/news/world-asia-india-57479761>.

'Italy Drops Probe against Marines Who Killed Indian Fishermen in 2012' 1 February 2022, *The Week*, available at: <https://www.theweek.in/news/world/2022/02/01/italy-drops-probe-against-marines-who-killed-indian-fishermen-in-20-12.html>.

'ITLOS Judgment' 23 September 2017, *Tullow Oil*, available at: <https://www.tullowoil.com/media/press-releases/itlos-judgment/>.

'Local Fishermen Encouraged to Meet Counterparts in Tobago' 24 August 2019, *Barbados Today*, available at: <https://barbadostoday.bb/2019/08/24/local-fishermen-encouraged-to-meet-counterparts-in-tobago/>.

'Netherlands, Russia Agree Deal on Arctic Sunrise Compensation' 17 May 2019, *Dutch News*, available at: <https://www.dutchnews.nl/news/2019/05/netherlands-russia-agree-deal-on-arctic-sunrise-compensation>.

‘Philippines tells China to “Back Off” after South China Sea Clash’ 18 November 2021, *Al Jazeera*, available at: <https://www.aljazeera.com/news/2021/11/18/philippines-tells-china-to-back-off-after-south-china-sea-clash>.

‘Philippines Tells Fishermen to Ignore Beijing’s Ban on Fishing in South China Sea’ 5 May 2021, *Reuters*, available at: <https://www.reuters.com/world/asia-pacific/philippines-tells-fishermen-ignore-beijings-ban-fishing-south-china-sea-2021-05-05/>.

‘Russia drops first Greenpeace Arctic 30 case’ 24 December 2013, *BBC News*, available at: <https://www.bbc.com/news/world-europe-25504016>.

‘Settlement of the Arctic Sunrise Case between the Netherlands and Russia’ 17 May 2019, *Greenpeace International*, available at: <https://www.greenpeace.org/international/press-release/22071/settlement-of-the-arctic-sunrise-case-between-the-netherlands-and-russia/>.

‘Ukraine Accuses Russia of Returning Ships “Stripped of Toilets”’ 21 November 2019, *BBC News*, available at: <https://www.bbc.com/news/world-europe-50501241>.

‘Ukraine and Russia Exchange Prisoners in Landmark Deal’ 7 September 2019, *BBC News*, available at: <https://www.bbc.com/news/world-europe-49610107>.

‘Under China’s Shadow, Philippines Clings to Rusting Maritime Outpost’ 29 November 2021, *Radio Free Asia*, available at: <https://www.rfa.org/english/news/china/philippines-southchinasea-11292021151419.html>.

Aurelio, J. M., ‘Duterte-Xi Fishing Deal Verbal – Palace’ 2 July 2019, *Inquirer*, available at: <https://globalnation.inquirer.net/177292/duterte-xi-fishing-deal-verbal-palace>.

Barker, A., ‘China and the Philippines’ Tense Stand-Off over Scarborough Shoal Leaves Fishermen in Fear’ 26 May 2021, *ABC News*, available at: <https://www.abc.net.au/news/2021-05-26/china-philippines-stand-off-over-scarborough-shoal/100145586>.

BGIS, ‘Barbados and Trinidad Sign Fishing Protocol’ 5 December 2014, *NationNews*, available at: <https://www.nationnews.com/2014/12/05/barbados-and-trinidad-sign-fishing-protocol/>.

Bodner, M., ‘Ukraine Seizes Russian Tanker in Black Sea in Retaliation for 2018 Flotilla Clash’ 26 July 2019, *Sydney Morning Herald*, available at: <https://www.smh.com.au/world/europe/ukraine-seizes-russian-tanker-in-black-sea-in-retaliation-for-2018-flotilla-clash-20190726-p52axd.html>.

Borger, J. and T. Phillips, ‘How China’s Artificial Islands Led to Tension in the South China Sea’ 27 October 2015, *The Guardian*, available at: <https://www.theguardian.com/world/2015/oct/27/tensions-and-territorial-claims-in-the-south-china-sea-the-guardian-briefing>.

Carter, G., ‘Fishing for Deal’ 4 February 2019, *NationNews*, available at: <https://www.nationnews.com/2019/02/04/fishing-for-deal/>.

De Castro, R. C., ‘Incident at Reed Bank: A Crisis in the Philippines’ China Policy’ 20 June 2019, *Asia Maritime Transparency Initiative*, available at: <https://amti.csis.org/incident-at-reed-bank-a-crisis-in-the-philippines-china-policy/>.

De Silva, R., 'T&T, Barbados, to Negotiate Fishing Treaty' 24 August 2019, *Trinidad & Tobago Guardian*, available at: <https://www.guardian.co.tt/news/tt-barbados-to-negotiate-fishing-treaty-6.2.917177.555001b133>.

Greenpeace, 'About the Arctic Sunrise', available at: <https://www.greenpeace.org/usa/about/shiptour-old/about-the-arctic-sunrise/>.

Grigg, A., 'Less than 20 Years after Independence, Timor-Leste is Running on Fumes' 30 April 2021, *Australian Financial Review*, available at: <https://www.afr.com/companies/energy/less-than-20-years-after-independence-timor-leste-is-running-on-fumes-20210429-p57nc7>.

Gupta, S., 'Beijing's Creative Compliance and Non-compliance in the South China Sea' 11 October 2021, *East Asia Forum*, available at: <https://www.eastasiaforum.org/2021/10/11/beijings-creative-compliance-and-non-compliance-in-the-south-china-sea/>.

Gutierrez, J., 'Philippines Accuses Chinese Vessel of Sinking Fishing Boat in Disputed Waters' 12 June 2019, *The New York Times*, available at: <https://www.nytimes.com/2019/06/12/world/asia/philippines-china-fishing-boat.html>.

Jagdeo, B., 'Address to the Nation by His Excellency Bharrat Jagdeo, President of the Republic of Guyana, on the Award of the Guyana-Suriname Arbitral Tribunal' 20 September 2007, *Guyana News and Information*, available at: <http://www.guyana.org/guysur/jagdeo_tribunal_award.html>.

Jakhar, P. 'Whatever Happened to the South China Sea Ruling?' 12 July 2021, *Lowy Interpreter*, available at: <https://www.lowyinstitute.org/the-interpreter/whatever-happened-south-china-sea-ruling> (accessed 1 September 2022).

Knight, P., '"Everyone Lost" in T&T-Barbados Fishing Boundary Dispute' June 2006, *Caribbean Today*, available at: <https://ufdcimages.uflib.ufl.edu/UF/00/09/92/85/00006/00006-2006_Page_08.txt>.

Ku, J. and C. Mirasola, 'Tracking China's Compliance with the South China Sea Arbitral Award' 3 October 2016, *Lawfare*, available at: <https://www.lawfareblog.com/tracking-chinas-compliance-south-china-sea-arbitral-award>.

Kuipers, A., and S. Khan, 'U.N. Favors Guyana in Oil Border Spat with Suriname' 21 September 2007, *Reuters*, available at: <https://www.reuters.com/article/us-suriname-guyana-idUSN2044982420070920>.

Mangosing, F., 'China Still Harassing Filipino Fishermen in Scarborough Shoal – US Navy Official' 13 February 2019, *Inquirer*, available at: <https://newsinfo.inquirer.net/1085307/china-still-harassing-filipino-fishermen-in-scarborough-shoal-us-navy-official>.

Muiruri, P., 'Kenya Rejects UN Court Judgment Giving Somalia Control of Resource-Rich Waters' 15 October 2021, *The Guardian*, available at: <https://www.theguardian.com/global-development/2021/oct/14/kenya-rejects-un-court-judgment-giving-somalia-control-of-resource-rich-waters>.

Murphy, H., 'Colombia Leaves Pact Recognizing U.N. Court Rulings' 29 November 2012, *Reuters*, available at: <https://www.reuters.com/article/us-colombia-icj-idUSBRE8AR11Q20121128>.

Panda, A., 'Reclamation, Arbitration, Competition: South China Sea Situation Report' 9 May 2015, *The Diplomat*, available at: <https://thediplomat.com/2015/05/reclamation-arbitration-competition-south-china-sea-situation-report/>.

Paul, R., 'UN Tribunal Rules for Bangladesh in Sea Border Dispute with India' 8 July 2014, *Reuters*, available at: <http://uk.reuters.com/article/2014/07/08/uk-bangladesh-india-seaborder-idUKKBN0FD15N20140708>.

Pedrozo, R., 'China Again Uses Force to Bully Its Neighbours' 10 December 2022, *Lawfare*, available at: <https://www.lawfareblog.com/china-again-uses-force-bully-its-neighbors>.

Robles, R., 'Philippines Says China Is "The Trespasser" as it Refuses to Move Ship from Disputed South China Sea Shoal' 25 November 2021, *South China Morning Post*, available at: <https://www.scmp.com/week-asia/politics/article/3157403/philippines-says-china-trespasser-it-refuses-move-ship-disputed>.

Sanders, R., 'Guyana to be Oil Rich?' 26 September 2007, *BBC Caribbean*, available at: <https://www.bbc.co.uk/caribbean/news/story/2007/09/070926_sanders240907.shtml>.

Shumei, L., 'China Ends Fishing Moratorium in South China Sea, Foreign Media Speculation Rejected' 16 August 2021, *Global Times*, available at: <https://www.globaltimes.cn/page/202108/1231625.shtml?id=11>.

Specia, M. and M., Takkunen, 'South China Sea Photos Suggest a Military Building Spree by Beijing' 8 February 2018, *The New York Times*, available at: <https://www.nytimes.com/2018/02/08/world/asia/south-china-seas-photos.html?>.

State Council Information Office of the People's Republic of China, *China Adheres to the Position of Settling through Negotiation the Relevant Disputes between China and the Philippines in the South China Sea* (2016), available at: <http://english.www.gov.cn/state_council/ministries/2016/07/13/content_281475392503075>.

Stevenson, A., 'How Argentina Settled a Billion-Dollar Debt Dispute With Hedge Funds' 25 April 2016, *The New York Times*, available at: <https://www.nytimes.com/2016/04/25/business/dealbook/how-argentina-settled-a-billion-dollar-debt-dispute-with-hedge-funds.html>.

Strating, B., 'Timor-Leste Runs the Risk of a Pyrrhic Victory' 11 January 2017, *The Interpreter*, available at: <https://www.lowyinstitute.org/the-interpreter/timor-leste-runs-risk-pyrrhic-victory>.

Thao, N. H. and N. T. L. Huong, 'The South China Sea Arbitration Award: 5 Years and Beyond' 12 July 2021, *The Diplomat*, available at: <https://thediplomat.com/2021/07/the-south-china-sea-arbitration-award-5-years-and-beyond/>.

TMT, 'Vessel Details – ROBERTO – Delisted', available at: <https://iuu-vessels.org/Vessel/GetVessel/71458ofc-od2c-4613-976f-4bd7d71a7dbd>.

Vidal, J., 'Arctic 30: Russia Releases Greenpeace Ship' 6 June 2014, *The Guardian*, available at: <https://www.theguardian.com/environment/2014/jun/06/arctic-30-sunrise-russia-to-release-greenpeace-ship>.

Viray, P. L., 'Manila Protests Beijing's Unilateral Fishing Ban in South China Sea' 18 May 2021, *Philippines Star*, available at: <https://www.philstar.com/headlines/2021/05/18/2099224/manila-protests-beijings-unilateral-fishing-ban-south-china-sea>.

Yiallourides, C. and E. R. Donnelly, 'Part II: Analysis of Dispute Concerning Delimitation of the Maritime Boundary between Ghana and Côte d'Ivoire in the Atlantic Ocean' 20 October 2017, *EJIL: Talk!*, available at: <https://www.ejiltalk.org/part-ii-analysis-of-dispute-concerning-delimitation-of-the-maritime-boundary-between-ghana-and-cote-divoire-in-the-atlantic-ocean/>.

Zhen, L., 'South China Sea: Countdown to a New Fishing Season in Troubled Waters' 13 August 2021, *South China Morning Post*, available at: <https://www.scmp.com/news/china/diplomacy/article/3144844/south-china-sea-countdown-new-fishing-season-troubled-waters>.

www.ingramcontent.com/pod-product-compliance
Lightning Source LLC
Chambersburg PA
CBHW031326230926
51848CB00001B/105
9789004689893